OUTSIDE THE MARGINS

Lessons from Walking with Communities of the World

Sharon Bieber

Outside the Margins
Copyright © 2020 by Sharon Bieber

Tellwell Talent
www.tellwell.ca

ISBN
978-0-2288-2448-0 (Paperback)
978-0-2288-2449-7 (eBook)

CONTENTS

FOREWORD

Have you ever wondered if the way you spend your life has any meaning? In quiet moments of self-reflection, do you sometimes long for a profession with some adventure or a little bit of risk and excitement? Do you wonder if your passage through time will count for anything?

Bill and Sharon Bieber are a couple that have followed the inclination of their compassionate hearts to serve those living on the margins (actually, many living *beyond* the margins) of the world. In doing so, risk and adventure and meaning have all followed as their lives have unfolded in remarkable ways. The communities and people in them where the Biebers have worked form the basis for these stories. The lessons these folk have learned and the useful principles they have integrated into their work and lifestyle are the heartbeat of this book.

William Bieber, a medical doctor, and Sharon were recently awarded the Meritorious Service Medal given to Canadians "to recognize the extraordinary people who make Canada proud" for founding a street clinic in 1988. Serving the homeless poor and addicts in Calgary, the clinic and its offspring are still helping people overcome the vicious cycles of poverty and regain stability by providing health care, education, housing support and more.

Worthy as this effort was, as the award given to honor it recognized, it is only a small portion of the impact the efforts of this remarkable couple have had around the world, efforts about which fellow Canadians have little inkling. Truly, like others with a similar calling—mostly unnamed and unsung—Bill and Sharon have chosen to live and work beyond the margins of the world.

Though hardly the kind of folk who sit and tally the numerical impact of their lives for the good on others, it would not be an exaggeration to conclude that thousands if not multiple thousands have been positively impacted by the unique approaches of this couple and the pioneering work of Medical Ambassadors International. This book, *Outside the Margins*, is a chronicle of what they have learned in their fascinating life journey that they will pass on to those seeking to impact their own worlds.

Believe me, these are ordinary people who have made a difference. As you read these remarkable stories, think about your own 'ordinary' life with its impossible dreams, and what it would take, exactly, for you to step outside of your margins.

Karen Burton Mains

INTRODUCTION

For many years my husband and I have spent blocks of time working with people in some of the poorest countries, seeking to help them find solutions to problems that oppress them. We continue to feel the urgency of that call and to feel inspired by those who live in difficult places with a simple longing to see their families and communities flourish. In this book our stories and their stories intertwine because we have been challenged and changed by each other's lives; we are never the sole authors of our own stories.

The idea to write came after my father's passing in 2011, when my sisters came across boxes of neatly filed letters—all the letters that each of us had written to our parents over the years. I was surprised when I saw my package of letters, handwritten ones and printed emails, carefully preserved by loving parents who likely read them many times over. They were the accounts of the years that my husband, Bill, and I spent working internationally, starting with our travel as a young couple. The letters then moved to our years working in Papua New Guinea (PNG) along with our two pre-schoolers, Tim and Tera. Bill initially was staff doctor for a large mission there, afterwards working for the PNG Health Department. Finally there were files of our years as volunteers in various places after semi-retirement from Canadian work life.

I told my friend Karen Mains, author of many books and serving at the time on the Board of Medical Ambassadors International, about the letters. She affirmed, "Sharon, those letters are gold!" I knew then that I had better mine the gold! I carefully filed the letters, vowing to read and savour them one day.

A rainy day alone at our cabin in the East Kootenays of British Columbia provided the right time to dive in. The first letters to my parents were written on blue 'aerograms', one-page thin stationery that folded to form the envelope for lighter weight and cheaper postage, now artefacts of a bygone age. What a good idea, I mused— when did they stop making these, and why? The format forced one to write small and only cram in the important details rather than writing volumes. This series of letters were bi-weekly starting from 1970, the year after we were married. Bill was fresh out of a medical internship and I had just finished my first year of teaching, when a year of travel was combined with volunteer medical work in the Caribbean and Tanzania. The letters continued through the 1980's in Papua New Guinea. The switch to emails started in the mid-1990's with our stints of one to four month trips in various community health projects with groups such as Samaritan's Purse and finally Medical Ambassadors International (MAI). The latter continues still, and in 2005 turned into an almost fulltime role as MAI Regional Coordinators for Southeast Asia and South Pacific.

As I read, laughed and cried through the words written from my own heart over the years, experiences that had been long forgotten came flooding back. As the reading continued, I realized that something else was dawning. My heart was responding to stories of our own lives as though I were reading about strangers. Through my own accounts I understood at a deeper level things that we had missed seeing at the time—cause and effect that had not been clear then but that hindsight was revealing. Patterns were emerging that had not been obvious in the snapshots of the moment. Seeming random events and challenges had deeper implications that shaped our future. Unexpected people became influencers that caused us to change direction. Indeed our lives had a bigger purpose than we imagined, creating ripples that still move outward.

Writing is my way of looking back in order to understand what we had seen and done and learned in the process. This book is divided into four mega-principles and ten chapters that represent the most significant life lessons we have identified. Interwoven with our experiences is some data to support these lessons and best practices in development, and to formulate principles about living and working beyond one's own borders. The book introduces some complex and weighty topics of inequities and injustices towards the marginalized but barely scratches the surface of the serious study the topics deserve. Hopefully it will serve to start conversations and deeper research for some, since in the book we have focused on people and practice but not much on theory. Our tutors were real people dealing with real issues, whose stories may otherwise never be told. Some of their names and places have been changed for privacy or security reasons.

Our hope is that our learning may benefit others that follow, especially those who may choose to serve outside the margins of their own culture or geographical boundaries. Another larger vision for this book is to inspire others to reflect on their own life stories, to look backward in order to look forward with greater focus on the things that matter. Embedded in all your stories too, are significant signposts that point to what is worth pursuing in life and what is not, what is of lasting value and what disintegrates. These are lessons that provide hope and help for others, worth passing on to those who also seek a meaningful life.

Bill and I would be honoured to have you enter our stories, to live with us and with the people of Papua New Guinea, the Caribbean and South America, India and Nepal, Africa, Southeast Asia and Kosovo. Enter and learn, identify with their concerns, and then go back to your own stories and live with gratitude for who you are, for what God has gifted to you and for what you can share with others. By recognizing the extraordinary gift that life really is, may we all be encouraged to make the most of it.

One note for our American readers—you may have already noticed that, as a Canadian, I have chosen to use the spelling style of British Commonwealth countries. This may seem unusual or even archaic, but thank you for accepting this as part of our uniqueness, which may be lost one day as social media homogenizes the English-speaking world!

A Timeline of significant events in our lives:

1969: Bill graduated Medical College at University of Alberta, Edmonton, we married and moved to Calgary for Bill's internship and Sharon's first year of teaching.

1970: A year of travel and volunteering in Dominica, West Indies and Tanzania, with travel to South America, Europe, Ethiopia, India and Southeast Asia in between.

1971: To Calgary, to the same school for Sharon, Bill started a private family practice.

1974: First baby, Timothy, changed our routines.

1976: Second, Tera-Lynn, completed our family, now living on a farm outside Calgary.

1978: Ukarumpa, Papua New Guinea, one year that became eight.

1979: Kainantu, PNG where Bill was Medical Superintendent at a small government hospital and Assistant Dean of the College of Allied Health Sciences; Sharon was at home with kids and did volunteer work as opportunity arose with medical students and hospital.

1982: Goroka, PNG for the job of Provincial Health Officer for the Eastern Highlands Province, responsible for all the health facilities, budget and staff of the province. Sharon again had many volunteer involvements as both kids were in school.

1982-84: Sharon did MA in Education by extension from Azusa Pacific Univ, Seattle

1986: Transition back to Calgary, Canada

1987: Opened a family practice in South Calgary

1988: Co-founding CUPS 'street clinic' in downtown Calgary.

1989: Opening of a multi-disciplinary medical clinic, Health Plus, in South Calgary. As part of this, Sharon and two physiotherapists ran a business called Health Plus Preventative Care.

1990: A two-week medical mission trip to Dominican Republic with our two teenagers

1992: Two-week trip to Dominica, West Indies, with five other teens, for a health research project looking at lifestyle related diseases

1994: First trip to Albania

1996: To South Africa to look at medical IT needs there

1997: Requested by Samaritan's Purse to teach at a 'Barefoot Doctors' School in Chiang Mai Thailand and to help with curriculum development. First introduction to Community Health Education (CHE) by a US couple, and we were excited with the approach and resources.

1997: First trip to Nepal, with Kelowna based Hope for the Nations

1998: Sent back to Nepal by Samaritan's Purse Canada, to teach church workers requesting health knowledge. On the way, at a conference in Bangkok, met Stan Rowland (founder of the CHE strategy) with Medical Ambassadors International and Darrow Miller then Vice President of Food for the Hungry. We were impacted by their teaching, which helped us see the impact of worldview and of whole people as integrated within themselves and their communities.

1998: Did the CHE training, in July near Victoria, BC.

1998: Third trip to Nepal, first of many trips to Myanmar

1999: War in Kosovo. With Samaritan's Purse Canada to their Albania refugee camp, then to Kosovo. We continued there for another year in three- to four- month blocks ending late 2000.

2000: After doing the CHE training, we began to connect more with Medical Ambassadors International (MAI). They asked if we would go to Papua New Guinea to meet with the Health Department to determine if this CHE approach would enhance their primary health goals. This began our long and positive involvement with MAI and the influence of their leadership team from around the world who we meet regularly.

2000: Facilitated the first Vision Seminars in Eastern Highland Province in two districts.

2001: Returned to PNG to conduct the first Training of Trainers workshop in Goroka. Also visited Myanmar to connect with groups that had started doing CHE there.

2002: On-going involvement in PNG to the present. Initially trips were twice a year for two-three months each time, plus several times to Solomon Islands, Vanuatu and Fiji at the invitation of interested groups.

2003: More trainings in PNG, a second trip to East Timor to conduct a TOT and to Kiribati.

Asked by MAI to take a more formal role as Regional Coordinators for Southeast Asia and West Pacific. This involved regular visits and training multiple development organizations in nine Southeast Asia countries as well as the Pacific. It also meant planning a yearly conference for CHE team leaders of the entire region where they could share and compare, and learn as new materials were developing.

2003: It became clear we needed to spend more time abroad than was realistic with an active Calgary medical practice. So Bill decided to retire early from his practice.

2004 onwards: Continued to serve up to eight months of the year, with Bill doing a few locums in the summer months either at the CUPS clinic or the Health Plus medical clinic.

2005: Organized a nation-wide HIV/AIDS conference in PNG for pastors and other leaders of every church organization in the country, with two keynote speakers from Africa.

2008: Initiated annual meetings of wholistic development groups in PNG, which later became known as the umbrella group EDEN (Effective Development Empowering the Nation). EDEN-CHE was accepted as the preventive strategy for Christian Health Services

2010: Nagaland, NE India twice, training Nagaland Baptist Church

2012: Mizoram, NE India to the Myanmar border to train Health and Hope Society

2014: Tacloban, Leyte Province in Philippines after the strongest typhoon in history, with on-going involvement there both at the municipal health level and Regional referral hospital.

2015: By this time local CHE leaders had become strong in the countries of Southeast Asia and PNG and our active training was less needed. Globally, CHE had spread through almost a hundred countries and over 200 organizations had adopted the model.

2015-present: Bi-annual visits to Southeast Asia and PNG to encourage and workshops as needed. Our current role with MAI is that of 'Technical Advisers in Health Systems and Special Projects.'

INTEGRATION

Integration is bringing diverse parts into a unified whole that is stronger than any of the parts alone. We are integrated beings—physical, spiritual, emotional and social—sharing the strength of others near us through common language, experiences and customs, while valuing differences. Human flourishing needs whole people in whole communities that reach outside the margins to the neglected, ostracized and ignored.

CHAPTER 1

Worldview Matters: Good witch doctor, bad witch doctor

Papua New Guinea, 1984

I had hoped that these sub-titles would stand out more. I had indented them in the original manuscript, but what about increasing the font size by 1 point or even .5 point? Will that work in the formatting? "I've got it!" exclaimed the consultant, stopping mid-stride as he and Bill walked down the sidewalk in main street Goroka. Dodging the clamouring vendors peddling carvings, reed baskets and colourful string bags to the few tourists who somehow found their way here, my husband, Bill, felt at home on these streets. This small capital city of Eastern Highlands Province in Papua New Guinea was where we lived and where Bill had served as a medical doctor and head of the Provincial Health Department for the previous two years.

"Got what?" returned Bill to the consultant's exclamation.

"I've got what made that tidy, clean village so different from the others!" He was looking triumphant now.

Bill and the Asian Development Bank consultant from France had been seeking 'facts on the ground' of the real health condition of people in the remote Eastern Highlands villages for which Bill as Provincial Health Officer was responsible. That had involved a morning in a helicopter, skimming the mountain ridges where villagers built to be safe from enemy tribes. From the hovering helicopter vantage point, the villages looked quite idyllic, invisible in dense jungle until suddenly spirals of smoke would be spotted, and grass-roofed bamboo huts would emerge. Coming closer, some of the huts would look like they were on fire as billowing smoke poured out the sides and roof. Bill had assured the visitor that this was just the smoke of indoor cooking fires escaping through the chimneyless thatch. The smoke, of course, has health impact—terrible respiratory effects for the women and children who sit in it for hours.

As the Canadian doctor and French consultant landed in village after village that had looked so serene from the air, evidence on the ground showed otherwise. Here they saw the kinds of conditions that breed disease and death—not just the smoke-filled dusty huts with dirt floors, but lack of toilets, contaminated water supplies, gardens three hours from the homes and often water for washing and cooking almost that far. All this resulted in overworked women and undernourished kids.

And the pigs! Pigs digging up the paths and gardens, defecating everywhere, pigs living with the people, even baby piglets being suckled by human mothers who should have been giving the precious milk to their babies. The children's skin reflected the lack of hygiene—scabies, fungal infections, oozing sores. The European visitor was appalled and discouraged. After all, the money coming into the country's health system was supposed to be changing this!

Then they came to a village that seemed to have been miraculously transformed, like it had been transported from a different world. The houses were the same, but they were organized into orderly compounds that were fenced from the pigs, with neat hedges and flowers growing along the pathways. There were windows for ventilation, clean and healthy-looking children shyly peeking out and giggling at the amusing white strangers. Clean water was being piped through hollow bamboo poles from a spring a couple of kilometers up the mountain from the village.

A church dominated Tainoraba village, but not just a church—in the back of the church building was a small health post. The pastor had been trained in health education and the dispensing of simple medicines. Pastor Danusa, a humble and unrecognized man, was the catalyst for the transformation. He had begun by initiating toilets to replace open defecation, and next the piped in water. These two seeming small activities sparked a generation of healthy children who before had been oozing with infections just like those in the other villages. What a breath of fresh air, finally!

On the journey back, the two men discussed how the fear of spirits, sorcery and taboos, which have so captivated the minds of the people, reflect in practices that lead to destructive behaviour—like isolating women in labour to give birth alone in a hut outside the village, or refusing to use toilets. Other beliefs prevent them from understanding that diarrheal sickness can come from drinking contaminated water or preparing food with dirty hands. To them, angering the spirits, or breaking a taboo or sorcery are more likely reasons for illness to occur.

Like these villagers, we all have our worldview biases as we engage in the logic of analyzing life's questions. How we go about determining causes and effects depends on what we have been taught from babyhood on, and this leads us to look for what will support those assumptions even if the evidence would bring different conclusions. The French adviser was still working through his own assumptions.

Later that afternoon, back in Goroka, Bill and his visitor were both deep in thought as they walked down the street, when the consultant had his 'eureka moment'. He knew the explanation for the difference he had seen.

"Oh yeah," Bill queried, "What do you think is the reason for the difference?"

His answer was not complicated: "That good village has simply exchanged a bad witch doctor for a good witch doctor!"

"Well," Bill mused, "that's an interesting kind of terminology, one the pastor would not likely have used to explain his hard work or the people's change of heart from his teaching!"

But it did give a simple black-and-white framework to explain the difference in a world where the spirits reigned.

Good witch doctor, bad witch doctor. In other words, the belief system that captivates our mind will work itself out in the way we live, eat, look after our bodies and care for our children. Ideas have consequences!

Over the next few years, these thoughts would continue to germinate, and ultimately affect the much longer journey our lives would take. At the time, our response was to initiate what we called a

Village Level Worker School, to train more of these village pastors in basic preventative health measures, water and hygiene systems and some agricultural improvements for their communities. It carried on while we were there to encourage it, and had some effect to be sure.

But this was 1984 post-independence Papua New Guinea in the optimism of the first decade as a nation free from Australia's colonial administration. The big push from all quarters was to see health statistics improve, which health professionals worldwide assumed meant more health facilities. As Provincial Health Officer for a large province of around 400,000 people, my husband was part of that push. The goal was to see a health facility of some kind within one hour walk of everyone, even though much of the mountainous province was so remote that villages could be accessed only by many days on foot or by helicopter. But how else, they all reasoned, would we see improvement in infant mortality rates of 77:1000 (as comparison, it is 4:1000 in Canada) or maternal mortality rates of 1:1000, some of the worst in the world. These kinds of measurements are reliable indicators of a country's health care system.[1]

World Bank. Asian Development Bank. Australian AID. They were all there and anxious to loan or give money to build health centres and training facilities. Bill had his Five Year Plan in place when this Asian Development Bank consultant had showed up to help draft a plan. "We already have one," Bill told him bluntly, "and if you are here to work with us on it then you are welcome. If not don't waste your or my time!"

The surprised consultant agreed to work with him on reviewing and implementing it. But first Bill wanted him to see from the air how spread out the villages were and how the geography had to be the deciding factor in planning where health facilities were to be located. This was somewhat different from the agenda of Asian Development Bank that thought a few big facilities were the answer.

The consultant was not quite prepared for what he saw that day from his brief bird's eye tour. Nor had his French education taught him about witch doctors! He had not seen them in action, nor did he really know what their influential role in the community might be. He could only imagine that a bad witch doctor did not have a healthy role, if the goal was to see healthy communities. True enough!

University of Alberta Medical Faculty in Edmonton had not prepared Bill for a culture of witch doctors either! The awareness of the deeper issues that had to be addressed was a steep personal learning curve. Who would have known that in so many tribal cultures, the sorcerer and the healer are one and the same person?

Traditional medical school had prepared Bill adequately for caring for the mainly white missionary community that first brought us to Papua New Guinea six years earlier, but not for what we found beyond the enclosed compound. The profound contrast between the westerners and the surrounding communities had intrigued us after a visit to the nearby government hospital. The abysmal condition of the hospital, the unfairness of the lack of good health care, the training of rural doctors that happened here, all presented an exciting challenge. We applied to the PNG Health Department to return at the end of our initial year and our lives did a right angle turn. What we had intended to be a one-year sabbatical turned into seven years and experiences that changed the trajectory of the rest of our lives.

Would the future hold more 'good witch doctors' replacing 'bad witch doctors'? That was hardly a defined goal, but we knew real change starts in the hearts and minds of people. On that day in Papua New Guinea all those years ago, Bill was able to show one French consultant what an 'idea in action' looked like. If one village could embrace a new idea with visibly life changing impacts on the physical, social and spiritual lives of its people, where else could such ideas take root? We had found our calling!

The seemingly unrelated random experiences of life are not just interesting excursions, they may be what change the entire trajectory of the rest of our days.

The Mentality of the Jungle, Venezuela 1971

It was a brief visit to the headwaters of the Orinoco River in Venezuela in 1971 that opened our eyes to the respect and influence of the tribal witch doctor, or medicine man, in a community. After our first year of marriage we had taken a year to travel and work our way around the world. Bill had finished his medical internship in Calgary, and I was able to take a year leave of absence from teaching with the Calgary Board of Education. We began 'cutting our teeth' for tropical culture and medicine with three months in a small rural hospital in Dominica in the West Indies. This was a medical assistance program jointly sponsored by Canadian Executive Services Overseas and the Canadian Medical Association. We thoroughly bonded with the people and the work and regretted when the three months was up. We had time afterwards to travel for two months before we were expected at a mission hospital in Tanzania.

So South America was next in the plan, but the remote headwaters of the Orinoco River happened by serendipity! We accepted the advice of a young couple we met in Caracas, Venezuela, who thought we should visit their colleagues working in a remote tribal area in the Amazon territory. It is hard to believe our presumption now, just dropping in like that!

The journey from Caracas to the south of Venezuela entailed a five-hour flight on a DC 3, rated in hindsight as our top worst flight ever! It seemed to last an eternity, the rough weather making the plane bounce and creak all over the sky until it felt like it was going to shake apart. We were sure this ancient plane had reached its lifespan and was going down! Besides, the flight attendant's announcement did not instil confidence. In the pre 9/11 era of loose security, the usual "fasten your seatbelts" was followed by "If you are carrying a gun or any other weapon, please check it with the flight attendant now and it will be returned at the end of the flight!" All spoken with a courteous smile!

Amazingly, the plane landed us safely in dusty, barren Puerto Ayacucho in the Amazon territory of southern Venezuela. The frontier town of about seven thousand population led to the dense jungle land bordering Columbia and Brazil. Here where many small rivers become the Orinoco River connected by a natural canal to the headwaters of the Amazon River, numerous Aboriginal tribes with strange sounding names like the Guiacas, Piaroas, Guujibos and Moquiritares had made their homes for centuries.

I had heard some of these names when I enrolled in an Anthropology of South America elective course in university, but little did I dream of someday seeing their cultures first hand and sleeping in a hammock in one of the longhouses the professor told us about! Neglected and often ostracized from citizenship, these were truly people outside the margins of their society. Still are. The health care and education of these tribes was at that time almost non-existent. After all, who wanted to leave the civilization of the cities to go into these isolated areas to bring basic health or education for people that were considered savages?

Who would do that? A small group of brave missionaries, that is who. They were trying to address these issues of neglect, first learning the languages and reducing the syllables to a written form. They knew that without a written language, advancing beyond warring and subsistence lifestyles was unlikely. Incorporating the Bible into their education approach would give the tribal society a vision for a humane ethic based on love and respect, rather than the treachery, witchcraft and killing that often characterized the heroes they venerated. We admired these missionaries, their sense of adventure, their commitment and their ability to make do without the usual comforts, as we experienced their generous hospitality and heard their stories for the next two days.

They told us about Frank and Bonnie (not their real names), a young couple of their group who had radio contact but rarely had been seen in Puerto Ayacucho over the past three years. They had just moved to a new location in the heart of Piaroa land and apparently had expressed a desire for medical help for the people. Nobody remembered a medical doctor ever coming to that region! They coaxed us to go, and before we could reconsider, they booked a Missionary Aviation Fellowship plane for us departing the very next day.

Unfortunately Frank's radio was broken, and could only receive but not transmit messages. Our hosts could not ask permission for us to visit, they could only inform! So the information of our visit was broadcast both morning and evening, hopefully ensuring that they would hear the message that a young Canadian doctor and his wife were flying in the next day! And, "Could you please send someone in a canoe to pick them up from the landing strip?"

Frank apparently screamed into the broken, now one-way radio "No! This is not a good time! Our canoe motor is broken! And this is a sensitive time in our efforts here, entertaining visitors will be a distraction." But his words were of no avail—the radio message just echoed in space! The two intrepid travelers were coming, ready or not, like it or not.

Fortunately a long dug-out canoe with a forty-five horsepower outboard motor was waiting to pick us up on our arrival. We found out later that they spent hours repairing the motor in order to rescue us from being left alone at the airstrip potentially for days, helplessly abandoned in the humid rain forest. We were glad to see them!

But jungle missionaries, we learned, are a resourceful lot, especially the second-generation kind like this lovely young American couple not much older than ourselves. They had just finished building their thatched palm, dirt floor house, and we helped them complete the outhouse when we arrived. They were anxious to start visiting the villages upriver. The opportunity to have a medical doctor on site may not happen for a long time, so they decided to make the best use of their uninvited guests and venture up the Paraguasa River where they had not gone before. These villages were the outermost reach of the Piaroa group whose language they spoke.

Frank in fact, had grown up in Venezuela, the son of missionaries. This was part of the territory he had explored in a helicopter search for the plane that had crashed four years earlier, killing his father. Up to that time, nobody knew that there were villages this far up river, but when they were spotted from the air, Frank vowed to return and make contact with them. He knew well the potential risks of new initiatives like this.

We were all well informed in those days of the murder of five such American missionaries fifteen years earlier in the epic event on a similar river in the jungles of Ecuador. Here the feared Waodani tribesmen speared and killed the men who landed their plane on the sandy bank near their village on an exploratory journey to befriend them, such as what Frank was intending to embark on now with the tribe on this river. The story had been told all over the world, and we knew that one of the wives, Elizabeth Elliott, along with Rachel Saint, a sister of one of the fallen men, had returned to live with the people who had caused the deaths of those they loved. The treachery and fear that had enslaved these people had been broken by the love of these courageous women. The story has been poignantly presented in a 2005 documentary movie, "The End of the Spear," by Steve Saint.[2]

Frank had studied and was now fluent in the language of the group he was living with, and already knew the longhouse culture—but also the dangers. Their lives had been threatened the last time they had ventured to a village further up river, as the seemingly friendly villagers started sniffing a 'jungle dope' called *yopo*, and worked themselves into a crazed all-night frenzy, debating whether they should kill the visitors sleeping in the hammocks at the far end of their longhouse. By the time an old woman came to inform Frank and his local guides of this plan, there was no escape even if they had wanted to brave the dark jungle at night.

Frank told us that he had remained anxiously awake the rest of the night, until the morning light finally dissipated the danger. When he asked his local guides, his own converts to the Christian faith, how they were able to sleep so soundly while he lay awake sweating in his hammock, they replied, "We knew if they killed us we would go to heaven, so why worry?"

Now several months later, Frank had decided to take his visitors along for the next encounter. But this time there was some white man's medicine to be of service! To us the naïve, it was another adventure. We grew up in rural Alberta, after all, where everyone could be trusted (well so we thought!), and a person's word was believed. Friendliness was next to godliness, and being a good neighbour taken for granted. What danger could there possibly be?

Late the next day, we found ourselves transported to another planet. We two white couples had set off in the long, dug-out canoe early that Sunday morning with several local guides, who were from a similar tribal group using a dialect of the language spoken up river. The day went by quickly with stops at several small villages, treating minor illnesses, and pulling the canoe through at least two sets of rapids. We relished the journey, and our companions let us try their six-foot long blow guns with the poison darts that they used to hunt the small animals that were their typical protein. We realized that we would require much more practice before depending on these for our daily rations!

Reaching the last remote village in the late afternoon, the world we found ourselves immersed in was even stranger than the clearing and jungle house of the missionaries where we had slept the two nights before. Here one longhouse, the communal home for the whole village, dominated the clearing and the only sign of life was a couple of small dogs.

After our guides called out greetings for a few minutes from the riverside where we had docked the canoe, a few children emerged from the longhouse. Then some women peeked out. Finally, deciding that no harm was apparent, the chief wandered towards us and others poured from the house. They were slight built people with black straight hair and high cheekbones highlighting sun baked brown faces. All were barefoot and clothed only in loincloths made from the cotton that they had grown and woven on primitive back-strap looms. The cloth was a natural off white in various shades of dirty, except for those dyed red to signify the menstruating women. There were about seventy-five people here, apparently large for a Piaroa village. The chief was known to be the fiercest along the river, stubbornly refusing to be influenced by tribesmen further downstream who had sold out to traders and loggers, choosing instead to live as they had for thousands of years. He introduced himself as Bonifacio, a name given him by some Spanish traders. We were invited up near the longhouse for the first very guarded exchange of words. He was fascinated that Frank spoke his language!

Soon curious children, the most trusting world over, were shyly trying to touch the two white ladies. Gradually getting braver, they took our hands, felt the texture of our clothes and touched our long smooth hair, such contrasts to the coarse dark hair cropped around their faces in a kind of 'bowl-cut' bob. Children, women and men all had the same haircut—conformity was obviously a value. At first we could not figure out why they were examining the underside of our wrists with such interest, and then we realized how unusual it must look to see white under the forearm and the tanned browner skin on top! In fact, the translators told us, they were calling us 'snake people' because of this two-toned skin phenomena! Also, when they listened to us speak English it seemed there were a lot of 's' sounds, which were less common in their mother tongue. Of course the nickname 'snake people' was perfectly logical!

After about an hour, the ice broken by the children and small talk, we were invited inside the longhouse for reprieve from the oppressive afternoon sun and some serious talk. Even in broad daylight, the interior of the one-hundred-foot longhouse was dark, both by the smoke of cooking fires and the lack of windows. In fact the only light in the building was from the open doorway and a few rays that shone through cracks in the thatched roof and woven bamboo walls.

Our eyes grew accustomed to the dim light and we were curious to observe the communal home. While the building was one big space, each family unit seemed to have their own area and their own cooking fire. This contributed to the constant smoke inside, as embers had to be kept alive day and night. Hammocks were tied back against the sidewalls during the daytime, with babies being rocked in the few that were down. Silently the people made their way to the area near the doorway where the strange visitors were gathered.

The only people given seats on the traditional small three-legged stools were the chief with his medicine man, obviously second in importance, on one side, with Frank and his 'medicine man' Bill, on the other! The chief's warriors and the rest of our entourage dutifully stood as though rehearsed, on their respective sides behind the leaders. It seemed surreal to me, like a scene out of a movie. Surely we must be just actors, part of a script that some clever producer had thrust into our hands? Somehow my mind harked back to Father Lacombe and the first settlers in our Canadian history, in their initial interactions with the local First Nations chiefs and warriors! Frank confided that without the credibility of having his 'medicine man' with him, there would have been much less cordiality here!

So first came the 'peace pipe' routine—in this setting it was a carved wooden bowl of cassava mixed with water. I wrote in my journal, *"Cassava is a root that is scraped, baked into a large flat cake and tastes like coarse sawdust soaked in water! This is their main staple, along with their hunting of monkeys, tapirs, laupas (large rat-like animals) and fish."*

Frank explained that the sharing of the cassava bowl was a good sign, as it indicated that our presence was being welcomed. The bowl was passed from person to person, and everyone took a sip of the chalky liquid (or faked it in my case!). The bowl kept going around and around until it was empty.

This was followed by short cautious exchanges of words that we assumed were explaining our purpose in coming: to get to know them and to offer help for any who were sick. While that offer was not readily accepted, still they invited us to sleep the night with them. Hospitality seemed easy in such a setting—as there were no partitions in the whole long building, all that was needed was to move their hammocks a bit to make room for us to hang ours! We had already eaten enough from the food we had brought along, so before the cool darkness of the jungle was upon us, between 6:30-7:00 pm, we all had our spots and were comfortably hanging in place. Quiet descended, as the noisy jungle birds, monkeys and insects had apparently also found their spots for the night.

The air grew quite cold, and as they had neither clothing nor blankets, the need for the all-night stoking of fires was obvious. I do not recall loud voices or noisy commotion as one might expect considering the number of people crammed inside—eighty or more of us! The adults spoke in hushed tones and it seemed that any loud talk or arguments must take place outside. Children and adults both settled in to sleep at about the same time, the rhythm of the setting and rising sun their only clocks.

That night, so long ago and so unlike any other, is still indelibly stamped in our memories. The ubiquitous smoke lasted the night, as small fires were tended for the warmth they afforded. The dogs seemed to never settle in one place, and at least one nearby pet parrot talked to us off and on, in an unintelligible tongue of course! There was the constant rustling of movement accompanied by hushed voices, as people got up from their hammocks to go out to relieve themselves, or to quiet a stirring child or to tend the fires. Soft breathing, noisy breathing, outright snoring…and then there was the coughing, the coughing and spitting! That is when we realized the extent of the respiratory illnesses here, whether tuberculosis or pneumonia we did not know, but we could see how the rapid spread of such an illness was certain in these crowded living conditions. Bill resolved that morning would bring the opening of his black bag and injecting some penicillin!

Sure as dawn, the long night ended and I wondered if I had slept! But that did not matter. The sense of shared humanity, of appreciation for the struggle to survive with just what they could make or grow for themselves, of the beauty of simplicity and the sufficiency of interdependence—my soul felt these in the darkness in a way I was unable to see in the light of day. Without need for books, study or even reflection, I was being impacted.

It is interesting now to ponder how, even with the quiet and calm of the early morning giving the appearance that all was well, we never questioned whether this tribe would be better off left alone as some would argue. Is it really better, we would now ask, to be left to murderous raids from neighbouring tribes wanting more land or slaves, left to the totally preventable diseases that rob the infants and children that should form their next generation?[3] Would they be better off left to their fears of evil spirits and numerous taboos, left to the mercy of outside forces that exploit their forests and land rights? Is survival of the fittest really the law of the universe?

Our answer now, even more than in 1970, would be to rebel against the 'leave the happy native alone' lie, which really means leave them to extinction. It is extreme cultural abuse, not cultural preservation that is at stake for groups that are left to retreat further into the jungles to be left alone. Sure, some well-meaning attempts to help have left too many western footprints or brought disease to which they had no immunity. But those greedy to exploit seem to still find them. Developers rape the rainforests of their protective canopy in many places and push the vulnerable hunter-gatherers from their habitat. Even after we have observed much 'botched aid' and mistaken efforts to help, we would still have to answer, "No!" We must not turn our backs and walk away with arrogant philosophical ideas that they will eventually work it out themselves. After all, our own ancestors could not have developed without printed language, schooling, healthcare advances and not least the lessons from The Book that transformed society once it was translated into the common languages.[4]

It is cultural abuse, not cultural preservation that is at stake with those who propose to "leave the happy natives alone". We must not turn our backs and walk away to let the next generations continue to suffer.

So morning brought the offer of treatment for the man who had coughed and spit all night, and he willingly agreed to the injection of long acting penicillin. The chief himself had a small sore that he asked to have treated. The medicine man was very intrigued with the process and wanted some of the medicines in Bill's black bag for himself. In the end, several people were treated, some antibiotic ointment and bandaging materials left with the medicine man along with some use instructions, and in exchange Bill went away with a monkey skull and some of the powders used by the medicine man!

It was not until much later back home, after carrying the relics in our bags around the world through numerous airports of the day, it occurred to us that the so-called 'dope', the white *yopo* powder the young men were sniffing outside in the clearing, might be an illegal drug similar to cocaine—so needless to say, we disposed of those powders from the medicine kit! In doing some study later, we learned that it is a hallucinogenic powder made from the crushed seeds of a leguminous tree, which is then mixed with ash and lime and sniffed. The women do not take part in the drug culture rituals, which some describe as a means by which the shaman keeps the men in their control both to maintain social harmony within the tribe and to work up courage for raids on their neighouring tribes. As in many cultures, the women are needed to maintain the real stability and act out of concern for their family's well being.

Long after leaving these jungles, we kept pondering the potential for basic health education training for people like this medicine man and the chief, who had obvious power of influence in their communities. That would have to wait for years later in our journey, as we were still steeped in the mindset of the Western curative medical model. We had miles to travel and much to learn before such thoughts for training basic 'practitioners' actually became strategies. As it turned out, Papua New Guinea was going to teach us!

First though, we would be thrust into another mission culture, that of an African Mission hospital in Tanzania, before being immersed again into the world we had grown up with—only now with confused wondering as to which was in fact the 'real' world? Had we been permanently changed in any way? Would we just go back home and continue with the busyness of our own culture, teaching Canadian teenagers and growing a thriving medical practice, starting a family? Many of us have great, meaningful cross-cultural experiences like this, but what long-term impact do they have? We desperately wanted to remain sensitive to global issues, but how quickly they faded as we were swept back into Canadian life.

Still as we look back, we could not have done what was to come later in Papua New Guinea without the credentials gained by the next eight years at home. For Bill that involved starting a new family medicine practice in a suburban strip mall office, constructing a clinic with a team of other professionals, serving as Chief of Medical Staff at a large Calgary hospital and being involved in teaching first year medical students as an Adjunct Associated Professor of Family Medicine. All these honed his people-skills, leadership and entrepreneurial experience that would become useful later. Life, as we will note again, like Lego building blocks that interconnect to form some interesting shape, is a series of experiences that each build on something that went before. Our futures are always connected with the past, informed by the successes, mistakes or acquired skills we gain. No experience, not even a failure, is ever wasted.

Ten years later—Kainantu, Papua New Guinea, 1981

The Kainantu hospital (called a *haus sik* in Melanesian Pidgin) in Papua New Guinea, was as basic as a small-town government hospital could be. We had returned on a government health department contract with our two adorable and inquisitive kids: Timothy, by then nearly five years and Tera-Lynn three. We looked forward to living longer in this beautiful and largely unspoiled land, following the previous one year 'sabbatical' on the large mission centre located just a few kilometers from Kainantu which we now called home.

This was the kind of work we had dreamed about, a job that seemed to suit Bill perfectly—CEO of the one hundred bed hospital and Assistant Dean of the College of Allied Health Sciences. The clinical instruction of second year paramedical students, who in two years would become the general medical practitioners of the rural health centres, was particularly rewarding. While this job would ultimately move Bill up the ladder to the Provincial capital of Goroka, and the challenging role of Provincial Health Officer, for these three years the work with students was exciting and fulfilling.

As a general rule, Bill had banned the local witch doctors from coming to practice their arts in the government hospital, which seemed reasonable enough. But on one occasion it appeared that the only way he could buy time to allow a woman with lethal cerebral malaria to stay on IV treatment in hospital, was to grant her family's wish that the village witch doctor come and try his solution. Bill did, however, insist that he would stay and observe so that nothing harmful would happen to his patient!

The health staff was keenly aware of the strongly-held premise of most village folk that all sickness has a cause—but not a cause such as bacterial as we have come to understand. No, it is due to a spiritual cause, a curse, a spell, an angry spirit, sorcery (locally referred to as *sanguma)* that has been worked against the sick person by someone who has a grudge to avenge. The so-called sorcerer may make a potion (which they call poison) of some kind, with leaves, bark, powder or even something from the person they want to curse, like nail clippings, hair of feces.

A premise held strongly by many village folk is that all sickness has a cause, not a cause such as bacteria as we have come to understand, but a spiritual cause, a curse, a spell, an angry spirit...

Some claim the sorcerer will put the person to sleep, cut them open and put stones or other foreign objects into them, which will eventually make them sick. Still other beliefs involve the sorcerer 'cutting out the heart of a person' while they sleep, in order to later eat it and thus gain more power.

Most often the person suspected of sorcery is a woman, and once identified, usually by divination of some kind, she is killed. They justify this action as preventing further deaths. It is another example of the terrible oppression and abuse of women in cultures such as this, which we will address further in another chapter.

The witch doctor and relatives who came to the hospital this day were determined. "The sick woman must tell who cursed her," they insisted. "Otherwise we will take her home."

The health centre staff knew that would mean death. Staying in hospital and receiving medication is all that could save her life. They were hedging their bets, hoping that by allowing the village traditional methods to fail, they would be able to continue her treatment.

So the witch doctor proceeded. After chewing up some 'magic leaves', he spit them out and made the woman eat the masticated slimy liquid. This he claimed was to give her clarity, to open her mind to remember who had done the terrible deed to her.

"Now think", he said, in their vernacular language, with the translator relaying it to Bill. "You were probably walking to your garden. Someone came along, grabbed you, put you to sleep and cut you into little pieces. She then put you back together and healed up the cuts so a few days later you got sick. Now who was it that did it to you?"

"No, that didn't happen", she moaned. "I just got sick."

"Who is mad at you for something?" he persisted. "That person hired a *sanguma* (sorcerer) to do this to you." Bill and the staff, who later confessed that they had been quietly praying, all held their breaths. They knew if she named someone, there might be two burials not one.

"No, there were no enemies. My head pains so much. I want the medicine from the hospital." She was desperate and lapsing in and out of consciousness, her fever raging.

The witch doctor gave one last attempt to convince her to focus her mind and remember who did this to her. "There are too many people and too much distraction around," he declared. "We need everyone to leave."

The staff and Bill relented and moved out of sight behind the doorway, where family members were also gathered. An interesting discussion ensued between them and Bill. Most of the people in that area were converts of the early Lutheran missionaries, so Bill asked them what the missionaries had taught about the divination that was being carried on inside the room.

"Oh, they taught us this was not right, and they would not allow us to do any kind of magic or sorcery," they all claimed. "They had other beliefs about where sickness came from."

"So what did you do? Did you leave your practices?" Bill questioned.

"Well not really, we just did it quietly, in secret, we kept our old beliefs and practices."

"So, you really did not believe the missionaries?" Bill's rhetorical question was met with silent acquiescence.

"After all," they continued, "this was what we had known from our ancestors, and at least it gave us some way to try to cure sick people."

Bill's reply stuck in his throat as the realization of their words hit him. There had not been a viable option presented to them, no alternative to a destructive belief system passed on to them from before time. Another defining moment in our own journey had just happened.

As the interesting discussion continued, the witch doctor finally emerged from the room. The patient had obviously not been forthcoming with the information he was looking for.

He turned to Bill. Speaking in the Melanesian Pidgin language that he knew Bill and the health staff understood, he announced, *"Dispela em i no sik b'long ples"* (This is not a village kind of sickness). *"Em i narapela kain sik b'long yupela."* (It's your kind of sickness). *"Em i mas stap long haus sik."* (She should stay in the hospital).

The husband and other family members were still standing around the bed, including the one who would sleep on the floor under the bed to be the hospital caregiver. They all nodded their approval. Bill and the health staff exchanged relieved glances and began to proceed with the life-giving medications that enabled her to survive. The witch doctor and village entourage left with due ceremony, back to the village.

As we later pondered that conversation with the villagers in the hallway, it seemed the villagers were emphasizing a very significant point for us. For so many in the developing world, animistic belief systems have provided for them their only options for explaining and attempting to cure the illnesses that they do not understand. How else could an otherwise healthy young man grow suddenly sick and die from what the medical people in the hospital call pneumonia, or TB or AIDS? There must be an explanation that they can get their minds around, something closer to home, something in their own life experience. There must be a way to control illness in the absence of 'white man's medicine'. Hence the very elaborate systems that get constructed in each culture, where their own belief systems, developed over centuries in the absence of other facts, explain events and illnesses in what we term supernatural ways.

An explanation of treachery leading to illness, such as described by the witchdoctor to the cerebral malaria patient in the Kainantu hospital, is to them as believable as our story of a 'bug' too small to be seen by human eyes that is carried and transmitted by a mosquito bite! In order to agree to take the prescribed malaria medicine, one must first have some faith in the story line. Mosquito is the villain, we tell them, not a vindictive or jealous neighbor who hires a 'poison man'. Why should they believe our story line above their own? Unless we attempt to understand the beliefs and values behind their practices, why should they listen to our ideas or try our cures?

Don't advance higher than your neighbour

Does this willingness to transition from the generational beliefs of the ancestors to the scientific view of the Westerner happen by education? Can education change beliefs? Maybe, but maybe it takes more than that, or so we have discovered.

More recently, in a lunch conversation with a couple of Papua New Guinean doctors who we had not seen for a few years, we asked how they were doing in their everyday lives. One, who was the chief health administrator of a province, told us that he was living on his traditional land, with good gardens but a rather run-down house. He had not upgraded his house even though he could afford it.

"Why is that?" we asked. "Surely your wife would like running water and a good stove!"

"Of course," he replied. "But the problem with living on our clan land is that we cannot appear to get ahead of others. That causes jealousy and someone will work sorcery to kill me."

"What!" exclaimed another of his colleagues, who himself comes from a district in the Highlands known for their strong sorcery. "Aren't we supposed to be educated people? And you still believe that?"

"Yes," replied the first doctor. "I know their power, and I have no power that can counteract it, in that I am not a church-going man."

We felt sad, knowing that he was the honest one, and that almost all of the others if pushed into a corner would bring their animistic beliefs off the shelf. These are the 'default' beliefs, confirmed biases, even though their intellect and reason tells them they cannot be true.

But are we much different, grasping at straws and anecdotal remedies when we feel desperate? How many supposed cancer 'cures' are tried to no avail? Who has not tried some untested potion just because it is 'natural' medicine? The billion-dollar food supplement business bears witness to our own anxious attempts for health without the work of nutritious whole food and exercise. So who are we to judge the strange and exotic, yet often harmful beliefs of our tribal friends?

Yet without addressing the worldview issues that are the real rulers in the way a culture reacts to events around them, progressive development towards full health and well being as we perceive it is impossible. How we think and what we believe really matters to the way we live.

The deeply rooted animistic belief system affects not only the aspects of life that cause or prevent illness, but also the way people work together, who it is that should be elected to positions of influence, where, how and why structures should be built, what crops to plant and where and when to plant them, what foods each person is allowed to eat, and who they can eat with, gender work roles...and the list goes on and on.

Worldview—Does it Matter?

Ideas shape the world of humankind. These ideas in turn have consequences on our world. As we look at where ideas come from and puzzle over how they shape and influence us, we have learned to look deeper, at roots—the worldview behind the ideas.

What is worldview, and why is it so powerful? Some describe worldview as the 'glasses' through which we perceive the events of our world. It is a set of perceptions of reality through which all events that happen around us are filtered. Without even realizing that we have a worldview, it affects the way we think and act about everything in life—our ideas about work, relationships, value of life, money, success, history, reality of God or a Supreme Being, death and what happens after, how government and leaders should function, morality and values like honesty, responsibility, loyalty, equality. It is the attempt in every culture to answer the two universal questions: Where did I come from? And why am I here?

Worldview goes even deeper than our values and beliefs. It is the trigger that touches our motivation, and ripples into what we treasure and desire most, to our behaviour and the consequences of that behaviour. We have come to realize through our interactions with cultures whose beliefs are different from ours, why an understanding of the worldview of the people where we are working is so critical. After all, the whole world may look different through their eyes than our own.

Personally, we had not given thought to the impact of worldview until we happened to attend a conference in Thailand in 1998, where Darrow Miller was the main speaker. He was at that time VP of Food for the Hungry International and had just authored a new book titled *'Discipling Nations: The Power of Truth to Transform Cultures'*.[5] He defined worldview simply:

> *Worldview is a set of assumptions held consciously or unconsciously in faith about the basic makeup of the world and how the world works.* [6]

Miller summarizes and simplifies prevalent worldviews into three categories: animism, theism and secularism. All worldviews, he states, can be found somewhere along a continuum with animism and secularism at either end, and with theism in the middle.[7]

In an attempt to give insight into the impact of worldview in the communities whose stories we share throughout this book, I will simplify even further. This is not an academic treatise, rather our observations in real life.

1. Animism: The first broad Worldview

Animism is the prevailing worldview of almost all pantheistic (a god or spirit for everything and in everything) folk religions of the world, as well as the more organized belief systems of Hinduism and Buddhism. Animists believe that the spiritual world is all that is real, and the physical world is simply illusion, or *maya*. Spirits inhabit everything in the natural world, and it is the spirits, gods or dead ancestors, that are in control. Animation, or life, is attributed even to inanimate objects such as rocks and rivers, moon and sun.

There are no 'accidents' to the animist. Everything has a spiritual cause, and anything negative that happens either individually or in nature, is a result of some action—angering or insufficiently appeasing a spirit, someone's curse, breaking a taboo. The ones who are the most powerful in these societies are those who have ways of influencing the spirit world, of interpreting it to others or of creating harm to an enemy—hence the power and influence of the witch doctor. Power is therefore of highest value, whether that is inherited or earned by influence, by heroics in battle, by treachery or even by bribery and corruption.

There are two other factors in animism that have made these cultures the least developed in the world. The first is fatalism, the idea that one's lot in life is pre-determined, and there is little motivation to move beyond that. Day to day survival is uppermost in importance, and dreams to improve life or advance out of poverty are not encouraged. In fact, to advance above one's peers, as we saw in the story of the Papua New Guinean doctor, risks upsetting the balance of the social structure.

The second factor is that the balance of power is towards the men, with women most often seen as of lesser importance. At worst, they are simply chattel to be used or abused and discarded. At best they are given fewer opportunities for education and advancement. We know now how devastating that is on society as a whole, as we will share in Chapter Five.

In applying animism at the community level, beliefs become glaringly important to health and well being in the population. If people believe that illness is caused by spiritual factors, then practical physical solutions will be a hard sell. If the worldview tells us that every individual is not equal, that men are more important than women or that a certain class of men are of more worth than others, then all our public health slogans of equality or women's health may go blindly unheeded. Health publicity campaigns and education talks in the marketplaces will have little lasting impact. Environments will not change without deeper motivation.

Nothing was a clearer description of the impact of an animistic worldview on a community than some brief interchanges we had while serving in Nepal.

The spirit of the highway wants blood!

It was 1998, and we had been asked to do some community health training in the central part of Nepal. The bus stopped for us to buy lunch at a small town en route, and we engaged in conversation with a shop owner. We remarked at the nice road that had recently been paved, which cut through the centre of the town. The shop owner looked sad as she told us, "Yes, it is nice, but on the other hand we have had so many children hit by the speeding cars and many killed, as everyone now drives faster through the town."

"So sorry to hear that," we replied. "How is the town planning to prevent this? Traffic lights, fences, speed bumps or what?"

"Oh no, nothing like that," she returned. "The people believe that the spirit of the highway is hungry for blood, so they are killing lots of chickens and goats and pouring the blood on the road. This we hope will appease the spirits and the children's blood won't be needed."

We were stunned! How could it be that a simple solution, like a fence and cross walk, or speed bumps, was not even a discussion point? The 'colour of the worldview glasses' totally blocked an obvious answer to what would continue to be tragedy for that community.

Some days later, in training a group of trainers we had worked with before in this area, more animistic worldview issues surfaced. We had decided that a practical demonstration of 'double-dig gardening' would be in order. Someone chose the garden plot to use, they accumulated some spades, others collected piles of composted manures, and the group was ready to start. The concept is to dig a trench the depth of the spade, setting the topsoil layer aside, then loosening the hard subsoil layer at the bottom of the trench with a fork (spade in this case as they did not have forks). This aerates the ground deeply so roots can go straight down. Compost follows and the topsoil is returned from the next trench, working this way all across the garden area.

One problem became obvious quite quickly: who would do the manual labour, the digging? The group was made up of several different castes, or the classes of their Nepali society! There was a Chetri, the upper priestly caste, a few high caste Brahman, and several of the tribal mountain groups which were considered low class. Who should work? We, as Canadians coming from a 'classless' culture, did not even realize there was an ideological dilemma going on. For us equality between human beings is not questioned, workload is based on physical strength and capabilities, not on an inherited or even conferred station in life. Especially not one ordained by the gods! Silly naïve outsiders!

Bill, being the eager and fit person he is, grabbed one of the shovels and started right in. I started mixing the manure. Others of the 'lower caste' in the group followed suit, with the rest looking on somewhat awkwardly. Someone joked about Bill's strong legs, as he was wearing hiking boots while they were wearing flip flops which just did not hit the shovel with the force that he did! We did not even realize the dynamics we had created until Bill decided it was someone else's turn to dig, and innocently handed the shovel to one of the high caste participants! It was obvious as he began to hesitantly dig in the trench that this was a totally new experience. There was giggling and good-natured jesting at his valiant good sportsmanship, but it was clearly not a job that was 'fit' for him! As I observed his upper arms, I realized with surprise that they were not developed with usual male muscle, but were thin and flabby. After generations of neglect, physical strength had long since disappeared from this class of men.

The inequality only got worse when we looked at gender issues. I had been watching manual roadwork being carried out everywhere we had gone in Nepal—by women. Not strong, well-nourished women. They were thin, frail, very sad-faced, yet resolutely carrying the large woven baskets of gravel or rock which hung down their backs by a large strap from their forehead. I truly didn't know whether to cry, to vomit, to yell, "foul" or to flee...I just knew it was deeply affecting me and I felt helpless.

So here in the village where we were doing the practical training, I watched as the building of a toilet was taking place. Rocks had to be stacked in the pit once it was dug to avoid it collapsing. Of course, that was the women's job and they seemed happy to do it, unlike the women I had observed doing roadwork for their living. The young women laughed and competed for how many rocks they could put in their baskets. When I asked to try, they put a couple of rocks in a basket and helped lift it to my head. My head almost snapped backwards with the strain it put on my undeveloped neck muscles!

"I see this is a developmental thing," I laughed, as I watched even the young girl children start carrying small loads with their small baskets. "I started at the wrong age!"

Walking the short distance with my pitifully small load, the rest laughed and loaded their ten or more big rocks. When Bill asked to try, and wondered aloud why only women did this work, they laughed uproariously! He of course did better than I did, but his neck still couldn't cope. And nobody got the point! Despite Bill's rather humorous demonstration that men might really be able to do the tougher physical labour, they were stuck in their generational pattern. Women were meant to bear the burden of the menial tasks of life. End of discussion.

Secularism: The second broad Worldview

The second broad and general worldview at the opposite end of the continuum is secularism, quite a natural fit for most of us growing up in the Global North world (as differentiated from the Majority world or Global South). While the animist sees reality as being ultimately spiritual, the secularist sees the physical world as the primary reality. The material world, the world of our five senses, that which can be proven by science, is all that is real. Morals are relative. Self- preservation is of highest value, and personal fulfillment overrules the common good. While consumerism has exploited both the people and natural resources of much of our world, our society feeds consumerism. Recent studies in Canada indicate that people are more concerned about buying cheap goods than about the working conditions of those who manufacture them.

At the same time as the addictive power of consumerism captivates us, fear of extinction, of using too much of the earth's limited resources haunts us. It is a tension of our own making.

In secularism, any spiritual world or 'supreme being' out there is unknowable and disinterested in the affairs of humans. While many secularists in our world today say that they believe in God, a Universal

Good, a Force or even a Christian belief system, the real 'god' is self. Man is the centre, and there are no limits to what we can achieve with enough effort.

Without a supreme God who is connected to humanity, or an eternal soul within each person, there are no absolute truths. Truth is relative for each generation. Morality is defined by each person or by the current drift of the societal thinking, often as promoted by media culture.

Many of us would be surprised if we were to really analyze our own motivation for showing compassion to others, for 'paying it forward' or 'giving back' in the current jargon. Is it still a selfish act—coming down to preservation of self or the world, an elevation of ego, or a belief that somehow good done will result in good coming back to me? Or maybe a touch of fatalism, a belief that our future 'karma' depends on ourselves and on what we do now?

Self-help books abound, and formulas for success in life have promoted the next step—to get whatever we want in life by associating with the people or situations that enhance us, to 'name and claim' the material things we desire. There are 'Universal Laws of Attraction' that govern our rise to success. Similarly, some confused Christian groups encourage this same ideology in the name of faith—now called 'prosperity gospel'. When taking these concepts to their logical conclusion, they may well begin to sound like a blend of the self-centeredness that embarrasses us about secularism and the animistic concepts of power and appeasement. The end goal is a distorted view of a God that can be manipulated by getting the formula right.

The current western Millennial cohort is being identified by self-centred individualism and materialism, while the same generation of materialists is growing even in countries that before were considered quite materially poor. Worldview shifts are happening—with economic and environmental impact yet to be determined!

Cambodia illustrates the point. Amidst the poverty of rural Cambodia, we have watched the educated young adults of the cities of Phnom Penh or Siem Reap spend their free time sipping lattes in one of the hundreds of coffee shops, their eyes glued to smart phones. These are luxuries, but elevation of status demands that one be seen in such places. We shudder at what we have brought to these countries! Rather than compassion for their disadvantaged country folk, or a passion to work for progress for the country as a whole, we have modeled self-focused comfort. Working for the common good is only good if it pays well!

Thailand, Malaysia, Indonesia, Philippines—all across Southeast Asia we are surprised by the high degree of consumerism, brought by our own generation of Westerners. We all worship the god of consumption that seems never satisfied. One only has to visit Chiang Mai or Cebu with their numerous opulent mega malls full of high-end shops, to realize that there is a growing appetite among the young secular generation to see the highest advancement of culture as being the pursuit of self. Who cares that the rich are getting richer while the poor get poorer?

Monotheism: The third broad Worldview

This third general worldview, I will call monotheism to be differentiated from general theism. It can be divided into several branches—Islam, Judaism, and Christianity being the main ones. All three share a common belief in one Supreme and compassionate God who created the earth and life in some manner. By creating man and woman in His image and likeness and asking them to care for His world, He remains intricately involved in His cosmos.

In the Biblical theism of the Jew or Christian, men and women were created equal, and the chief goal and purpose of mankind is to learn to know and love this God, and to grow more like Him. This Creator-God values creativity, reason and choice. He desires people to choose good over evil, to advance and develop the talents and abilities they have been given, to use their intellect for the common good, to work hard for family and community, doing good to others as they would do to themselves. He extends grace, second chances (or more), understanding and forgiveness. The concept of grace, defined as undeserved and unearned favour experienced and extended, is glaring in its absence in other get-what-you-deserve worldviews. It seems backwards to claim that joy in life is derived from giving rather than consuming, from serving rather than being served, from building others up rather than elevating self. These are the qualities that God identifies in Himself, and by emulating these through the help of His Spirit, humanity is living in fulfillment of their purpose in life. They become bearers of His image and likeness on this earth, His caretakers of the natural world.

Hope for the present and the future characterizes this worldview. There is no room for unabated pessimism, for despair for the world or its resources, or for neglect of those less fortunate. The task of humanity is to seek relational restoration of what God intended, which must direct us then to reconciling relationships between ourselves and God, each other and the natural world.

As we reflect on this description of Biblical theism, the link with human development is fairly obvious. Ideas have consequences—equality for all, the elevation of the status of women, caring for the environment while seeking improved ways of planting crops or building homes or treating the sick, developing the arts and music and scientific advances. After all, the God who seeks to know and be known has given creative and intellectual powers for mankind to develop with peace and goodwill. The world of reason and science flourish in this worldview.

Islam shares similar versions of the two Great Commandments to "Love the Lord your God with all your heart and with all your soul and with all your strength and with all your mind" and "Love your neighbour as yourself". These are articulated in the teaching of Jesus[8] as well as in the Muslim oral tradition (*hadith*) where Muhammad states that "None of you has faith until you love for your neighbour what you love for yourself." [9] However, in the more systematized approach of Islam, the prescribed routines and set ways of following what they interpret as the will of Allah, there is little need for reasoning what His will might be in each situation.[10] Lack of encouragement of creative problem solving or of doing old things in a new way has slowed development in most of the countries where Islam dominates. Fatalism and gender imbalance, as in animism, have impacted development in the Muslim world.

Ideologies on the move

So the lines between these three over-generalized worldviews are blurred, as animism influences many theistic countries, as the pervasiveness of secularism touches the whole world and as the movement of people today carries divergent worldviews everywhere. Theists in Muslim,

Christian and Jewish camps are in many ways 'functional' secularists, living in real time differently than what they claim to believe. In other places Christianity is a thin veneer over an animistic underlying centuries-old foundation. The actions determined by all these belief systems impact health and ultimately how we live together.

There is a definite correlation between what a society believes at its core and its process of development. For modern secular societies that have been founded on theistic roots, growth and development has flourished. For coming generations, as these roots are forgotten or ignored, we can only guess what their future will look like. Countries like China on the other hand, which tried unsuccessfully for several generations to wipe out religion of all kinds, has looked at developed countries and realized that they could never have evolved in an ideological vacuum. Ideas matter. Evidence of that searching is growing; today in China there are millions of Christians, estimates impossible to determine accurately but ranging from fifty to one hundred million, possibly more than the number of Communist party members. There are burgeoning worldview changes with huge implications—but that story will be for our children's children to write.

Confronting Cracks in a Worldview—Papua New Guinea, 2010

There are times in our lives when we come against a brick wall, an issue that stares us down so we cannot move beyond it. Such was the case of a group of leaders in the Duna valley of Papua New Guinea who knew that their lack of development was largely the fault of beliefs that were keeping them in poverty. They were beginning to understand the concept of integration, the interactions between the physical, the spiritual and the diverse social dynamics of life.

They live in a world of sorcery, where someone must be blamed for a death or misfortune in the community, resulting in senseless revenge killing and endless rounds of compensation payment demands that keep the communities cash-poor. Tribal warfare also requires money, as villages endeavour to buy more illegal guns than the others. Useful productivity is compromised as capital is hard to come by and conflict wastes valuable time.

Our daughter and son-in-law, Tera and Zach Jones, worked here for two years under the direction of the Governor of the Eastern Highlands Province. Their initial focus in the Duna Valley was to bring reconciliation and development to an area of continuous tribal fighting—a tall order. The Governor dubbed it the 'Happy Valley' development project, and money was to bring the solutions. We all realized that was too simple. The foundations of Community Health Education, where each community takes ownership of their own issues under the leadership of a committee, was a necessary first step to any lasting change.

Unlike some of our initiatives where one responsive village is singled out for attention and training, it was apparent that all thirty-two villages had to be simultaneously involved or jealousy and conflict would be unavoidable. So the project began with leadership training for a committee of the respected headmen of each village. Just getting them together was an effort, as the road that ran through the valley was only partially passable; several bridges needed reconstruction, and many of the villages were several hours walk from the road.

We were impressed with the sincerity of this leadership committee, made up of men and a couple of women, who were tired of fighting and living in backwardness and who desperately wanted to see peace and progress. They had begun to understand that their animistic beliefs were not serving them well, and asked that Bill and I come to do a workshop on animism. Most of them were Christians, some even pastors. They wanted to confront their ancestral beliefs, lay them out in the open, and brainstorm how to deal with them!

In preparing for a workshop that aims for maximum group participation, we follow a set format—starting with an impromptu role-play using a humorous scenario reflecting a real problem relevant to them. That is followed by an animated discussion as they recount what they saw in the role-play, and how the same situation occurs in their own context. The scenario was not difficult to come up with, as we knew many of the local customs and beliefs. For this particular role-play, the two ad-lib actors were men leaving church and discussing the great sermon. Then one of them remembered that he had to hurry home before dark to shut up all the windows. This was urgent, as the previous night a firefly had flown in an open window, surely a bad omen for his family and possibly heralding a death. The other man agreed, and the two parted. End of story; beginning of very lively discussion!

Next we divided participants into four groups to talk and list all the practices and beliefs from their various villages under four main categories: animistic beliefs and rituals around death; beliefs about the spirits of the dead; spirits of nature; practices of magic, sorcery and healing.

Everyone got right into the task! We just walked around the room, watching as these 'Christian-animists' filled up large sheets of flip chart paper in writing their lists. They laughed nervously at themselves as now they were seeing in their own handwriting the practices that even to them were so bizarre. Some of the beliefs were fairly common to all of them, others were unique to one particular clan and were totally unknown to the others. Some were scary and occultist, some just crazy superstitions, some were deadly. They were sparing nothing, as each gave courage to the others to talk openly, bringing everything into the light.

After each group posted their papers on the wall and explained their lists, there was silence in the room. The gravity and the weight they began to feel as the multitudes of beliefs were spoken aloud was almost palpable. Somehow seeing the practices all written on paper in black and white took away the mystery, the secrecy, the fear. Instead they were disgusting.

Then as these leaders discussed the physical, emotional, social and spiritual impact animistic practices were having on their families and communities, they became convinced that they had a responsibility to become the agents of change. These beliefs, they decided, were the main factor keeping them in poverty. One of our trainers shared the effect in her own family of a grandmother who had borne the accusation of being a sorcerer, and of her Christian father who renounced all such beliefs. He forbade the children to listen to accusing 'sorcery talk' or to try to frighten each other with the scary stories of the village. We could see that her personal story was having impact, as all present knew and respected her father, and observed her confidence and freedom to move from place to place as an educated woman teaching others.

As they were Christians, we had one of them read the list of occult practices from Deuteronomy 18, which God declared detestable. Israel was being warned not to follow these practices when they settled in their Promised Land after years of nomadic wandering. The Duna leaders were stunned and sobered as they realized that all of those "detestable practices" were found in their communities:

> *When you enter the land the Lord your God is giving you, do not learn to imitate the detestable ways of the nations there. Let no one be found among you who sacrifices their son or daughter in the fire, who practices divination or sorcery, interprets omens, engages in witchcraft, or casts spells, or who is a medium or spiritist or who consults the dead. Anyone who does these things is detestable to the Lord; because of these same detestable practices the Lord your God will drive out those nations before you. You must be blameless before the Lord your God. (Deuteronomy 18:9-13 NIV)*

Not long after the workshop, one of the women who had attended met us on the street in town. She was eager to tell us that she had gathered her family together to tell them about the workshop. Her announcement to them: "There is no *sanguma,* it is all a lie to frighten us, keep us poor and hold us back from achieving what we should."

"They were so excited!" she told us. "No *sanguma!*" her children were incredulous. "We don't have to be afraid of spirits, of the dark, of bird calls or fireflies!" What liberation!

In fact, all the leaders had gone back to their villages with the same message. Gradually we heard that peace was starting to come to the Valley, that truces and reconciliation meetings were happening, that progress was being made. Not without slips and backwards steps of course, but a general slow movement in the right direction.

We had observed that day the power of Jesus' words, "you shall know the truth, and the truth shall set you free" (John 8:32, NIV Translation). We had seen that darkness cannot stand up to exposure to light, that fear and faith are incompatible. Worldview can change, in small steps taken and modeled by courageous leaders who are willing to revise their beliefs in light of self-discovery of the impact of these beliefs. We could all learn from such humility.

DISCUSS AND REFLECT:

1. What was new or significant for you personally in the stories of worldview and how it impacts development?

2. Identify a few of the current deeply held beliefs of your generation and culture. Which of them are lies that keep progress or equality from happening?

3. How might these beliefs shape the way we think in other areas, like how we spend time and money, what gives us feelings of significance and meaning in life?

4. Have you had an experience when you tried to accomplish a task without understanding or considering the worldview of the participants?

CHAPTER 2

Listen to the People: Engaging communities on their terms

"The first service one owes to others in the community involves listening to them… We do God's work for our brothers and sisters when we learn to listen to them… Listening can be of greater service than speaking." [11] *--Dietrich Bonhoeffer*

Whom do I listen to?

A community is defined by its stories. All of us are the sum total of our stories—our family of origin, the places where we lived, our childhood experiences, the positive or negative words that were spoken over us. As we reflect on these, we learn why we respond to situations or people as we do. There are emotional triggers, drivers in our own lives. In the same way, reflectively listening to a community with both our ears and our hearts will tell us why they are where they are and where they may be heading. This is part of the integration we refer to, seeing the big picture, the whole person in their whole community.

Most of us are slow to listen and quick to give advice! In conversations, we are preparing our own response in our minds well before the other person is finished speaking. The skill of listening without giving smart answers is one that must be practiced and developed in order to make it our habit. Those of us who serve in other cultures are often the most obvious offenders, as we are quick to see the outside 'objective' solutions. Instead of listening to the community, we have listened to the so-called experts, who tell us what needs to be fixed, what the needs and priorities of a developing society should be. This has been conventional development thinking, and the experts abound. Of course it leads to projects that go nowhere in the long term as they will be seen as 'owned' by the outside group that brought the ideas.

Instead, being quiet and listening has the desired result of the community feeling both respect and ownership, as they own the ideas and potential projects. The community engagement processes that we have learned, among other positive outcomes, has given us a pattern that forces us to be quiet and listen to the community! We are instructed to first 'look and listen' before engaging the community in any way. This can involve days or even weeks of just walking the streets with the people, going to their gardens with them, playing with children, visiting with groups of women or men. As we observe life on many levels, we find out where the balance of leadership and influence lies and we get to know these leaders. We identify with their everyday workloads and the burdens they bear. This is not a quick and easy process we might add, but well worth the time in sustainable results.

This may involve putting aside our timelines or 'Key Performance Indicators' and placing relationships over projects as we step out of our cultural mindset of defining productivity in terms of work accomplished. In cultures where spending time with people in order to understand each other is a priority, getting the tasks done are of lesser importance than building relationships. Learning to listen well, to really attend to people, is a skill we could all benefit from practicing. Listening with our hearts rather than just hearing with our ears does not come naturally for most of us.

In the corporate business world, we now see seminars advertised such as The Art of Hosting, The Art of Listening and Facilitating, Open Space Meetings. Listening to others is seen as a way to accomplish tasks or meet challenges with more creativity and enthusiasm than what could be done around traditional boardroom tables or with outside experts. The same simple tools and facilitation approaches that our trainers use in communities composed of oral learners, which simply provide opportunity for the collective wisdom of a group to be heard and conclusions drawn, are being sold in sophisticated settings with the same results. We get the feeling that we can learn a lot from oral cultures about the benefits of truly listening to people.

The Gift of Listening to the Unheard Voices

Only after listening to the community's stories and enjoying the rhythm of their lives do we have the right to ask more specific questions about their hopes and dreams, their assets, their concerns as integrated human beings. This is usually done in community meetings, where small groups discuss a question and then share opinions with the trained facilitators and the rest of the community. The process of facilitation and group participation is what gives opportunity for all to be heard. The power of this group process to generate enthusiasm for their community and to plan for its growth is exciting to witness. Just by being there to facilitate this listening process, we feel like we have given them a gift of more value than money. In reality we have done nothing but be there to let them hear each other.

> *Facilitating listening feels like we have given a gift of more value than money...we have let them hear each other.*

For many in communities around the world, from isolated rural villages to those in urban overcrowded settlements, there has been little opportunity for the lone or dissenting voice to be heard. Leaders tend to be the more extroverted or outspoken males, or those who have done well in the eyes of their society. Women in particular may have intelligent understanding and knowledge that is totally overlooked. When group interactions around common issues include women and even children, their status rises immediately as their answers are wise and relevant.

In one such community meeting we witnessed, the children were taken by a facilitator into their own discussion group, mainly to keep them involved and quiet. The discussion that evening was an exercise known as the 'Road to Health' where roadblocks to community development are identified. The group of pre-teen children decided that the biggest block to community advancement was not a physical one, but the discord and fighting between the adults. When it was their turn to share their conclusions, we could almost see shock waves ripple across the room! But their answer was given equal relevance to the others, because everyone knew it was true. And the smiles the children gave me as they walked out of the room later in the evening showed that their self-esteem had just grown immensely.

We will look now in detail at the story of two communities, where the lessons of listening can be illustrated in real life.

A Strong Start—Lufa District, Papua New Guinea Highlands

The community in Lufa District of the Eastern Highlands could be described as the backside of the province, about as far away from anywhere that one could get in a four-wheel drive Land Cruiser. It is made up of fourteen small hamlets, separated from each other by 20-30 minutes walking distances. We had come at their invitation, and they insisted that we had to see them all!

We were here with their local health trainers and Peter, the District Administrator responsible for this area. He had been our good friend since the days when he was a new college graduate. As a Papua New Guinean, he was used to these roads and his rugged white 'ten-seater' Land Cruiser was built for them—just muddy trenches of muck, ruts and holes too big to be called potholes! Peter himself had not been to this area for two years, but this time he wanted to witness the changes he had heard reported and to do a survey for a water source in the mountain, which would bring a much-needed water supply to the hamlets.

The lively conversation about Peter's years as a government administrator in out-of-the-way places such as this made the gruelling three hours from his district headquarters go much faster. One of his main duties before any development could proceed was to see that tribal wars were resolved and peace restored. Having grown up in the next province where he walked three hours to school each way, sometimes through enemy territory, he was not easily deterred or frightened by anything. His faith in God was likewise unflinching, enabling him to calmly face sorcerers and angry tribal chiefs alike. His innate intelligence combined with a good education and good mentors, produced a very successful chief administrator, honest and capable of developing infrastructure on behalf of the neglected rural people.

This particular community had been targeted as 'ripe for change' by four of the local health workers who had come through the first Training of Trainers in Community Health Education (CHE) that we had conducted in Papua New Guinea the previous year. The hamlets were peaceful, industrious and most inhabitants attended one of the two churches in the community. Although in the training our suggestion had been to choose a community within forty-five minutes by vehicle or foot from where the trainers lived, they insisted on this one although it was two hours when the roads were dry. Their medical patrols had walked from village to village immunizing the children and observed these people to be cooperative and motivated to see positive changes occur. They were the experts, so we had to listen to their recommendation!

In the Community Health Education model, after trainers have gone through a week-long Training of Trainers workshop, they begin to interact in their chosen community. The trainers are taught to ask questions and listen to the responses, not to give directives. Next, they facilitate several evenings of community meetings, where most of the community members show up and participate in lively discussions about their community.

This community was ready to implement the ideas discussed in their community meetings. As they had learned together through role-plays, shared dreams for the future and realized that a healthy community was more than simply physical health, they were anxious to change. Along with engagement in their issues came the growing awareness that they could work together with their own resources to see the dreams become reality. They then appointed a representative committee to receive further training to identify and prioritize issues that needed to be solved.

One of the first issues the committee wanted to address was toilets— they had learned that vector-borne disease spread by open defecation around their villages was contributing to the rampant diarrhea that constantly plagued them. Just a few simple measures of hygiene such as toilets could eliminate this. According to surveys previously conducted by Peter and the health team, only three per cent of people in this part of the district had toilets. They told us it was a 'spiritual issue,' we call it worldview. Their deeply rooted belief in *sanguma,* or sorcery, where human excrement might be used to curse a person, meant that depositing one's waste in one place was not a good idea. Also, the fears of spirits that might linger inside enclosed spaces filled them with dread. But when the trainers had spent time listening and discussing how their animistic fears were holding them back, and the committee decided that the God they claimed they believed in had power to release them from those fears, they felt free to do what 40 years of government health educating and top-down directives forbidding open defecation had been unable to do. The committee members themselves were able to lead the way with convincing boldness as they began to build and use toilets! One toilet per family was their rule so that they would be responsible to keep them clean, and the distance from the homes was also prescribed and enforced. When we came, we observed in every hamlet dozens of the small outhouses perched along the edge of the ridges on which their homes were built.

We were surprised when Peter himself observed, "There has been a mindset change here! In most villages in this area we still rarely see toilets. It is obviously a spiritual change!"

For us, this was one of the first times to observe how the power of the community acting together gives individuals the courage to make changes that they would not otherwise make on their own. We realized that we could not underestimate the value of a community structure where the people have vested some authority in a committee that will listen to their collective voice, and in turn be listened to by the community. This form of 'direct democracy' is key to bottom up change. And it starts with listening, not talking!

There were other noticeable differences from typical nearby villages in these hamlets scattered over the pristine mountain slopes. Immediately we noticed their tidy family compounds, swept clean and lined with hedges, flowers, pathways and steps carved in the hillsides. They looked like mini botanical gardens with the variety of colours and walkways! They felt so proud when we admired the results of their hard work! Each home had a fence around it to keep pigs from wandering in, destroying flowers and depositing their waste, which attracts flies and intestinal worms. Each had a newly built dish-drying table exposing dishes and pots to the disinfecting rays of the sun, rather than the usual 'wet stack' method. There were refuse holes and compost piles for household waste, clotheslines for drying rather than laying wet clothes on the ground or shrubs to dry, outdoor kitchens to keep the open cooking fire smoke out of the houses. Gardens next to the house were beginning to offer some easily accessible nutrition, rather than relying only on those an hour or two walk away. These FAITH gardens—Food Always In The Home—represent a shift in their knowledge about the importance of adding various colours of vegetables and legumes to their staple sweet potato *(kaukau)* diet.

No wonder they all wanted us to visit their homesteads, to be noticed and commended for their hard work! So we agreed to split up, with half of our visiting group going to the hamlets on each side of the valley. Fortunately we love to walk, and the moderate temperature of the Highlands provides a pleasant temperature to do that. These are days to love and remember.

The healthy physical and behavioural changes we noted were amazing, and yet deeper spiritual shifts were evident in the conversations as well. Most of the people attended one of the two Protestant churches in the community, but until now they had not understood how their spiritual and physical lives connect.

When asked what had motivated them to make these changes, we heard comments like the one expressed by an old man: "In the same way that we attempt to make our spirits clean, we want to make our physical environment clean."

Or another, "Before we used to think that stories like the creation and Garden of Eden were just stories. Now we realize that we can learn lessons about our own life and that we can live in an environment like the one God created us to be in."

On our ride back, we talked more about how spiritual change could result in physical change, and vice versa. We were amazed that something as simple as toilets represented a big hurdle for them. This breakthrough, this first small step, gave them energy and conviction to change their whole way of life! Why? They did not have to be fettered by the fears of spiritual forces that were powerless over them once they refused to believe their power over the God they claimed to serve. We have no understanding of how liberating that might be. Our own horizons were being stretched...the world we had hoped to change was changing our own paradigms! Physical and spiritual, social and intellectual, these are all inextricably linked. There are no neat compartments as our Western mindset suggests. Integrated human beings, that is what we are, linked through our God to each other and to our land and environment in an inseparable package.

> *There are no neat compartments...we are integrated human beings, linked through our God to each other and to our land and environment in an inseparable package.*

I wish I could give a glowing story of happy forward motion forever for these genuine people living in their beautiful hillsides far from the public eye and so motivated to change. Long term change is hard, requiring ongoing leadership development and encouragement. The health workers who had initiated training, who had targeted this area as 'ripe for change,' were not able to continue after two of them were transferred to different health centres. Their ongoing presence had been essential, even though it was some distance away. These communities, made up of largely illiterate agrarian people, are fragile. Even after seeing their illness patterns, deaths and general hardships sharply decline, and enjoying peaceful and pleasant environments, they can be swayed by dissident voices.

In the case of this community, some of their educated young people who returned home for Christmas holidays were the dissidents. Rather than being excited about the changes they observed, they brought discouragement and jealousy. Their accusations that the health workers had personal motives for encouraging them to change, that they were being paid extra and given promotions based on the success of this community were of course completely untrue. They based this on the fact that photos had been taken, which they claimed were being used for international fund raising. So the community believed the lies—they listened to the wrong people. The trainers were made to feel unwelcome in their next visits, and the committee disbanded over time as their suggestions went unheeded.

The reasons why young educated people such as these would deliberately try to sabotage positive progress may lie in belief systems beyond our cultural understanding. There may have been issues of power being seen to transfer to the committee rather than traditional leaders. There might have been jealousy issues by some who had their own aspirations for successful development in the village. Or maybe underlying conflicts between clans had not been addressed, that only they knew about. In tribal societies it is important to include all the clans or communities in simultaneous development—so there may have been a group excluded without the trainers realizing it, and the young college 'spokesman' was from that group. Who knows? Any of the above could have easily thwarted the good that was happening. Listening to the community in more depth may have avoided the disappointment. Maybe.

Even the water system that Peter had approved and funded did not come to be! The contractor was paid to get the supplies and supervise the community work, but absconded with the money and was never seen again in the community. Of course they were discouraged. We would be too! And, as often happens when people have not been trained to know their power in a democratic society, the perpetrators were not pursued and brought to justice.

One step forward, two steps back! Development is a generational effort, and how many false starts does it take to build many good things? The majority may be diligent in all the various physical, social and spiritual aspects of building and then from the sidelines they are thwarted by a few discouraging words.

There is hope though, for the backside of Lufa, as they have tasted the pleasure of positive lifestyles and they have experienced better health and life for their children. There will be another brave health worker or community champion who will decide to try again, to return and encourage them again. There will be one of their youth who will come home with positive dynamic leadership rather than jealousy. There will be children who will remember, and who will motivate their parents. There will be.

We have learned good lessons from this story—both for ourselves and for those we train to go into similar communities. Life, as always, is the best teacher. But only as we reflect and learn from it.

Consistency and presence—that is what we now try to instil in those who seek to engage communities in positive change. Listening to their stories and to the pain and joy of their day-to- day lives does not occur in a few brief visits. Even for those who seem most ready and 'ripe for change', there are few who can maintain that forward motion without the encouragement of an objective person from outside the community who consistently shows up in the community to encourage and engage them in meaningful discussion. For some the process seems too slow, and it is easy to say the project is finished and move on. Alas, there are few quick fixes anywhere.

Breaking the Mould—Eastern Highlands of PNG

Sava (not the real name) was a community in another district of the same province that was fortunate to be located near a keen and diligent trainer who brought consistent presence. Esther was a young Community Health Worker (a two-year trained nurse, often responsible for running a rural health centre) in the church-run Health Centre near Sava village.

This village had recently returned to their land after spending fourteen years in the mountains as refugees following the tribal war that had destroyed their homes and burned their crops. Many of the men had been killed. A peace treaty had been signed with the enemy clan, but their land had no trees for building houses. In 2002 they began rebuilding their lives back on their land with small hovels made of the reed-like *kunai* grass. The village was near the main highway, so we often drove by and wondered who lived here in what looked like animal shelters. They were a broken but determined lot.

When Esther attended the Community Health Education Training of Trainers course, she was quiet and did not stand out as the mighty health warrior she was to become! Returning to the health centre near her home, she decided to implement what she had learned. Looking for a community to begin, she thought of Sava, which was close by and motivated to establish their community once again. Esther knew that unless their community began with a positive approach, it was likely that the young men would form marauding gangs of highway robbers, or plant marijuana for a quick cash crop. They were tough, embittered by their unfortunate past and already boasted some notorious criminals.

Esther approached some of the leaders with a proposal for training them to rebuild their community in an orderly and positive way using the creativity and the resources they had, rather than looking for what they did not have. They agreed—they had nothing to lose.

She began with community participatory meetings each evening, which included impromptu drama, role-plays of their own lives, lots of laughter and serious talk sometimes well into the night. Starting with affirming their self-worth, their 'made in the image of God' identity, they began to see themselves as having resources and creative abilities. If indeed men and women were both equally created in His image, then the women should have some say in developing the village too, and would sit on the committee they would form to plan and govern. What a paradigm shift that was!

Next came discussions on the meaning of health and what makes a healthy home and community. They talked of themselves as whole beings, physical, social, mental, spiritual, and of the need to maintain harmony with self, God, each other and our environment.

Did they want to wait for handouts, or to take charge of their own development? That was their next question. Esther pointed out the fallacies of aid and of growing dependent—they would become 'beggars'. They were seeing it all clearly now—the only way for them to be healthy was to understand simple preventative primary health measures, and the only way to sustain this was to be willing to own it themselves.

An indigenous plan was taking shape. They were fortunate as a community to have been blessed with fertile soil and adequate moisture in their traditional land, and they all knew how to garden. First using only sticks as implements, they made the soil burst forth with vegetables that could be sold at the markets. This helped buy spades, and then posts for the houses to be built one by one. The walls were made of woven bamboo growing nearby and thatch for the roofs.

We were surprised when we heard of the changes that were taking place and that a quiet young woman was leading this community so renowned for their fierce warfare! When she invited us to a community meeting, we were even more impressed to see her in action. About five hundred people from two villages sat in a clearing to listen. If she had been a visiting celebrity they could not have been more attentive and responsive! How had this happened? What had transformed this timid Community Health Worker in a culture where men listen only to men? She had caught a vision for whole and healthy communities built on truth rather than lies, where everyone was valued and given a say in working together for the good of their community. She believed them, the people trusted her and were willing to participate.

Esther told us of the community meeting where she had asked them to express their dreams and visions for their community's future. The group was silently contemplating when a ten-year old physically disabled boy asked to speak. His mother was surprised, as he had never spoken up in public before! Esther gave him the 'floor' (the ground!), and he described a village that was peaceful and clean with rows of trimmed hedges along walkways, with grassy areas for the children to play on rather than dirt and of multi-coloured flowers. "Not just yellow flowers," he added, "but red ones and blue ones and purple ones and orange ones!"

Everyone was stunned! Soon tears were flowing—to think that this child whom the village viewed as unimportant had such dreams! To think that children cared about the environment where they grew up, what the adults did and what legacy they were leaving for them to inherit! Of course the adults all listened! Of course they started that very week to make pathways, and hedges and flower beds! They could all dream, and they could all make it happen. After all, if they were going to build a new village, they now had reason to make it orderly and attractive right from the beginning.

Somehow this also sparked creativity as they talked about the styles of housing that were traditional in the area. Typically there were no windows, only a door, and the cooking fire was in the middle of the one-room round house. The women and children might sit in that smoke for two or more hours a day, not to mention the smoke from embers all night long. Esther explained to them the need for ventilation in their sleeping and cooking areas. Now we know that two hours of breathing wood smoke like that is equivalent to smoking a pack of cigarettes a day in the damage done to the respiratory system. Children breathing the smoke will have on-going respiratory issues, ear infections, and almost always have runny noses ("number 11" as the mucous trail is nicknamed in PNG!).

So new houses began to be built one by one, as the vegetable gardens flourished into cash. The cash bought trees from neighbouring villages for construction. We were intrigued at the new styles—all of them had windows, partitions inside, cooking shelters outside, some even had verandas with hexagon shaped openings for decoration. They were anything but traditional Highlands huts where the pigs freely ran in and out! Outside were grassed lawns, clothes lines, dish drying tables, benches to sit under thriving banana or papaya trees. The children all had smiles on their faces! Esther's father helped them put in a gravity-fed water system piped from the spring a few hundred meters up the mountainside to a series of communal faucets throughout the village. Such liberation from the drudgery of carrying water, a daily job allocated to the women and children.

One woman said, "I have learned that God made me for something better than living with my pigs! I have more value than that." This, remember, is from a culture where women are considered chattel, purchased with bride price to be treated as a commodity.

This is truly a breakthrough—in any culture or language!

Early on in the process of community engagement, usually after about six evenings of general community sessions, the community group appoints a committee to represent them and to receive further leadership training from Esther. This initially went well, and Esther eagerly trained them in the leadership lessons she had been taught. But after a few months she observed the dynamics change and the community was arguing again! Bill, as an outsider was asked to come and mediate. The whole community was there to talk! After asking a few simple questions about who was supposed to take responsibility in resolving these disputes, and whether the committee was doing that, Bill quietly observed as they launched into a heated vernacular discussion. In this case he listened, but obviously didn't understand!

Undaunted, he sat and 'listened' anyway. He was pleased to observe their animated engagement in the process!

After about thirty minutes, the chatter suddenly stopped, and someone announced to Bill, "We have it settled!" The original committee it seemed did not really represent them because they had chosen the most outspoken people. "We will appoint a new committee," they decided.

End of discussion, and everyone went back home agreeing to meet the next day when a new committee that truly represented the whole community would be appointed. And they did—this time a committee with women, youth, and all the clans represented.

Training of peer educators, called CHEs or Community Health Educators, came next. Appointed by the committee and trained in regular short sessions, they are most often the mothers who are recognized for their concern for the children and community. We have seen many women rise to leadership as they are empowered through this process. Because they are right there in the warp and weft of the community, listening to the heartaches of their neighbours' families and sharing what they are learning from the trainers, they become invaluable tools for sustainable development.

Nobody is too poor or too old or too uneducated to be part of the process, or even to become the CHE. The heart to listen to others and to see transformation in their community is the main qualification. Every community has these people, and their unrecognized leadership and abilities are what will give strength and resilience long term.

Not long after Sava had appointed and trained their CHEs, they were honoured by the provincial Governor as the first official 'Healthy Community' in the province. This was attained because of their progress in rebuilding according to the ten Healthy Home standards that the provincial training team had decided would be the key indicators for good health. The criteria:

- A toilet for each home
- Safe drinking water
- Smoke free, ventilated sleeping area
- Clean home environment inside and outside
- Refuse pit for non-decomposable waste

- Dish drying table for sun drying of dishes
- Nutrition garden near the home
- Children fully immunized and attending school
- Beautification and care of natural environment
- Family prayers/worship in their home

It is noteworthy that the list includes not only physical indicators, but mental, social and spiritual criterion as well. In order for them to be declared a 'Healthy Community,' at least 80% of the households had to meet the ten criteria; they also had to demonstrate progress on addressing negative social and cultural issues like sorcery and tribal fighting, and all school age children had to be attending school.

The Sava people were excited and honoured to have the Governor and many other dignitaries come to visit on this occasion to present the 'Healthy Community' award. To formalize this recognition they were given a large signboard to mount by the highway with the name of their village, and a shield design bearing the words they chose in their Kemano tribal tongue, "We did it ourselves!"

When the HIV/AIDS epidemic hit in full force around 2005, Esther began teaching in earnest in the hopes to promote marital faithfulness and avoid certain death toll. In a culture of polygamy and lack of respect for women, this was a hard but critical topic. The community responded with genuine desire to change. When she came to the lesson on caring with compassion for People Living With AIDS (PLWA's), there were tears as they told of some who had already been ostracized before their untimely deaths. In fact, there was one woman who right now had been banished to a small hut outside the village where she would stay until her death. The very next day they went and brought her back, washed and cared for her and began to show her love. Her health improved somewhat and her skin lesions healed. While she did not live long, her last weeks were filled with a feeling of inner wellbeing and love from her family and community, rather than the total rejection of aloneness.

The value of education became a priority, and all the families sent all their children to school—both boys and girls. They went on to high school, and now many to university. The general health and peacefulness of families continues to be held up as a standard to other

communities who come and look at the changes, even take notes on the
'new styles' of houses that have been built! Their two local churches,
Seventh Day Adventist and Lutheran modeled cooperation as they
worked together to re-build the damaged roof of the Lutheran church.
Both churches began to thrive with the new attention to spiritual
health and encouragement for families to pray together and discuss the
teaching of the CHE volunteers.

As in any real-life community, they are rarely 'happily ever after'
forever. In this saga, one of the community leaders, the chairman of the
committee for several years, was somehow enticed back into joining the
criminal gang he had led before he helped to 'reform' the community!
Within a few short weeks, the report came to us that he had been
shot and killed by the police while undertaking an armed robbery in
the nearest town. Such a waste of a life that had been on track for the
common good for a number of years, and such a loss to his community.
We only hope this has been a warning to the younger men who might
look at a life of crime with excitement.

It seemed after this shock, the community carried on with new
vigour and registered an official association, built a large building for
a resource centre for adult education classes and other community
meetings. It continues to be well utilized, and we heard that the fifty
adults who had missed out on schooling during their fourteen years of
dispersal graduated from adult literacy class the end of 2016.

The Sava story was told in 2012 to a group from the Starkey
Foundation, which was looking for 'Operation Change' stories to film
for a series on the Oprah Winfrey TV network.[12] So in 2014 Esther
and husband Jesse were invited to the premiere showing in Los Angeles
to acknowledge Esther's part in the community transformation story!
What an amazing ten-day experience that was for two Papua New
Guineans—and what an eye-opening back story they took home as
they told of the 'street people' they had stumbled onto, listened to and
befriended around the upscale hotel where they stayed! Listening and
learning apply anywhere!

We have learned much from Sava that we can apply to other
communities. Local initiative and ownership are critical, as are good
leaders who are willing to accept outside mediation when adjustments

are needed. A consistent encourager present for a period of years is one of the most important lessons. The transformation of this community came about when a young local health worker was willing to take the initiative to listen, to love and to be present with a struggling community week by week for a number of years. Their sad stories of war and loss took time to hear, but out of that catharsis emerged the dreams that could be fanned into reality when they learned to use what little resources they had. Sustainable community ownership also takes time. It will ebb and flow as individuals come and go, but Sava will keep moving forward.

Listen to their Folk Stories—Western Highlands of PNG, 2010

Emma, Community Health Education (CHE) training coordinator in Papua New Guinea, had been invited to introduce CHE training to a community, in Western Highlands Province near her own tribal home. Her contact was Las, a pro-active and educated man with training in agriculture and business who was determined to see his community move forward. Emma knew that having a trusted 'champion' like this within the community, who could motivate others by his enthusiasm, was one important ingredient for success. So she finally agreed to Las' persistent requests to go and conduct the community awareness sessions for six evenings.

In introducing the Community Health Education program to a new community, one session of a typical series is called "The Power of Story". The community is encouraged to tell its traditional cultural stories in order to see how these might be instructive to the younger generation in understanding their current lives. Many of the youth have not even heard these stories and songs, so it becomes a hilarious evening of fun as well as an honour for the older people to have their stories heard.

As Emma came to this session in her training, they began telling their traditional creation story about their legendary ancestor Minimbi. They explained that they are known both by others and themselves as the People of Stone. They do live in a very rugged stony place, called in derision the 'back page' of the area, which has shaped the way they have come to think of themselves as backward and of no value. But the real reason, they say, is that their forefather Minimbi is believed to have hatched from an egg placed on a stone. As the 'stone people,' they even use a stone to place their hand on to swear to the truth ("touch stone, I'm telling the truth!")

Emma pondered this for a moment, as a question came to her mind: "Who in the Bible is called a stone?" she asked, praying as she did for insight as to where this might go.

Having been somewhat schooled in the Bible they knew the answer. "Jesus is," they replied. The room was silent for a time, as they grasped for the analogy.

Emma's thoughts raced to 1 Peter 2:4-5. "Let's read about others called stones in the Bible", she continued. Here they observed that Christ, the living Stone, had been rejected like them, but was precious to God. Then they read that they, "like living stones, are being built into a spiritual house to be a holy priesthood".

The excitement in the room was building! "We ARE stones, important, living ones!" The room was buzzing with chatter now and their faces were alive.

"And that means we are valuable, not the back page! We are children of the King, being built into a house for Him to occupy!" Their importance and significance to God was becoming obvious to all. "We are not worthless people, we are royal priests for God."

"So we really came from Jesus!" someone else stated. "And when we touch a stone, it is Christ the Rock that we are basing our truth upon."

Emma just sat and listened in amazement as the talk went on, sometimes in their own language, sometimes in Melanesian Pidgin. The transformation in their thinking was so tangible it was almost hard to imagine that something so simple had become like a runaway train. She could only think that God had been at work all along in their culture through their own stories, and now He had revealed that to them.

Now someone else wanted to share a Minimbi story:

> Minimbi had been invited by the People of the Clouds to go up and share a meal with them. So he tried to build and climb a banana tree ladder to get up to the clouds, but his ladder broke

and he fell to the ground. So the People of the Clouds felt sorry for him and threw down a pig for him to cook.

His neighbours were the seven mountains around him. When he started to cook, his first mountain-neighbour smelled the smoke and came over to join him. They both ate only the vegetables and were too full to eat the meat. So Minimbi gave the meat to the neighbour to take home and told him to cook it the next day.

That day the third stone-mountain came to eat with the second mountain, but again they ate only the vegetables and the third stone was given the meat to take home. This went on for seven days until finally the seventh stone-mountain, named Mitiku, cooked but nobody came to eat with him so he ate the pork himself.

Feeling very full and sluggish, he went to the stream flowing from his mountain for a drink. As he did so, healing properties went into the water from the meat he had eaten that had been a gift from the People of the Clouds. From then on the people believed that the stream of water they call Mitiku River had healing properties to heal their wounds.

The group began to see this story too in a new light. With Emma interjecting a few questions, they intersected their story with God's story of the redemption of mankind, until an amazing 'redemptive analogy' emerged.

Minimbi, they said, represented mankind, created for fellowship with God, the People of the Clouds. Trying to reach God in his own way, he failed. But God in His love, even at the time of man's rejection, gave the promise of the Way to God that was for all people. God sent Jesus into the world of humanity, but for the Minimbi it took many generations for them to avail themselves of His gift. When they did, Jesus became the river of life for all mankind to find healing from their brokenness as they partake of Him.

The Minimbi people, once thinking of themselves as despised and worthless, now believe that they are so precious to God that He has used their own culture to finally bring them to knowledge of His true intention for them as a people. Their stories, intertwined with their knowledge of God's story have enabled them to find a new narrative for their community; they have dignity, and a new purpose in life much greater than just existing. A new identity has emerged, this time one which is transformative. They are in the process of moving, we might say, from an animistic to a Biblical monotheistic worldview that gives them a new way of looking at themselves and the reality of the world. They have the power to change, having been released from the fears that had them bound.

Since that time, the community has continued to progress, building a community training centre where Las has helped to organize regular classes in such things as basic budgeting, sewing, agriculture skills or carpentry. Their coffee gardens are cared for, productive and are providing income for them. They are helping needy community members, and even reaching out to influence neighbouring communities in a peacemaking role during recent tribal warfare.

Emma's questions prompt us to ask some. Has God been at work all along from the beginning of every culture? Could it be that embedded into every culture on earth are keys like we observed here that lead to an understanding of their true identity and purpose on this earth? The Apostle Paul's interactions in Athens as recorded in Acts 17 seem to support God's involvement in shaping cultures in order for them to seek and find Him.[13] If this is so then it begs us to listen for the deeper story within their story. We need to listen to the culture both with ears and heart.

Nobody ever asks... they only tell us! Port Moresby, PNG

Pepa had become a close family friend as a young man in 1980, as one of Bill's Health Extension Officer students in Kainantu. Now having risen in the Health Department in PNG's capital city, Port Moresby, he had just gone through one of our CHE Training of Trainers workshops. We were together now in a notorious Port Moresby slum, and Pepa was facilitating the discussion. He had just asked a question to the large group gathered in the light of the circle illuminated by one overhead light bulb. "Do you think men and women were created to be equal?" he asked.

We were in the central open area of the slum settlement, where one of the church groups had decided to try the methods for community engagement that we had taught them the month before. They had grown discouraged after spending time listening and learning what they could about this community of about 2000 population, misnamed 'Garden Hill.' Yes for sure it was on a hill; it was anything but a garden!

What they had known was that this was one of several over crowded, under serviced squatter settlements where much of the criminal element of the capital city was accommodated. What they did not know was that sanitation was almost non-existent, with only three or four toilets for the whole settlement, as documented by their house-to-house surveys. The real 'toilet' of the community was the hillside field outside the fence, which was military land so they would only go under cover of darkness! Everyone collected water in containers from a single pipe that came into the compound, making proper hygiene next to impossible. The only electricity as we had now discovered, was from the one small trade store. Those living close to that would run a pirated extension connection from the store.

The hill was in fact on top of an old city dump site. One of the reasons for the lack of toilets, as our friends soon realized, was a result of this location—the few inches of soil that had accumulated over the years just barely covered the old garbage below. In some spots there were batteries, bed springs or bottles still showing through to the surface. It was not possible to dig even a few feet to install a pit latrine, and there were no collection services for above ground bucket toilets. Of course there was not even the thought of a sewer system by the city to service illegal settlements such as this.

Life was hard, and cash income was either from minimum wage jobs, street selling of cigarettes or betel nut (an addictive locally grown nut which is mixed with lime and chewed for the mild stimulant and euphoric effect), or goods such as peanuts, bananas or second-hand clothes. Sadly many women sold themselves to have means to feed their children.

Most homes were made from pieces of galvanized sheeting or bits of wooden planks and plywood found in the landfill—the typical urban slum look all over the world. A few homes were more properly built, but even those residents knew they were vulnerable to city planners giving them the ultimatum to move as they made way for development.

As the information unfolded, it seemed most makeshift homes had two or even three shifts of residents, each sleeping at different times of the day! It was thus impossible to get an accurate assessment of the population, much less to talk about improving the health of each home.

This was not a choice environment in which to bring up children, but many in this world do not have choices. Some in fact define poverty in terms of lack of choices. We prefer to define it in the broader terms of broken relationships—with ourselves, with other people, with God or with our natural environment. Whether Garden Hill was defined in material terms, or in the brokenness that was so apparent here, this community was off the scale.

No wonder these church members, in spite of their good intentions for community development, were feeling overwhelmed and had asked for some back up support to begin!

The relative cool of the muggy evening, the solo light on the pole in the centre of the community and the obvious curiosity the people felt towards outsiders coming into the settlement, had drawn a crowd of a couple of hundred observers. Pepa's question had created a low buzz of murmuring, both inside and outside the circle of light.

It was the men who quite predictably, began to share an opinion first. "No, men were definitely meant to be more important than women." One man was giving voice to what seemed the general agreement.

This group, like almost all of Papua New Guineans, had been raised with some Christian teaching in their village church or in school. "Adam was created before Eve," one man chimed in. "And Eve came from his rib!" Some of us smiled, but it seemed to them a valid argument.

"Eve sinned, not Adam," another emphatically added.

Pepa wisely just smiled and said, "Thank you, does anyone else have an idea about this?" He knew that trying to correct such misconceptions at this point would only lead down the proverbial rabbit trail.

I had noticed a couple of young women in the shadows, whispering to each other and obviously disagreeing with the opinion being circulated. Finally one of them tentatively raised her hand and spoke up. "We do not agree with what the men have said. If God created both men and women in His own image, He created them to be equal. And it's time the men in this society start recognizing that women are of equal importance and begin treating us that way!"

The surprised crowd went silent, and Pepa took that as opportunity to express agreement with the comment, then skilfully moved on to ask some less controversial questions. The discussion turned to focus on some of the positive things they could tell about life in their community. Surprisingly there are always quite a few, even in a place like Garden Hill!

I moved over beside the two young women during a lull in the discussion, and commended them for having the courage to speak up with a dissenting view when all the men were agreeing on their dominance. The girls made an interesting comment that touched me deeply.

"The reason we spoke up is because this is the first time anyone has ever come here and asked us for our opinion—all they do is come here and tell us everything we are doing wrong and that we need to do something about it. They never ask us what we think! You have made us feel like real people by asking for our opinion, and that is why we knew we had to speak up."

I was startled by the comment. I felt the sadness associated with the hopelessness that they must feel when told by outsiders, mainly government health authorities, how bad their living conditions were and that they should clean up their act. I could not imagine how it must feel to know that your opinion never counts, that your side of the story has no credibility. Of course they felt compelled to speak when given the chance.

Who will dare to go into these difficult areas outside the margins, to ask, and then to listen in the hope to understand their hearts? Who then has the right to "speak up for those who cannot speak for themselves, for the rights of all who are destitute... to defend the rights of the poor and needy"?[14] And who will go the next step and give them their own voice to speak up for themselves? Only those who have first listened to them.

Listen to the Governing Authority Structures

Likely because of our years of working inside the government health care system, this seemed the natural place to start when Medical Ambassadors International asked us in 1999 to go and check out PNG as a potential place for their Community Health Education training. We found the door wide open, and in fact it was their mandate to train communities to take responsibility for their own health. The new initiative from World Health Organization for the Pacific Region, called 'Healthy Islands' was just a concept, but without wheels to take it to the community level. We came at the right time—it seemed there was a role for a maturing doctor-educator couple!

From the first floundering attempts to pick a province and begin training some trainers, there is now a strategy in place to cover the country with this community engagement process and to train peer educators to carry the integrated health messages—physical, social, mental and spiritual—right into the homes. This fits the mandate of Public Health as directed by the World Health Organization definition of health:

> Health is a state of complete physical, mental, social, spiritual
> well-being, not just the absence of disease or infirmity. [15]

The vehicle for this strategy is the rural health centre, over 80% of which are run by a variety of church agencies under the umbrella of Christian Health Services.[16] While owned and operated by the church agencies, the funding for staff and supplies comes from the National Department of Health for curative work. The CHE preventative plan came after all the church agency groups that were doing some form of health promotions at the community level had formed a network and were meeting annually to share stories and best practices. The network formalized under a banner called EDEN: Effective Development Empowering the Nation. In 2015 the government approved funding for a Christian Health Services health promotions department and a country coordinator.

The learning that came from this experiment in large-scale strategy reinforced the need to first listen to the government! What are its plans, goals and initiatives? All countries have a current Health Plan, as well as Education Plan, and likely a National Plan that may span a decade or longer. Have we ever bothered to read them? How do the goals of our organizations fit? How can we be of assistance in helping the government achieve its objectives and the key results it is hoping for? Where might we need to seek permissions to work? When we spend time listening and learning, just as we do in communities, we may be amazed to find areas where cooperation is obvious, and even where program funding is available.

In 2010 Papua New Guinea set forth its National Vision 2050 Plan, with the goal to reform the mindset and attitudes of the people, institutions and systems to become a "smart, wise, fair, healthy and happy society by 2050." [17] The subsequent Development Strategic Plan for sustainable development will strive to bring the nation to the status of a "prosperous middle-income country by 2030".[18] All of these are goals we can appreciate and work towards with them, especially in that many of them concern health and lifestyle issues.

One of the architects of this Vision 2050 Plan was a wise and respected gentleman from the Prime Minister's Office whom we grew to know and appreciate as he came year by year to simply listen in on our annual EDEN meetings. He realized that listening to grass roots reports from community trainers gave him hope that the country really could change. One year he chose between our simple annual meeting and the National Health Conference—"all those statistics are lies!" he emphatically asserted. "I just get discouraged listening to them! Here I get real life stories and go away encouraged."

Listen to the Faith Communities: Listen to God!

Within most communities worldwide, the faith leaders are the most respected people, no matter which religion they represent. If we do not make the effort early on to seek them out and become friends with them, we may never hear the real pulse of the community. For several years Bill made a point of attending the Pastors' meetings in various places in Papua New Guinea and always found them welcoming and informative. Numerous cups of tea and bowls of soup with the Catholic priest in Goroka cemented a deep and enduring friendship that continues to the present even though he has retired in another city. Listening to the faith leaders in friendly dialogue is always worthwhile.

While we do not claim to be experts on the topic of listening to God, though numerous good books have sought to teach us through a lifetime of trying, there are times when His voice does break through. Often it is through others whose life experiences and attitudes touch our hearts. We have heard God through the simple village pastors who so passionately cry out to God for help to change their communities. Sometimes we have found ourselves sitting on hard benches or on even harder dirt floors of small churches, and have been more personally touched by the heartfelt words of an uneducated pastor than by a polished theologian in our own country. When tears spontaneously overflow as we soak the words and the simple context into our souls, we know that it is God speaking. Time to listen.

Such was the day when we attended Pastor Zoro's village church outside Goroka. We have repeated his sermon on the call of Moses from within a burning bush over and over again in other contexts and many of the PNG trainers now use it too. After all, who does not wonder why the heavens seem silent in the face of injustice? Where is God in those hard times? Why does He not act? Or is He waiting for us to act? Moses listened:

> *I have indeed seen the misery of my people in Egypt. I have heard them crying out because of their slave drivers, and I am concerned about their suffering. So I have come down to rescue them... So now, go. I am sending you to bring my people out of Egypt.*[19]

And who does not feel inadequacy as their first response when thrust into the ring to become the change agent? *Moses said to God, "Who am I that I should go to Pharoah?"* We are yet to find anyone who cannot relate to these words.

Sometimes in moments when we rage inwardly at the unfairness of life and the evils of injustice that dominate so much of our world, we identify with the Psalmists' lament, "how long oh God?" Then the small inner voice of calm reminds, *"Be still and know that I am God."*[20] And we remember that the final chapter is still not written. Hope that keeps us optimistic that right will prevail—that hope is the whisper of God. Beauty shining everywhere we look reminds us that love wins in the end, and that too is the finger of God.

At other times we feel such an urging within us to do something about a problem we have seen that we cannot keep quiet. Or we take some first hesitant steps towards starting something that seems impossibly crazy, and then unexpected energy and creativity begins to surface and help is offered from others. We sense within us that the whisper of God has broken through to our often-deaf ears.

We listen to the voice of God through children who seem to see the obvious that we completely miss. "It was God that turned the steering wheel!" declared our six-year-old son when our jeep, idling on our sloping Kainantu driveway, began to roll (thankfully nobody was in it). I knew it was futile to race beside and try to jump in, so just watched in horror as it headed towards the embankment that would take it crashing into the houses below. Then, just as though an invisible hand really were on the wheel, it turned, finished its unbidden journey on our own level lawn and came to a stop. As we later pondered Tim's emphatic declaration of miraculous intervention, I thought of one of Jesus' statements in the famous Sermon on the Mount: "blessed are the pure in heart, for they shall see God." [21] Still I cannot read that verse without remembering the Hand on the steering wheel.

We have our rational explanations for everything, but only the pure in heart, those who really see and hear, have the pleasure of Divine encounters at every twist and corner of life. The secularist may see these random events as mere chance, which presupposes absence of purpose or meaning; the pure in heart see purposefulness in unpredictable, seeming-random events. "Too amazing to be chance" really means a God-factor was evident. When God is there, meaning is there too.

Elizabeth Barrett Browning almost two centuries ago expressed the longing to be among those who see God in a famous quote from *Aurora Leigh*:

> *Earth's crammed with heaven*
> *And every common bush afire with God;*
> *But only he who sees takes off his shoes,*
> *The rest sit round it and pluck blackberries,*
> *And daub their natural faces unaware.* [22]

"God is listening!" Cambodia, 2011

One of the most memorable moments of that Cambodia training week, well actually two moments, was when nature spoke the still, small voice of God. Like Moses and the burning bush, our shoes were already off. We had been asked by a large secular Buddhist organization, all Cambodians, to train their senior staff of mostly doctors, in moral values. It seemed a strange request indeed, born from a desperate longing for moral and ethical rejuvenation in a broken land.

It was our second training for this group, and they decided it would be appropriate to hold it, not in a nice hotel in Phnom Penh as the first one, but in a forest at Angkor Wat among the ruins of their 1000 year old Buddhist civilization. For a week we all sat on mats on the ground with only the trees to shade us from the hot sun, and no amenities. This was obviously uncomfortable to the participants too, accustomed as they were to their air-conditioned offices, but the CEO had decreed it and we would all comply. "After all," she explained, "it is symbolic of the need to rebuild the ruins of cultural values and restore our humanity after the degradation of the Khmer Rouge and Pol Pot regime." The genocide of the 1970's had wiped out a quarter of the population, and almost all of the educated and religious teachers.

We soon noticed with curiosity that the translators used English instead of Khmer for key words like compassion, kindness, respect and love. They explained to us that there is only one general Khmer word for all of these, which would lose the meaning in the moral landscape we were trying to help them understand. One woman told us, "we have heard these concepts but have no words to describe them, which is why we need your help in order to teach others."

On the afternoon that our Singaporean colleague, Min, facilitated the lesson *Forgiveness: Healing the Wounds of the Past* using the Prodigal Son story, the power of the pain and horrific memories they carried became obvious. Buddhism after all, does not provide for them the means to extend or receive forgiveness and grace. As a conclusion to the lesson, we were asked to think of a person we needed to ask forgiveness and someone else we needed to forgive. As Min strummed the melody of *Allelujah* on his ukulele, we quietly sang "Please forgive me, please forgive me..." and then "I forgive you, I forgive you..." As the group then stood silently in the circle, an uncharacteristic wind broke the sultry stillness of the air, causing papers to flutter and the trees above us to move in a circle as dry leaves dropped on top of us. We looked up, but the wind had passed, and I heard someone murmur, "Where there is forgiveness, God is there." It could not have been any clearer.

As the last session on Friday concluded, the 'thank you's' were stretching on as we were all reluctant to leave this intimate circle. I looked upwards adding, "And thank you God, for this beautiful place in your creation where we have met this week." For the second time the stirring above us drew our eyes to the treetops, now swaying in a soft wind as dry leaves rained on the mats where we sat. Then it was gone. A hush fell over the group, then someone uttered an incredulous but reverent whisper, "God is listening to us."

What if God really does listen? What if He promised to answer all who call out to Him, but we are just too busy to bother?

What if we don't listen?

Listening does not come easily to most of us, whether that is listening to the everyday voices around us or to communities where we live and work or to the quiet voice of God in our world. So what? What if we do not ask the questions that encourage discussion and introspection? What if we ask but then do not listen to the answers? What if we do not hear the stories, the heart beats of people within communities? Simple answer: we will continue to bring projects they have not asked for and therefore will not own. We will miss the mark in elevating others to positions of strength and self-determination. We will attempt to work for them, but not with them, to give projects to them but not let them develop. The cycle of dependency will be perpetuated again and again for another generation. We will be planting well-intentioned seeds that never develop roots, never flourish and never bear fruit. That frankly has been the all too frequent pattern of the past and likely of the future.

Not listening, not asking questions, not waiting for the response. It is common to most of us and not exempt are the global workers who enthusiastically embark in their new country with all the knowledge and right answers! We saw this in living colour in one of our ventures to Nepal. While walking through some villages near the place where we were doing a workshop, we noticed quite a number of brand-new-looking outhouse toilets. Looking inside, we noted that they were sparkling clean, no smell that would indicate use as a toilet, and most had rice or other vegetable crops stored inside. We realized they were being used for storage rather than for their intended purpose. Why? The latrines had been built for them, we found out, by a well-known NGO, without any community discussion and without any questions of why the people preferred open defecation in the cornfields. It was a spiritual reason here too, as it turned out—they were afraid of spirits that might inhabit areas where human waste accumulated. We know that story!

No doubt the NGO reported great success in the numbers of toilets built and the enthusiasm of the people to help, but had they returned to check the next year if health standards had improved, they would have been surprised to see their lovely toilets had been changed into granaries!

One of the most humorous 'TED talks' we have heard describes this dilemma by one who has been there and is able to poke fun at his own attempts at doing things for a community without listening. It is called, *'Want to help someone—Shut up and Listen!'* by Ernesto Sirolli.[23] In the hilarious talk he tells his story of working with an Italian NGO in Africa, and deciding that they needed to teach the people how to grow gardens—tomatoes of course, as they were Italian—on the fertile land of the community. Naturally the people willingly cooperated in the endeavour, as they were being paid to work the gardens. Harvest time drew near. But just the night before they got in for the harvest, hippos got there first—and ate the whole crop!

"Why didn't you tell us there were hippos here waiting to eat the gardens?" the distressed Italian workers questioned. "You never asked us!" was the terse reply.

The Italians then noticed that the Americans, the British, the French—they were all making the same mistakes. "But at least," they consoled themselves, "at least WE fed the hippos!"

Sirolli identifies the two fundamental ways we Westerners tend to deal with people:

- Paternalistically, or treating people from another culture or economic status as if they were our children.
- Patronizingly, treating other cultures as if they are servants and can be commanded.

Instead, the first principle of helping is respect. To do that, he claims we must "shut up and listen." Study the local passions, leave those alone who do not want to be helped, become a servant of the people who have dreams, sit and visit with them where they are most comfortable, only offer to help them find knowledge when they are truly seeking it.

This story of the hippos in the gardens could be repeated over and over throughout the Majority world or Global South. We have seen examples of good aid money being poured into construction of aid posts and other health facilities, without engaging the community in planning or ownership. What happens when something breaks down? Call the group that built the facility to come and repair it. Or worse, as we observe in PNG during times of civil conflict when they burn the government aid post of the village as an act of warfare. After all, it did not 'belong' to anyone anyway!

DISCUSS AND REFLECT:

1. What importance do we give to listening to the life stories of those we work with or those we demonstrate compassion to? Why is it so beneficial?

2. When has your opinion been drastically changed by listening to the 'other side of the story?' Or when have you changed your perception of someone after hearing their story?

3. What groups are there within our community, or within our government system, that we need to research and link with to achieve some common goals? Who will get the credit if there is success?

4. Listening exercise: Share with each other (or with your journal) a 'life story' in your own journey that has deeply impacted you—maybe shaped your worldview or changed a course of direction in your life. Focus on the other person and truly listen.

SECTION TWO

COLLABORATION

Collaboration: a joint effort of multiple individuals or groups to accomplish a common goal or project. The common goal takes precedent over individual differences, enabling diverse groups to work together to combine their strengths and resources.

CHAPTER 3

Leader as Follower:
We did it ourselves!

"Go to the people, live with them, learn from them, build with what they have. But with the best leaders, when the work is done, the task accomplished, the people will say, 'We have done it ourselves.'" *--Lao Tzu (6th Century BC Chinese philosopher)*

Leaders from Within

These words, spoken millennia ago by an ancient philosopher, are as fresh and relevant today as they were then.

The 'Healthy Community' signboard awarded to Sava in the Eastern Highlands of PNG was painted with words they were proud to declare to the world, "We did it ourselves" in their native Kamano tongue. This means much more than the four simple words indicate; it means that the community as a whole decided to work together to be involved in their own development. It means that both men and women were participants in representing the wishes of the community. It means that they decided what their priorities were and how to accomplish them with the resources available to them. They were all the leaders.

The process of community ownership and collaboration, as described previously in the Sava story, involves a committed and frequent trainer like Esther. Community discussions where everyone can participate, leads to the growing belief that "We can do it!" The appointment of a committee, and mentoring of these people into leadership, cannot be over emphasized. They will be the ones to take the lead, to decide on projects and secure the resources to see them accomplished. Their mentoring will include training and discussion of integrity and responsibility, as well as tasks undertaken together such as social and asset mapping of the community. The latter involves drawing a 'bird's eye view' community map with homes, public buildings, schools, roads, crops that are being grown, any local industry, where people meet together, markets and so on. Planning for change grows out of this assessment of what is and what might be missing, not out of what the outsiders think should be the priorities. The trainers, who come to facilitate these discussions and walk alongside the committee and the peer educators (we call them Community Health Educators, CHEs), remain in the background. The committee becomes the leadership team who will be the real agents of change.

Pointing out the obvious: Oro Province, PNG 2005

We like the definition that describes a consultant as "one who borrows your watch to tell you what time it is!" Often we have observed that ideas or resource solutions so obvious to us are missed or taken for granted by a community that sees them all the time. Sometimes it takes someone from a step outside to point out the obvious, and then to move aside. Being part of that process is delightfully rewarding!

The Barai people group, who live in remote villages in the Owen Stanley mountain range of the Oro Province in Papua New Guinea, seemed motivated to change their lives. We were invited to come and do the Community Health Education training by an Australian couple, Peter and Bev, who were translating sections of the Bible into the Barai and related languages. They had also taught literacy for many years. The couple were now ready to retire, and were leaving behind a Barai Non-Formal Education Association and some enthusiastic, well-trained young people. The integrated approach to health training that CHE offers seemed to them a great step in their forward movement.

The first two visits, about six months apart, had produced a training team of a dozen or so mostly late teens to mid-twenty-year-olds, headed up by John who was also in his twenties but had an air of maturity that the others respected. The team had the time and inclination to walk from village to village sharing what they had learned. We had seen visible results in the general health and cleanliness of the villages.

This was our third visit, and as we flew over the dense, green, rainforest-clad mountains, we recognized the four landing strips where the Airlines PNG Twin Otter would touch down before arriving at Itokama. We watched small villages pop out of their hiding places as we flew over them, and marvelled at the many streams and waterfalls that graced the area. Finally, our strip came into view and the plane dropped us on the bumpy grass landing field, the pilot quickly unloaded cargo, and off he flew to the next stop. This was a weekly route, so we hoped to see the plane the same time a week later, weather and other conditions permitting! Now the familiar setting brought a welcome from many friends and it felt inviting rather than daunting.

However, the training module this week would involve some harder issues that the young training team would need to address. Throughout PNG there was growing alarm at the rising incidence of HIV/AIDS, but it was still a new and little understood disease in these remote rural areas. We knew that they were vulnerable, and the time to discuss it was before it reached epidemic proportions. But the discussions would need to touch on the root beliefs that had been perpetuated for generations, especially their beliefs about the superiority of men over women!

The training was held in the open-air style Anglican church, which made the whole community feel they could stop by and lean in the open windows from time to time to listen in on this very interesting seminar! While the actual participants numbered around forty-five, the reach was much broader because of this community dynamic! Each day as discussion groups posted their summaries on the walls on large pieces of paper, many lingered to read and discuss what was written on the papers, especially such topics as 'Consequences of extramarital affairs' and 'Effects of HIV/AIDS on a community.' All of the words written on the papers were from their own friends' lips, a strong point of this group participation process. When a person voices an opinion or offers an answer to a question, they 'own' that information—and the action that must be taken.

One morning coffee break, a participant came to us and said that an old woman, the mother of a pastor from the next village, wanted to share a 'vision' she had experienced while watching the group earlier that morning. Knowing the importance to these people of dreams and visions, and of our being willing to listen to the community, we agreed she should tell the group about it right after the break. Here is the summary of her words:

> I saw a picture of the group of you walking down a road. Bill and Sharon were behind the rest of the group, following along. Then you came to a large roadblock, a fallen tree across the road. You didn't seem to know if you should remove it or step over it, so you looked back and Bill and Sharon just motioned to you. They didn't say anything, just looked, and you all picked up the tree and carried it together easily to the side of the road. Then as you walked on, they pointed to show you that there were banana shoots sitting beside the road. These were ready to be planted, so you all dug some holes together and planted the bananas. A bit further along were sugar cane stalks lying by the road, and you planted them too. Then you kept on walking, and I didn't see any more. I wondered about the meaning of all this, so I wanted to tell you.

The group looked puzzled for a minute as they thought about the strange story. Especially in that they saw us as 'the teachers,' and in her description we did not say a word, just pointed to the obvious things that everyone else could see as well as we could.

Then people began to smile, as they realized just what the old woman had described—the process of community ownership they had learned, where the 'outsiders' were simply helping them to see the resources they already had. They had been ignoring many resources, or just did not have the will to work together to solve problems. We simply came along in the background to give them encouragement to do what they had the creative ability, knowledge and resources to do. What a great picture-summary of leading from behind she had described!

The old mother felt pleased that her story had been explained and had a good meaning, and she became a very loyal supporter of the CHE program. As we came to know her better, we appreciated her spirituality and wisdom, and her heart to serve others in her role as a traditional birth attendant for the local women.

Since that time, we have often been reminded of the 'standing in the background' story and the wise advice it represented. When we have been tempted to run out in front with solutions that are so obvious to us, but which may be totally premature or even inappropriate for the context, we remember the wise old mother who put us in our place, at the back of the pack!

As the week of HIV/AIDS training continued, another dream as amazing as the first, was shyly whispered to us. This time it was one of the young men, Aaron, who had such a vivid dream that he awakened the other guys sharing the one-room house with him while attending the training. Again, their concrete-thinking minds puzzled over the meaning, worried that it might indicate something harmful about to happen to us. Still, they decided they had better share it with us. Hence the hushed tones of the bearer of the message to us at morning coffee break.

This time the dream was a scene from the training classroom and it was the last day of the training.

> *The training wasn't finished, and yet the distant hum of the approaching plane coming to pick you up could be heard! There were still more questions, more important discussions! Somehow, we had the sense that you would not see us again and were feeling the urgency to learn all we could. The plane bounced down the landing strip beside the Anglican church where we were meeting, and we all jumped up and helped put things in your suitcases and ran out to the plane.*
>
> *We waved goodbye and went back to clean up the classroom. The walls were still full of papers, the results of the discussion groups. One paper at the front of the room seemed to stand out with large letters. It simply read: Acts 20:20. What does it mean?*

The night-time group knew it was a Scripture verse, so they had lit the kerosene lamp, read it and looked for clues…the context seemed to indicate that the Apostle Paul was saying a final goodbye to a group he had worked with for three years. It would be his last time to see them. But the verse in question remained a mystery to them. We were anxious to read it ourselves, so quickly went and looked it up.

Getting more excited as we read it, we told them, "This exactly describes what CHE does, the methodology and what we have been doing this week!" Paul too had been teaching things that were hard, that involved mindset changes for those under his teaching. He too was not staying, but entrusting leadership to them. Here is what we read:

> *We have not hesitated to teach all that would be beneficial to you, both publicly and house to house. (Acts 20:20 NIV)*

Indeed, the beneficial lessons we were passing on to them in this very public training would be carried from here to smaller gatherings of CHE volunteers, and then house-to-house. This is the CHE process—trainers from outside or within the community facilitating discussion of a couple of lessons each week with the CHE volunteer peer educators. Each would share this physical, social, spiritual, agriculture, environmental or lifestyle knowledge with neighbours. A whole community can be saturated within a short time, with dramatic changes evidenced.

Again, the people we had come to teach had taught us. Their simple awareness of the significance of dreams and visions, not so common in our own cultural mindset, had given us a new set of 'sound bites' for describing the work we do—we called it our 'Vision 2020': no hesitating, this is urgent; teaching all that is beneficial, an integrated approach; using both formal and informal contexts in public groups and then peer educators informally sharing in their homes. This said it all!

Our coffee break excitement transferred to the rest of the participants, as the night-time discussion group shared their discovery with the others. They concluded that they must be on the right track if we were following the lead of someone as influential in human history as the Apostle Paul! Indeed, they are on the right track and continue to this day.

Who gets the credit?

I remember a poster I put up in my school office years ago: *"There is no limit to what can be accomplished if it doesn't matter who gets the credit."*

This principle is especially relevant when working with governments who desperately need to meet certain targets. When we are willing to work toward somebody else's goals and help them meet their initiatives, giving them the credit when success comes which makes them look good, we are achieving true leadership. We understand that for governments, meeting targets and achieving their own indicators means continued funding from national coffers or from large international sources. This is, of course, in all of our best interest as these governmental institutions bring strength and order to society. These are society's 'walls' that we must help repair, rather than setting up parallel systems that compete and show up the weakness of the government system.

In the same way, collaborations between various Non-Government Organizations often stall out because each one wants to build its own empire and get credit for successful results rather than sharing that credit. Headquarters ask for statistics to justify budgets, and personnel need proof of results to gain promotions. Each organization protects its turf and wants to claim good outcomes as its own.

One of our favourite tales about giving credit to another comes from the now classic story of a young man, Bruce Olson, who in 1961 went to live and learn from the Motilone tribe of the remote Columbia rain forests. His approach has become a model for sustainable development for the generations, like us who followed. In his book, *Bruchko,*[24] he tells of an epidemic of eye infections that ran rampant through the community. The local healer, or witch doctor, did her incantations and rituals to no avail.

Bruce had antibiotic eye ointment, which he knew would work, but she proudly refused his offer to try it on her patients. "White man's ways are different," she claimed.

So rather than shaming her by giving the medicine himself, Bruce knew that keeping her on his side was essential to the balance of power in the community. He waited until an idea came to him—he would give himself the eye infection, which was easily done as so many were already infected! Then he asked the healer to try her incantations on him, again to no avail. He returned to her after a day or so and asked if she would do her routine again, but this time put the eye ointment in as well! Of course, this time it was successful.

He then gave her the medicine and suggested she use it for all her patients, along with her own methods of course. Within a few days the whole village epidemic was over, she got the credit and her importance in the community was elevated. She became a close friend and a future ally to be trained in the dispensing of other health measures for the community.

While his method may not be appropriate in many cultures where shamans bring harm not healing, we have been personally impacted by this great illustration of giving credit to another, and of true leadership-- the leader who stands in the background.

Swallowing Organizational Pride

Collaboration—it is becoming obvious that this is the way of the future in international efforts in both Faith-Based Organizations (FBO's) and Non-Government Organizations (NGO's) of all kinds. While many organizational leaders balk at working closely with other groups, already we are beginning to observe more multi-organizational teams, especially in difficult to reach areas of the world. Each brings different strengths, training and support to the mix. An effective team approach results when strong leaders are comfortable and willing to stand in the background rather than on centre stage, affiliating with others who may not be exactly like their own group!

Why is collaboration such a powerful tool? Collaboration may be defined as *a joint effort of multiple individuals or groups to accomplish a common goal or project.* The common goal takes precedence over individual differences, at least to the extent that diverse groups are enabled to work in unity to bring their strengths and resources together. Resources such as personnel, knowledge, training, strategies or finances may be shared in order to reach the goal. Materials become 'open source' rather than income generating. Because no one agency or organization has all the solutions or expertise, the synergistic effect of working together makes all the groups stronger. As well, by appearing to have a united voice, larger entities like governments or large funders will pay attention and may even provide additional resources.

No one organization has all the solutions or expertise, but the synergistic effect of working together makes all the groups stronger.

One of our experiences with this type of collaboration is the EDEN network in Papua New Guinea. Formed in 2009 at a conference of faith-based community development groups, the network idea was born and dubbed 'Effective Development Empowering the Nation.' We have met with them annually ever since, adding new groups each year. In a country where geographical isolation is the norm and travel expensive, there is little opportunity for local workers to attend conferences or receive new training. The EDEN network offers to train new groups in the Community Health Education methods, sharing materials and becoming an advocate to link community projects with government assistance. Helping each other succeed rather than hoarding knowledge or resources is an important value. No longer do these groups feel alone in their struggles. Their collective voice has become clearer and is recognized by the national health department as offering hope for their primary health care initiatives.

EDEN comes under the larger network of Christian Health Services, which is a coalition of churches that together provide the majority of rural health services in the country and is funded by the government. The health facilities that are part of the EDEN network are encouraged to be diligent in recording statistics from their preventive programs, some of which are showing remarkable results. For example, in some health centres in the East Sepik Province, a six-fold decrease in skin diseases, five-fold decrease in malaria and a three-fold decrease in pneumonia over five years has been documented. These health workers are reaping the reward of working with communities that have taken charge of their own issues to see this huge health improvement. Because of their increased ability to work together, we can predict that a community like this would be able to respond in a more organized way to a crisis like an epidemic, natural disaster, or even the threat of a tribal fight. They would also be more resilient, able to bounce back after such a crisis.

As we have observed in the EDEN network, for collaboration among organizations to be effective, they must have enough similarities for them to feel comfortable with each other, and a shared goal that takes precedence over procedural or philosophical differences. The uniqueness of collaborative projects is the fact that each group can maintain its differences, rather than trying to be the same in all aspects. So rather than criticize or argue with each other over differences, they celebrate these differences and know that all are needed.

Our plea is thus for cooperation and unity among faith groups, for willingness of all groups to work with governments, for secular NGO's—and all of us—to leave empire building and turf war mentality at home and just serve in the trenches together. Leading from behind— that means it really does not matter who gets the credit as long as the task gets done!

A group of Papua New Guinea Church Leaders Become Servants

The Goroka pastors' group broke the norm in cooperative initiatives when they decided to spearhead a city garbage clean-up! Most of them had gone through the CHE Training of Trainers workshops that had been offered in their city and were convinced that the Gospel means more than preaching. Their leadership had to set examples of faith in action in all aspects of life. The physical environment, rat-infested garbage to be precise, was a good place to start.

They began by purchasing and painting forty-five-gallon fuel drums for garbage bins, which were placed in strategic places in the main shopping streets. Pressure on the town council and governor's office to actually do regular collection of the waste from the bins was a bit tougher, but it has gradually taken hold.

The pastors then decided, as a model of servant leadership, that they would all gather with shovels and trucks on a Saturday morning to clean up the huge pile of organic waste outside the main vegetable market. This had been allowed to fester and feed rats and loose pigs for a decade or more. As they shovelled up the stinking, maggot-filled pile until they had the whole area clean, they said they felt that they were symbolically digging out the filth of the society and were seeing a vision for the renewal they all longed for. Like no other teaching message had done, they were feeling the link between the physical and spiritual worlds in their very souls.

One Sunday soon after this, we attended a church service where the pastor announced there would be no sermon that day. Instead, they had disposable gloves, plastic bags, shovels and a truck ready for action. Everyone was to go out and clean the streets in a three or four block radius! It did not take long for the three hundred or so people, with the speed and effect of a whirlwind, to have the streets clean of debris, and the piles of waste in the shop areas shovelled into the truck. I had prepared flyers for them to give to the mystified people who were, as always, hanging out on the streets, to teach about the reason for churches to be involved in issues of cleanliness and environmental concern. The demonstration had more impact and reach than inspiring teaching would have had. More such action-packed sermons are needed in this world!

Demonstration has more impact than inspiring teaching.

It did not take many days for the streets to be dirty again of course, but the message had gone out loud and clear. Over the next few years, others would repeat the process, with groups doing clean up in specific areas, businesses promoting cleanliness as their Corporate Social Responsibility, and the town council beginning to do their share. Time and the persistence of diverse faith groups working together paid off, and Goroka had been transformed from a city strewn with garbage to an exceptionally clean city for Papua New Guinea.

Importance of Invitation

How to decide where to get involved when there is so much need is a perplexing issue. Spending time, building friendships, asking questions, listening to the heart of the community is a critical first step. Enthusiastic leaders often miss this step as they see the need and want to respond. We have learned that random selection of a community or a simple process of elimination with a set of criteria to predict success is not enough, even though we do use and teach that as a tool for objective selection. But more important is a clear invitation from the recognized leadership in a community for any development there to be effective. They will be the ones who step to the front while we fall in behind them.

A group of the Community Health Education trainers in PNG was asked by a large NGO if they could be contracted for community engagement with a village where the NGO wanted to do a water project. They were beginning to realize that some groundwork should happen in the community if their European Union funded water systems were going to be properly used and maintained by the community.

The trainers deliberated and then agreed. After all it was a way to supplement their meagre incomes. What they had not counted on was the resistance of the community to do anything for themselves. They were very willing to be the beneficiaries of a water system if someone delivered it, but to take ownership was another matter.

The trainers later described the week they had spent in the community as a "waste of our time," largely because the community itself had not asked for the program but had been told that this training was part of the package! For them to be inspired to take ownership, to organize a committee structure, even to understand their role in prevention of common illnesses that could easily be prevented at the home level—they were not ready for that kind of change! They only wanted water to flow through a pipe!

There was no real desire for collaboration and no local champion to inspire the people to say, "We did it ourselves."

DISCUSS AND REFLECT:

1. What leadership qualities that we admire would stand out more clearly if the leader led from behind rather than leading from in front?

2. How can we, in our various spheres of influence and responsibility, simply point the way for others to excel using their own gifts or resources?

3. Who in our lives has come alongside and encouraged us, fading into the background in order to let us succeed?

4. When have you found it difficult to let others take the credit for something you have had a large part in accomplishing?

CHAPTER 4

Living Beyond the Tribe: And the models that inspired us

"He is no fool who gives up what he cannot keep to gain what he cannot lose."

--Jim Elliot

Outside the Comfort Zone

When we elect to leave the comfort zone of the culture and the place where we feel we are grounded and belong, we suddenly become outsiders. Some thrive in the wonder and adventure of learning to love another culture and place; others barely survive. Cross-cultural blunder stories could fill volumes, but fortunately in the end most are not too serious, and most cultures are quite forgiving to their guests!

For our purposes here, we will define 'the tribe' as our family and place of origin, our cultural settings, and even the homogeneous groups to which we belong. Bill and I have lived outside our tribe for much of our married lives. Maybe some of our experiences and insights will be of help to those readers who are considering spending time outside their boundaries whether at home or abroad.

Living beyond the tribe does not have to take place far away. Some choose to step out of their social or geographical setting within their own culture, identifying instead with the disadvantaged of the inner cities, with new immigrants, refugees, recovering addicts or other sub-sets of our own cities. Issues such as cross-cultural tensions and collaboration between diverse groups can apply at home as well as abroad.

The successful sojourner beyond the tribe is the one who can look back with humour at the experiences that have at the time seemed excruciatingly tough or embarrassing! We often tell young would-be cross-cultural workers that a well-developed sense of adventure is a pre-requisite—and the definition of an adventure is "misery remembered!" Those camping trips where you woke up to a snow-covered tent, or your sunny cycling trip that became an endurance test as driving rain soaked your packs, or the day hike that finished with headlamps in the pitch darkness of night—those experiences will stand you in good stead in life wherever you go!

We admit there are painful parts to living beyond the tribe, often for the most vulnerable members of the family. Illnesses that we were never prepared for, the feeling of being outsiders no matter how hard we tried to become insiders, perceived social or educational disadvantages for our children, potential criminal attacks, long distances separating us from loved ones during times of celebration or bereavement, concerns about being relegated professionally or financially to the backwater of our own culture—all costs to realistically consider.

The obvious question that many ask is therefore, "Why do it?" If the personal cost is so high, is it not more reasonable to stay in your comfort zones?

To answer the question, we come back to worldview—if we see advancing one's self to the highest status possible as most important in life, then this question is valid and any reason to expend this kind of effort on those outside our tribe may be absurd. However, if life is not

---

Why not just stay home in your comfort zone rather than take personal risks? The answer comes down to worldview.

---

for self-enhancement but if it is for the generous sharing of our time, skills and resources for the common good—after all none of us deserve these in the first place—then the question is much easier to answer.

Could it not be as simple as discovering joy in the possibility of seeing others, from the very young to the elderly, flourish as they fulfill their God-given potential in life?

Surprisingly, we do not personally lose out as we might suspect. We all win, even if we see just an inkling of harmony emerge where it did not exist before in the four critical relationships—with self, community, the environment and with God. Indeed, the personal joy we feel goes beyond any material or social satisfaction, while diverse friendships have enriched our family beyond measure.

Inspired by Heroes

We have been urged on by the inspiration of others who have dared to live out their lives on distant shores. In the medical field alone there are many who risked life and limb to save others' lives, and still do.

Bill and I and many others, have been inspired by Dr. Paul Brand, a British orthopedic surgeon who devoted much of his life to lepers in Vellore, India. Recounted in the book *Ten Fingers for God,*[25] his efforts to bring new life to lepers discarded from their society resulted in advances in reconstructive surgery that restore deformed hands and limbs. His techniques developed in the 1950's remain current today.

Dr. Denis Burkitt, an Irish surgeon who served in Uganda for years, identified a pediatric cancer still named after him, the 'Burkitt lymphoma'. He also did pioneer research related to bowel inflammatory disease patterns, correlating this with the difference in diets in Africa and the developed world. His personal sacrifices still count for good worldwide.

A more current inspiration is Dr. Ken Clezy and his wife Gwen. While in Papua New Guinea we had the privilege of forming a deep friendship with this humble and courageous Australian couple. They had rejected a stunning career, choosing rather to dedicate their lives to serving the least fortunate. Skilled in general surgery as well as brain and spinal tumours, Ken was a professor of surgery in Port Moresby for years and an exceptional hand surgeon (he had studied under Dr. Brand in India). In his 70's, instead of retirement, Ken served as surgeon for a mission hospital in Yemen. When three colleagues were shot dead, he was spared only because he had gone home for breakfast following his early morning rounds. Others left the country, but he and Gwen stayed on and were most disappointed when the mission decided to close the hospital. His book *Now in Remission*[26] reflects a brilliant and dedicated man who recorded with surgical precision the details of his life, joys and tragedies. Now a widower in his 90's, he is still a church organist, occasional Bible teacher and has just finished writing his second novel!

Another couple from California whom we met our first year in Papua New Guinea, Dan and Marjorie Goodwin, soon became surrogate grandparents to our kids and mentors to us. They were dorm parents in the mission boarding school but realized much like us that their real calling and interest was with the people of the surrounding villages. This led them after a couple of years to establish themselves in a village not far from Kainantu where Bill by then was Medical Director. They lived as much like the people as they could, cooking over a fire, walking to the stream for water, getting along without electricity or a vehicle, while focusing on adult literacy in the area. They often came walking to our house with a bag of laundry or to relax with a hot shower and play with our kids. We admired their dedication and willingness to live the simple life in PNG rather than a life of ease with their grandchildren in California. From PNG they went to a Hmong refugee camp run by World Vision on the Thailand–Laos border. As camp manager, they were given the right to live on site while the other staff stayed in a nearby town. They were comfortable with that after their village life in PNG. We were privileged to visit them there and share their basic home, made from bush materials like the rest of the refugees. They always pushed the system, always held justice and compassion above pragmatism or tradition even when it put them at odds with their peers. We maintained our close friendship right until they both passed on, Dan in 2012 and Marjorie in 2016. They never failed to encourage us and motivate us to live with less and not to give up when the going got rough.

Such are the unsung heroes of our times, men and women of the kind of courage and conviction that dares them to act on their belief that all men and women have rights to equal treatment and compassion. While many of us believe this, few leave the comfort zones to live beyond the tribe. Our own lives pale in significance beside these most exceptional people who have shown us what it means to be fully human.

"Enough for our need, but not for our greed"

Another of our heroes was a humble, home-grown Papua New Guinean poet-writer-theologian and a dear friend, Kumalau Tawali, who was willing to push the margins of his own culture. When Kumalau died in 2006, the country lost a courageous voice of freedom. Kumalau had determined to live life beyond his tribe. As PNG's first Poet Laureate, and an avid writer of newspaper columns and stories of PNG life, he was not afraid to call the nation to integrity, or to point out corruption becoming rife in political arenas, or to address issues of the ecological impact of resource development. We have noticed that when these kinds of fearless prophetic voices are silenced, either by disease and death, or by political muzzling such as imprisonment or martyrdom, even the physical environment groans.

Kumalau wrote poetry that throbbed with the pulse of the waves lapping the shore of the islands of his boyhood. It is obvious from reading his poetry that the sea was his blood, the rhythm of the waves his heart beat. He would have loved to have lived his whole life fishing on the reefs in the days when the coral was still alive, the myriads of fish flashing colour between their waving branches. But he saw the day when greed would overcome beauty, and his lone voice could make a difference.

He became a spokesman for truth, for justice, for equitable treatment and preservation of the land and the people in it. As a young man he advocated for environmental care, long before it was on the front pages of our media. His articulate columns in the National newspaper were always pointed, speaking out against government corruption and other societal issues with no fear of political backlash.

Kumalau had a favourite saying, a quote often attributed to Gandhi, but apparently spoken earlier by Rev. Frank Buchman: "There is enough in the world for everyone's need, but not enough for everyone's greed." He had come to realize personally that looking out only for our own family and clan is a form of greed that will work to the detriment of everyone. So, while still fiercely loving his native Manus Islands

Province, Kumalau's concern extended beyond his island shores to the whole country and even further to all of the South Pacific Islands.

He once told us the awesome responsibility he felt when given the opportunity to be the mouthpiece of God Almighty! His poetry was a mouthpiece, as was his preaching, teaching and regular newspaper columns. He loved to interact with students of all ages but especially those at university, the next generation of leaders. As a camp and conference speaker, he traveled around PNG with his thought provoking and not-easily-forgotten messages. In his later years, his heart was broken by the destruction wrought on the generation of young people impacted by HIV and AIDS—we remember seeing him weeping on the stage during a nation-wide HIV and AIDS conference.

In 1988, he and his young family headed to Canada and a Theology Master's program at Regent College in Vancouver. Our family had returned in 1986 to settle for a few years back in Calgary, so it was natural to invite them to visit for semester breaks. On one of these visits, he connected with our First Nations neighbours—just ten minutes from where we had lived for years! This connection amazingly came through a New Zealand Maori friend he had met years earlier and who Kumalau knew was in Canada for a cultural exchange. We were invited to dinner for the first time in our lives to the home of a Tsuu T'ina Nation family, and then reciprocated with dinner at our home. We maintained that congenial friendship across a cultural divide that few are able to breach for a few years following the Tawali's visit.

Why do some have the eyes to see beyond their own tribe, while others of us find it so uncomfortable? We need more models to prompt us, like we had from Kumalau. But why, we wonder, are the Kumalau's so rare?

Our culture wraps around us and teaches us the kinds of attitudes that determine the way we live. Need or greed, self-preservation or generosity, hoarding or living with open-handed abandonment; the tensions go on and on. In PNG, as in many cultures, loyalty to the tribe takes precedence over all other obligations.

Whose hammer? Kainantu, PNG, 1980

Some of us who choose to live beyond our tribe are always outsiders struggling to become insiders, or even to just co-exist gracefully. Trying to fit into another culture often meets with limited success. Seldom do outsider Westerners feel totally accepted as part of a community, though some even go through adoption rituals and cultural protocols that promise 'insider' privileges. Those who can truly assimilate in living among a new group are the exception. There are good cultural reasons for this aloofness, even for adopted tribe members.

Cultural barriers that are hard to breach go deep, rooted in the voices and models from our infancy through childhood to adult life. For example, one cultural norm we are steeped in comes from our view of 'me and others' in our individualistic, nuclear family society. Our sense of obligation to others is often very narrow, extending to immediate family and close friends. In a traditional collectivist society, the loyalty is first to family, then clan, then tribal or language group, followed loosely by identification with province (or state) and finally the nation. Openness and trust of others beyond the tribe poses a challenge for good governance as well as the rule of law. Election time makes this very clear, as the tribal group puts forth a candidate that everyone is expected to support. If successful, this candidate is obligated to put the tribe first in government funding or development.

When it comes to possessions, we individualists believe what we own personally is ours to decide what to do with. What we earn we keep. This is not the case in much of the rest of the collectivist world where sharing is of higher value than possession. We learned about the cultural value of sharing from Yamu very soon after we arrived in Kainantu, PNG in 1980. Yamu and Juliepe, along with their children Albert and Helen, lived in a typical Highlands small, round house made of bush materials behind the big house next door to us. Yamu was caretaker of the house and grounds of the politician who owned the house but resided elsewhere.

Our kids, Tim and Tera, at that time ages three and five, quickly befriended the family and spent lots of time hanging out around their cooking fire. They loved the *kaukau* (sweet potato) roasted on the coals and quickly spoke the Melanesian Pidgin with a local accent! Yamu taught me the traditional way to dig and plant a vegetable garden on a steep slope with deep ditches between plots to avoid erosion during the heavy tropical downpours. They called us their *'wantoks'* (term for a clan member who speaks the same language, often generalized to mean a good friend).

One day Bill was searching for his hammer, and then remembered that he had loaned it to Yamu a week or two earlier. "Why had he not returned it?" Bill wondered aloud. He went next door to ask for it. *"Yesa, hema bilong yumi!"* (Oh yes, our hammer), Yamu replied, fetching it.

"What do you mean, our hammer," Bill thought. *"Em i hema bilong mi tasol,"* (It is my hammer!) is what he replied.

As he carried it home, Bill realized what had just happened in that short interchange--Yamu was treating him like a *wantok* where everything is communal and circulates around as needed, not hoarded by the person who had bought it! Bill was breaching his trust by emphatically calling it his own hammer, not to be asked for again.

In the collective cultural norm, personal worth is measured in interdependence, and success by fulfilling a role in the group. Wealth involves the loans given to others that incur their indebtedness to us! We on the other hand, find our personal identity in getting ahead as individuals, seeking self-fulfillment in our careers, valuing independence. Quite a contrast.

> *In the collective culture, personal worth is measured in interdependence, and success by fulfilling a role in the group. Wealth is in the loans we give others to incur their indebtedness.*

Our kids learned to love beyond their tribe more readily than we did. They played naturally with Yamu and Juliepe's two kids in the colour-blind fashion of children. Story telling around the open fire in the middle of the grass hut is central to the culture, and they fit right in. We did get nervous as we observed Yamu coughing and spitting in the fire, knowing that tuberculosis was rampant and that the sweet potato our kids loved to eat came from coals of that same fire!

One day when Juliepe adopted an unwanted baby from a clan member, Tera surprised us by deciding that she wanted to give away her treasured 'blankie' as Baby Hennie had come with barely a stitch of clothing. Yes, learning to love starts young. We realized that Tim's eyes had been opened to the disparity in living conditions one rainy night when he was saying his prayers: "Please God, keep Albert dry, because there is a leak in their (thatched) roof right over his bed!"

Oh, for the open eyes of a child. Oh, for a heart that learns to be bi-cultural at an early age. To be able to move from our time-bound cultural norm to the open view where time is unlimited and relationships are all-important. The kids' time around the fire listening to stories and singing songs was knitting them to a people who understood slow living, but not 'wasted time!' After all, time is not a commodity in this place.

"Don't share your drinking water!" Kainantu, Papua New Guinea, 1980

The myths and story-trading that are passed around expatriate groups living in other cultures are numerous and embarrassing. We found it better to associate mainly with our PNG health colleagues and students in order to keep our perspective and optimism. That is advice we continue to give to people aspiring to work in another country—listen to locals, not the expats!

Our water source was a large 3500-gallon galvanized tank that collected rainwater from the roof. Called 'sky juice,' it was generally fit to drink if the tanks were cleaned occasionally. Rain could be counted on quite consistently in the Highlands for most of the year, even in the so-called dry season. If the tank water ran out, we would be in trouble. Getting a truck to bring river water and then boiling water for drinking was tedious. The previous inhabitants of our rented house therefore told us that we should put a lock on our tank to prevent the people walking by from filling up their bottles on their way to the village at the end of our street! We somehow could not bring ourselves to do that.

As predicted, the local villagers helped themselves to our water as they walked by, mostly when we were not home to notice. There was no rain for a couple of weeks and we began to tap the rings in the metal tank to determine the water level and monitor the declining supply.

We knew in a few days it would be gone. Finally, there was one day's supply left.

That night the floodgates opened and it dumped rain for two solid hours! Before breakfast, Bill went out to tap the rings and was incredulous to find that the tank was at least two thirds full, or around 2500 gallons, a huge amount of water for a short few hours of rain.

With a great sense of relief, he set off walking the ten minutes across the airstrip to the hospital. When he got there, he commented to the staff how relieved we were that the night's rain had almost filled our tank. They looked at him with confusion. "But we only got a few drops in our part of town!" they all claimed.

We still have no explanation for what seemed at the time a gracious impossibility, but whatever happened, it changed us, we hope forever. The principle seems undeniable: hoarded stuff seems to develop holes or rot or disappear, while shared stuff multiplies.

Jim Elliott's now-famous words are a motto to live by: "He is no fool who gives up what he cannot keep to gain what he cannot lose." Elliott himself gave up his life in 1956 in Ecuador while attempting to make contact with a previously unreached tribe of Auca Indians. [27]

The principle seems undeniable: Hoarded stuff may develop holes or rot or disappear; shared stuff multiplies.

You won't have any Trouble—You're Part of the Community

Our first few years in Papua New Guinea were a steep learning curve—adapting to a culture just a generation away from the Stone Age, learning to recognize and treat tropical or other end stage illness that medics never see at home, learning to feel at ease with our personal security. Hearing stories from other expatriates didn't help!

Some like the water tank we could ignore, but others got closer to home and we knew they were real security risks. Bill would often worry about leaving the family at night when the nurses called him to the hospital for an emergency delivery they could not handle alone. He would often phone and wake me up if the complicated procedure was taking longer than he thought, just to see how we were! Naturally we were fine until the phone call woke me up!

One day he confided these concerns to Matthew, the Hospital Secretary. He and his wife Susie, both from Bougainville Province, had become close friends and we often enjoyed evening visits or meals together. Without hesitation, Matthew answered, "You won't have any trouble."

"Oh yeah," Bill wondered. "Why do you say that?"

"You are part of the community, and so are the *raskals* (word used for robbers/criminals). The community controls them, knows who is inside and outside the community. You always have locals in your home, you attend a church, you mix with the staff and they know that."

Thankfully he was right, we never experienced any problems during those years.

One night though, he tested his own theory. We received a phone call in the middle of the night. It was Matthew, hoarsely whispering into the phone, "Bill, there is a *raskal* in our house!"

"Where are you Matthew?" Bill asked.

"We are all in the bedroom with the door locked. He is walking around out in the hallway."

Bill asked the obvious question: "Have you called the police?"

"Yes, but you know how they are," came the breathless whisper. "They may not come for hours! They usually wait until they know the trouble is over."

"OK, I'll come over, but I don't know what I can do!" Bill responded.

He quickly dressed and got into the vehicle, even though it was just a couple of minutes away. He thought maybe the sound of the noisy Land Cruiser would frighten the intruder at least. The last thing he wanted was to encounter an armed home invader face to face.

Surprisingly the police had already come and had apprehended the inebriated offender.

"The damn guy claimed that he was looking for his own place and just wandered into the wrong house!" the policeman explained. The police, thinking that was a reasonable explanation for a home invasion, would have let him go on his way. Bill thought otherwise.

"Do you know who this man is?" he asked the culprit, pointing to Matthew.

"Yes, that is Matthew Hapoto," he replied.

"So, you do know where you are!" Bill stated. "Seems you are not so drunk that you do not know the owner of the house you are in. Certainly you must know you are in the wrong house."

"Take him to jail," the policeman told his partner. "He can explain his story to the chief in the morning!"

Another night a similar "Help!" call came from the house where several single nurses lived. This time the drunken would-be invader turned out to be the manager of the Electrical Commission, normally a very responsible guy.

When Bill drove over to investigate this time, he saw two sets of legs and the butt of a shotgun silhouetted at the back of the house, which was raised on pillars off the ground. He almost turned the car around and fled but stopped when a head he recognized poked around the corner. The gun, as it turned out, belonged to the neighbour, who happened to be the District Commissioner authorized to have a firearm at home. Hearing the commotion, he had come over.

"I almost shot the bugger," he told Bill. "It was fortunate I recognized him just in time!"

The intruder this time was sent home with a reprimand and the embarrassment of being caught in his compromised situation by two people he knew and respected.

This was the 1980's. As the years have gone by, it is unfortunate that the number of illegal guns coming into the country has made armed robberies, home invasions and murders a serious problem. Today we would not entertain the idea of investigating a call in the middle of the night without the presence of the police.

Most villages today have an arsenal of high-powered weapons. Hospital emergency departments, which before removed arrows from the victims of tribal warfare, are now confronted with fatal bullet wounds. Violence against the hospital staff on night duty has forced out-patient closure from time to time. Even the camaraderie and trust amongst the staff suffers, as violence begets violence in a downward spiral that seems unstoppable.

We are glad that we had the opportunity to live and raise our family in Papua New Guinea during the years that we did, when it was relatively safe. Not without incidents, but quite safe.

More recently we had our own hold-up experience while walking down a normally busy Goroka street on a quiet Good Friday. With no others in sight, two young men jumped out from a hedge, flailing a homemade sawed-off shotgun. It was like a slow-motion movie, hard to believe it was really happening to us! The two were young, nervous and, we both sensed, quite inexperienced in this activity. One of them gruffly ordered, "Your money or you are dead!"

The accomplice was busily looking up and down the road to make sure we were still alone. We were not carrying much money, but even so Bill was not about to give it to them. He capitalized on their hesitance, realizing they were almost as uncomfortable as we were, as we were still too surprised to be scared. Besides, he told me afterwards, in looking at that amateur gun it could have just as likely killed them as us had they tried to fire!

He let out the breath he had sucked in and began in his best 'Father tone' voice: "This is not a good thing you are doing," he chided, stating the obvious in the Pidgin language they understood. "You two look like you could think of better ways to earn a living than this." It was almost laughable to watch, as now the faces of the two boys had the look of surprise! They had been nervous holding up this older white couple and now to hear an unexpected lecture rather than a quick opening of the wallet was not what the script said was supposed to happen.

Just then the 'spotter' saw someone walking over the crest of the hill in the direction we were walking, gave a signal to the other and the two disappeared back into the hedge as quickly as they had come. We looked at each other silently before one of us spoke, "What was that—did that really happen?"

As we continued our walk to the house where our daughter and son-in-law had recently moved, we both knew that what had just happened to us would be a warning to her. "I am so glad that happened to us and not to Tera," we remarked to each other. We knew she had walked alone to work on that street several times, and that this incident would mean they would need to figure out something different. Indeed, good often comes from an intended evil.

Grieving for a pet the cultural way

As in most homes with young children, pets are part of the package. We had a few of them during our years in PNG—Gladys the black cat that seemed to have more than her share of nine lives as she lived with three families over two decades. Then there was a possum whose baby we called Night Rider. Their presence necessitated building a huge cage around a tree in our back yard. Three dogs in turn were part of our family. Each of course had its own story of beginning and end and was special to us. Candy, a Golden Retriever cross breed that we had raised from a puppy and brought with us when we moved from Kainantu to Goroka, had an unforgettable ending… I ran over her!

She always recognized the sound of our truck coming from a block away and would run down the driveway to meet us. On this particular day I bounced over an especially deep pothole in the driveway and swerved just enough that the tire caught her in the ribs as she ran alongside. I heard her yelp, as she ran in front of the car and fell after a few more strides. She was breathing her last gurgling breaths as I rushed panic-stricken to her side.

Bill heard the yelp from his open third floor office window in the building across the street and saw that I was standing there sobbing. Guessing what had happened, he came rushing down. Fortunately the kids were both at school and had not witnessed the event—but the neighbours had! The provincial Premier with his three wives and children lived next door, and several teenage boys came running over to commiserate with us. Bill asked if they would help me bury the dog while he returned to work so it was done before the kids came home from school. They carried the dog to the back of the house, where I chose a spot under some banana trees for her grave. I left them to dig the hole while I went inside to compose myself. After a very few minutes, a knock at the door took me back outside where one of the boys stood looking uncomfortable and obviously wanting to say something.

"Yes?" I asked.

"Our Papa," he began hesitantly. He was scrambling for excuses as I knew their father was nowhere around. "He is asking if you could give the dog for us to eat?"

Instantly I saw what was happening through their eyes: a chubby well-fed dog, already dead but still warm was about to be wasted by putting it in the ground to rot. What sense was there in that? At the same time, I felt as if I had been punched in the gut, and the emotions, already close to the surface, burst. "No!" was about all I could get out, my head shaking emphatically. The shocked look on the boy's face as he backed away from the sobbing white lady could have been funny if I had not been so upset.

I closed the door and ran to pick up the phone. "Bill," my voice squeaked between sobs. "They want to eat the dog!"

"They want to eat the dog?" confirming what he thought he heard. "I will be right over."

Moments later I watched as he again walked up the driveway and spoke quietly to the boys. "In our culture," he explained, "a pet becomes like part of the family and it is upsetting to think of eating it." I saw them nod soberly and resume digging the grave as Bill returned to work.

Another knock at the door. "We have finished digging the hole. But we have no box to put the dog in. Maybe you have a blanket we could wrap it in?" Now my suspicious mind jumped back into motion. I was sure they wanted to return after dark and dig up the dog, so they did not want it matted with dirt. I was not going to give that to them.

"No" I replied. *"Plantim em nating."* (Bury it just as it is.) Their puzzled faces seems to say, "how can she value this dog as part of the family, yet not even wrap it in a blanket?" I watched as they put the dog in the ground and shovelled the earth in a mound over it.

The next morning I secretly went out to inspect the dirt to see if the mound looked in any way disturbed. We will never know.

But who visits them? Brisbane Australia, 1982

During Bill's time of teaching Health Extension Officer students, the future rural doctors of PNG health centers, he became aware of a huge gap in their understanding of hygiene. They had grown up in thatched homes with dirt floors, so to supervise cleaning staff who would keep the brand-new flooring of the hospital sparkling clean was just not going to happen. Clean was relative; hygienically clean, not in the least way within their frame of reference. After all, cleaning staff mopped the floor regularly—using one bucket of dirty water for several wards!

As our family discussed this over the dinner table, it became quite clear—if they had never seen clean floors, how does one describe a clean floor? In addition, a serious cultural difference was apparent. Their norm is to accept the way things are without question. We, on the other hand, have grown up seeing challenges as opportunities to problem solve.

Bill issued a challenge in class the next day: "If anyone can raise two thousand kina (on par with US dollars at that time) in two months, at the end of the school year we will go on a trip to Australia. We will tour some health facilities, see clean hospitals and lots more."

We did not ever imagine that any of them could come up with that much money in a short time, but we were wrong! Out of the woodwork came the money (no doubt borrowed from uncles who knew they were future wage earners!) and a dozen of them got their passports and tickets. Off we went, along with our two, Timothy and Tera, then eight and six years old. It was just the right number to rent a fifteen-seat van in Brisbane for the drive to Sydney and then Canberra, about a week in each of the three places.

Most of the students, at around twenty years of age, had never even been to Port Moresby, the capital city of PNG, let alone to another country! In Port Moresby they experienced an elevator for the first time, which initiated gasps and giggles from some, and the 'brave and cool' look from others. Looking out the windows from the dizzy height of four stories terrified them. Three weeks later, at our last stop in Canberra, this motley crew who had been queasy on an elevator, were now freaking us out by leaning over the open balcony at the top of the Canberra tower, the highest in Australia!

Being billeted in the homes of Australians, organized ahead through our Australian friends serving in PNG, was in itself a great education for them. At first shy, their naturally winsome personalities and the friendly hosts soon overcame that. Most of the host families had never had opportunity to meet Papua New Guineans either, so the education went both ways.

At Royal Brisbane Hospital, the sparkling clean floors that we had come seeking were right there in plain sight. In fact, it was the same tiled linoleum that had just been installed in the recent renovations of the Kainantu Health Centre—and this gleaming specimen of a floor was apparently ten years old! It looked newer than our year-old floor. Mission accomplished!

At the end of the tour, we decided that one last institutional visit was in order, a long-term care seniors' residence. It was a beautiful building, new and spacious, the staff was friendly, the residents willing to chat. In fact, it was hard to get our group away as they loved visiting the elderly and hearing their stories. Some of the residents of course were silent, spending their days mindlessly watching the television screen.

Then one of the students asked a staff person the tell-tale question that was on all their minds, "Where are the families of these people?"

"Oh, they come to visit," was the noncommittal reply.

"How often do they visit?" the student persisted.

The response still echoes in our ears, as true today in Canada as it was there. "About one third of families visit regularly up to several times a week. Another third visit on their birthdays, Christmas, special occasions. The other third of residents never have visits from family."

When we left, the group was unusually silent, musing on what we had just witnessed and the words of the caregiver. They had been so impressed with all they had seen up to this point in Australia, but now a huge flaw in Western civilization had become obvious to them. We could actually leave our elderly in the care of strangers and rarely visit them? It was unthinkable. Where were the children these people had raised? Where was the rest of 'the tribe?'

Australians see Papua New Guinea as a scary place: now these students saw abandonment of the elderly in that home as the scariest thing they had ever seen!

The thought of growing old in Papua New Guinea was now attractive to them, in spite of lack of comforts or poor medical attention in the rural areas. They were glad to be going home.

Kumalau lived in death as he lived in life

Yes, growing old in PNG. There is no ideal way to become aged, but this is when being close to a tribe is advantageous.

We began this chapter with one of PNG's unsung heroes. The final chapter of Kumalau Tawali's life, while sad, became an object lesson for all of Papua New Guinea, and especially for the Christian community. Kumalau suffered a massive stroke at the early age of forty-nine years. He was left without speech, without his memory, without his ability to read and write. For an articulate writer and speaker, it appeared his purposeful life was finished. He was pastor of a church and part of a large pastors' fellowship group. One by one they came to visit. They did not know what to do with a one-way conversation, or how to respond to such a brilliant man who was reduced in their eyes to a child. So, one by one they left, and few returned with consistency.

In PNG, the tribe is supposed to come close at times like this. But what if the tribe is on a remote island province, a long boat journey or expensive flight away? Kumalau had chosen to be a son of the nation, not just of his tribe. He had counted the cost of living beyond his tribe and was prepared to pay.

So here he was stuck, and who would show love beyond their tribe to this family in physical and financial distress? The Church, sadly inexperienced in reaching out beyond its own group, did not pass the test. A few friends helped, some giving them very basic accommodation in small quarters at the back of their homes. Kumalau's wife Sisilia had a drum oven made from a forty-five-gallon barrel and started to bake buns for enough cash to meet the family daily needs.

Sisilia was determined that Kumalau would again walk, talk, read and write. She began teaching him preschool style by putting pictures on the wall and repeating the names of objects. They went on to photo albums to rebuild memory. Next came reading. When we first saw him after his stroke, he could talk and read haltingly. He explained that he remembered us only from what Sisilia had told him as she rebuilt his memories from the photo albums!

Kumalau lived until 2006, ten years after the stroke, and regained much of his previous life and wit, even preaching and writing occasionally. But he was never reintegrated back into his previous position of influence.

Still, messages from his newspaper columns continue to ring true: *"If everybody cares enough and everybody shares enough, would not everybody have enough?"*[28]

"Today was brought to birth by yesterday."

"Our obsession with making too much money too quickly in too short a time has begun to make us a heartless society."

Our world and his world in PNG desperately need to hear such words again.

Kumalau chose to be buried where he died so as not to incur the huge expense of flying his remains back to his home province as is customary. The extended family, steeped in animism, objected and even threatened, as their belief was so strong that his spirit should go back into their native soil. The common belief is that this would pass on his strengths to others at home.

Sisilia stood her ground as she knew Kumalau's wishes and his broader view of himself as belonging to the whole nation. We know the pressure she felt, and were proud of her bravery.

Her comment to us after the huge memorial service with the many glowing accolades from the other pastors was, "If only they had said those things to him while he was alive!"

In recent years we asked a well-connected national church leader if anyone was speaking against the blatant corruption that is crippling the nation.

His reply: "No one. Since Kumalau died, there has not been another courageous and articulate voice willing to speak out like he did!"

Fingerprints and ripples

Sharing our home and family became more and more the obvious thing to do as we got to know hospital staff and students. Barbecued meals on an open fire, making Saturday morning pancakes in the student mess, having an open door for the students to come for a visit or to a weekly Bible study—these were some of our efforts to live beyond our own tribe. As the students graduated and went to health centers around the country, they returned for visits or wrote to us from their isolated posts.

Some returned to work in the province where Bill became Provincial Health Officer and we had the privilege of seeing them marry and begin families of their own.

When we left to return to Canada to see our kids finish school and university, it was fourteen years before we were able to return. We were amazed to meet former students in places of authority in the Department of Health everywhere we went.

When we remarked about this, one of them smiled, "Yes, you have left your fingerprints all over this country!"

Fingerprints—like the pebbles we throw into a pond and watch the ripples move on and on until they impact a different shore than where they started. Is that how our lives are meant to be? Nothing we do is insignificant, no matter how small. No word, no action unnoticed.

"We were watching you all the time," another former student told us. "After all, we grew up in polygamist families, and we had no idea how a husband should treat his wife or how parents should guide their children's development."

Really? If we had known that, we might have tried harder to be better models! However, that short conversation has continued to replay in my mind as I picture the fingerprints, or maybe the footprints, that we all leave in our walks through life. I follow the footprints of my own mentors, whether parents, teachers or friends. Those that went before have guided me as I looked for positive people that left clear and strong footprints worth following. Will those who come behind me find clear footprints leading them on good, straight and secure paths that will serve them well right to the end?

Living beyond our 'religious tribe'

When tribalism is transferred to a religious group, we see insiders and outsiders becoming defined according to the norms of that tribe, judged by externals and expected actions, not by the things that really matter. New tribal allegiances are formed, not of blood and common geography but of religious preference.

Names like Protestant, Catholic, Charismatic, Conservative, Liberal, Born Again, Evangelical, Fundamentalist, and on the list goes...Each tribe with its methods of baptism or confirmation, sacraments and liturgy, policies on ordination of women clergy, even style of music. As always, the issues that divide are usually very minor in the beginning. Part of the personal mission we have had in our lives is to see such walls broken down, to work across denominations and across all faith groups.

This became clear to us for the first time in our 1971 travel and work year. It was then we realized how thoroughly these denominational divisions had been exported. We were young and new to working abroad. The country of Dominica in the Caribbean had a joint project with the Canadian Medical Association to rotate doctors through one of their rural hospitals, Marigot. We quickly bonded with the local staff, and with the community where we were one of only three expatriate couples. After attending both the local churches we felt that we wanted to get to know people on a more personal level, and decided to invite some people for a weekly Bible study in our home. Of course we asked people from both churches. We had no idea that might not be the 'religiously correct' thing to do!

The group was surprised the first night to see who was there, and even more surprised as the discussions went on to realize that they all really did think alike on their basic beliefs! One lady confided in me afterwards that she had no idea there were "real Christians in that other church."

Looking back, that was one of those defining moments when we knew we were being changed, our whole mission in life was being affected. From here on we would try to associate with people of every faith–stripe or creed wherever we went.

> We knew we were being changed, our whole mission in life was being affected. From here on we would try to associate with people of every faith-stripe or creed wherever we went.

That group in Marigot solidly bonded, and after we left it continued for some time with one of the local farmers, a dedicated Methodist, taking leadership. We returned five years later, and then again with our teenage kids twenty years later, to find many of those people who still counted us among their friends and mentors. One elderly lady told us that she had just that week been sharing with one of her neighbours something I had taught her twenty years before, a simple acronym for 'grace': God's Riches At Christ's Expense! As primarily oral learners, memories and stories are passed on and on, little ripples spanning time.

They were poor folk by the standards of our world, but rich in relationships. Lucina, a widow with several kids, felt sorry for us after we returned to Canada where she knew the long winters prohibit growing vegetables. She decided to send us a box of vegetables, by ship of course, as airmail was too expensive. She did not know the long days at sea would rot the vegetables or realize that Canadian customs would not allow for such a delivery anyway!

One day the post office phoned us and said they had a parcel for us. "We have no idea what is in this box, but it is dripping, and it smells to high heaven!" When we went to pick it up, they said, "Please, just get it out of here!"

Upon opening the putrid box, we found the oozing rotten vegetables, which by now had been three months in tropical oceans, on docks and train from Vancouver! We could see the remains of squash, taro, yams and okra, all their favourites. Intact in a plastic bag though, was a package of home grown spices—whole nutmegs, chunks of cinnamon bark, nuggets of cacao to grate for hot chocolate! I keep those in a glass jar in my kitchen pantry as a remembrance of her generosity to this day! They seem too priceless to use, knowing what that box cost her to ship.

I sent some clothing for her kids, along with a note to thank her for her care for us, for the spices, and to gently remind her that the length of shipping time is longer than fresh vegetables can survive! Thankfully she did not try it again!

Crossing the Catholic-Protestant divide

The importance of working cross-faith has grown even stronger over the years. In fact, when we train the trainers who will go to villages that have invited the Community Health Education (CHE) program, we tell them not even to start unless all the faith groups are willing to work together. Whether Christian and Muslim or Buddhist or simply several denominations of Christian churches, without this first step of cooperation, experience has shown us that it will be a struggle to see community initiatives take off in anything but a small or superficial way. We will always be trampling on someone's turf if the time is not taken to gain their support.

The same applies in urban settings. Often there is an association of pastors as in the case of Goroka, PNG. Father John, a forty-year Irish Catholic veteran in PNG, was active in this group. The Catholic church responded with great enthusiasm when the CHE provincial trainers offered to train pastors or lay leaders from each church. Father John shared the dramas and lessons from the CHE training in mass each Sunday and would conduct Saturday seminars for CHE volunteers. Their small home groups began to be revitalized and even the squatter settlement dwellers caught the enthusiasm of becoming 'healthy homes.' He offered small prizes to make this award special—prizes bought from a personal Christmas gift of money that a friend from Ireland had sent him ("After all," he confided, "what do I really need to spend money on anyway?") To his surprise, over one hundred and fifty homes qualified—and he personally inspected each of them! He had discovered that human flourishing incorporates the whole person—physical, social, mental and spiritual, and that God is interested in every part, not just the spiritual. He later told us that if he had known about this CHE strategy when he first came to PNG, his whole ministry would have been different.

"Usually," he told us, "a priest is only invited into homes of the parishioners to pray for someone who is really ill, or to give the last rites. But for this healthy home initiative, I have personally been able to visit all these homes for a happy occasion, and they were all proud to show me their homes and what they have done."

As the Catholic church grew and showed excitement for change, it inspired other churches as well, and greater unity between all of them became evident. By training leaders from all the churches together, they saw how few differences there were to divide them.

A huge demonstration of unity between the churches of Goroka was their working together with us in 2005 to put on a week HIV and AIDS conference for church leaders from the whole country. The two African speakers accepted the invitation to come, and for probably the first time ever in PNG church history, every single denomination, both large and small were invited to send delegates. The University theatre where it was held was packed, and the participants forgot their differences as they united around a common desire to battle a looming disaster that they had the power to address.

One of the greatest honours we will ever receive came when Father Ryan told us that we were to come for something special to St. Mary's church one Sunday in October 2006. We were to receive some kind of recognition, it seemed. As it turned out we were acknowledged, along with five or six elderly nuns who had served there all their lives, with a medal from the Office of the Papua New Guinea Governor General. The letter of recognition, signed by the bishop and archbishop, thanked us for our years of working for unity between churches in the country! What a humbling and truly surprising award!

Go to the margins and beyond

We know now that living beyond our tribe does not come naturally. It takes a willingness to be an outsider, to make mistakes, to forgive and to ask to be forgiven. It takes seeing our own cultural norms in a different light, not as right or wrong, but as just our norms. It takes acceptance of differences as we determine to collaborate with diversity out of genuine passion for human dignity. Jesus understood, and gave us this picture of going outside the margins:

> *When you give a luncheon or dinner, do not invite your friends, your brothers or sisters, your relatives, or your rich neighbours; if you do, they may invite you back and so you will be repaid. But when you give a banquet, invite the poor, the crippled, the lame, the blind, and you will be blessed. Although they cannot repay you, you will be repaid at the resurrection of the righteous." (Luke 14:12-14 NIV)*

The rewards, He says, will not be immediate gratification for the host, but long term gain in satisfaction for everyone involved. "Greater good for greater numbers," said our mentor Kumalau, who loved the whole world, both people and nature, and who listened with his heart not just his ears. Clear footprints; the pebbles he dropped ripple to the shores of eternity. His wife Sisilia gave me permission to print this poem as a tribute to our dear friend. Listen with him to the voice of the sea:

Voice of the Sea

That was it,
The old man and I sailing.
He with the knowledge of years,
I with nothing
But a sense of adventure.
He took the steering,
While I, as he said,
With my good seeing
Would keep my eyes ahead.

The sun had just gone to swim
After its day's work.
The seagulls were flying home
In groups of four and five,
Singing those ancient songs
Of ceaseless bread-seeking.
And who knows
Whether those stomachs
May be full or empty.
Then silence.

As the sail moved it,
The canoe slashed its way
Through the fiery water,
Giving those sounds
Pleasing to the ears of the old man.
But then my eyes could see no further,
As the sky was covered with darkness.
So, I thought of the old man's eyes,
And the countless times he went through safely;
What was his secret?

Remember son,
When darkness comes, and you are sailing,

Listen:
To the voice of the sea
With its endless chorus
Of water splashing on the rocks
And the see-sawing sounds
Of waves on sand bars.
Then safely shall you guide your boat
Among the sharp rocks of these reefs,
Without seeing.

Kumalau Tawali, used by permission

DISCUSS AND REFLECT:

1. Who is my tribe, those I feel obligated to defend, those I can run to for help?

2. What would be involved in going outside my tribe, to the margins, even in my own city or workplace?

3. Describe some of the advantages of 'living beyond our tribe.' What might we gain personally? On the flip side, what might we lose?

4. Who are the people that have left fingerprints on my life?

CHAPTER 5

Equal Dignity: How much is she worth?

There is no tool for development more effective than the empowerment of women

--Kofi Annan, former UN Secretary General

She is worth far more than rubies... Proverbs 31:10 (NIV)

How much is this little girl worth? Itokama, PNG 2005

Jacinta stood with her wide trusting brown eyes staring, as forty other pairs of brown eyes looked back at her. My question hung in the space between us, as if suspended in the sultry air. "So how much is she worth?" I had asked the group.

By this time in the week this group had already felt the sobering weight of their cultural gender inequality as we had spent time discussing issues that impact the spread of HIV and AIDS in a community such as theirs. One of the topics that had come up in the discussion of gender equality was 'bride price'—the practice common in most of PNG of paying for a bride in large numbers of pigs, yams, money, or nowadays cases of beer, given to the woman's clan. Previously shell money was the accepted currency of transaction, but in recent years the cost has become one of the most crippling cultural obligations the tribe faces, as sometimes even a vehicle is demanded as a bride price for a well-educated girl.

The debate on the pros and cons of bride price has gone on for as long as we have been involved in PNG. Still it remains as a deeply ingrained cultural tradition that will not be easily replaced. Many modern generation girls don't like the idea of 'being bought', and young men feel that the demands of the girls' clan are excessive. But the older generation of parents accept the practice as a given, especially if they are on the receiving end!

One thing we can say is that the practice can provide the motivation for girls to be given educational opportunity, as this increases their value! Bride price does cement the marital transaction, but on the other side, it often gives the husband the idea that he has paid for his wife, so he has the right to treat her as he wishes. She feels trapped, without recourse of returning to her family if the marriage becomes abusive, as the family has accepted the bride price and does not want to return it.

As the debate had continued in this particular group with views on both sides, I felt myself getting agitated. My eye had caught sight of Jacinta, the young daughter of the Anglican priest as she bounced her ball outside the church where we were conducting the training. Without any further thought on how this might play out, I had gone outside and asked her if she would come and help me for a minute. The group all knew her and smiled as she entered.

"So, what do you think Jacinta is worth?" I asked, feeling like an ancient slave auctioneer, and not knowing what they would say or what I might say next! I just somehow thought this might help them see how ridiculous it was to put a value on a person!

They looked surprised at the question, but soon the ideas were bantering back and forth. She was only seven but would likely be attractive and well educated, they decided. That would increase her worth. Numbers of pigs and other monetary values were being tossed around.

Surely, I reasoned, someone in this group of forty leaders would come to the obvious conclusion that worth is not to be measured in material terms. But it was not to be so. I could see there was little insight coming, and I could feel emotion welling up within myself as I hugged this beautiful bright-eyed little girl, feeling like I was holding her back from some evil bigger than either of us.

As they tossed ideas and forth, I fought the tears unsuccessfully, and soon felt very embarrassed. The group grew silent, shocked, wondering what they had said to elicit this kind of demonstrative emotion from me! I wondered too!

Trying to stop my blubbering, I managed another question. "How much do you think God would say she is worth?" A whole new ball game; stunned, questioning looks, then lights going on.

"We are all worth the same to God," came a quiet response, as someone finally spoke up.

"And how much is that?" I pressed the point, and observed the room again go quiet. It took what seemed forever for someone to speak.

"She is worth God giving His life for her," came a somewhat reverently subdued voice. "That means she is priceless!" Jaws dropped. We had discussed where worth comes from, not from what we look like or accomplish but from God's love for us as made in His image.

Then her Anglican priest father, who had appeared somewhat askance through the whole process, chimed in, recognizing the lesson being portrayed. "Her mother and I have already agreed that we will accept no bride price for our girls. It is not justifiable from Scripture."

We did not try to draw any further conclusions to that insight. After all, these cultural dilemmas can only be resolved from within the community. As the old mother of this community had observed earlier, our role is just to point out the obvious. We knew they would talk late into the night and maybe, just maybe some minds would change.

We broke for tea, and I thanked Jacinta for joining us. She happily went back to her play.

Religion and the Oppression of Women

We dare not continue this chapter without having an uncomfortable discussion on how religion has over the centuries contributed to the oppression of women. This applies not only to women in animistic cultures, or to those behind the veils of Islam, but to Jewish and Christian societies both past and present.

Having stated earlier that the monotheistic worldview upholds equality because of the belief that both male and female are created in the image of God, very often practice has not borne out that belief.

Within Christendom, many over the years have pointed out such Scriptures as Paul's statements about women remaining silent, or not being qualified to teach in the church.[29] To us, along with most others in today's Christian churches, this reflects cultural norms for women of that era, who were less educated and therefore less able to teach.[30] Literal interpretation of such Scriptures has resulted in the stifling of women leaders who might have been well utilized in teaching and leadership roles. A book I have found helpful, *Why Not Women?* by Loren Cunningham and David Hamilton, is a good treatise on the subject of women in church leadership roles.[31] The authors deal with the cultural contexts and the Greek connotations of some of the controversial sections in Paul's writings, concluding that he was in no way disparaging of women leaders. He recognized and honoured them as equals, addressing some of the issues that were creating discord in the multi-cultural melting pot of the early church.

The ideas of inequality which some attribute to Paul has led in past decades to other restrictions for women in the kinds of positions or careers to which they could aspire. Even the right to vote was suppressed in North America until a century ago, by the argument that women did not have the education or interest to have influence outside the home.

To relegate women to a lesser role based on misunderstanding of a few passages of Scripture leads to ignoring others such as Peter's stern warning that if men do not treat their wives with respect as equal heirs in God's kingdom, they cannot expect God to answer their prayers.[32] That sounds serious!

The argument against such suppression of female leadership would come strongest from the example of Jesus himself, whose interaction and appreciation of women was not bound by the tradition of the day. So we might conclude that oppressive views of women do not come from the correct interpretation of Christ's teaching, but rather from the misinterpretation of that teaching and modeling. Anyone who seeks to be a true follower will want to delve into the reasons behind any kind of inequality or injustice that we might observe in the world. They will not find those reasons in the teachings of Jesus. His own close circle included many women, who were loyal at His death and His resurrection. Even within the Judaism of His day, women had influential roles; in fact, the description of the 'ideal wife' of Proverbs 31 is that of an empowered and honoured woman leader.

Unfortunately, when Christianity was taught in countries where animism was the dominant worldview, suggestions of women as submissive and under the authority of men played right into and reinforced the animistic view of women as less important than men. Some churches, rather than elevating women and giving dignity through leadership, or urging parents to educate girl children equally with boys, remained silent on the issue. Thankfully we see this changing.

In discussing the view of women within the other dominant monotheistic faith, Islam, change is not so forthcoming or obvious. One of the spokespersons calling for change is Ayaan Hirsi Ali. In her controversial book *Heretic: Why Islam Needs a Reformation Now*[33], Ali describes growing up in Muslim Somalia with questions about the difference in her treatment from that of her brother. Even though questioning the faith was discouraged in her family, she claims "the questions never stopped coming, eventually leading to this one: 'Why would a benevolent God set up the world like this, marking one half of the population to be second-class citizens? Or was it just men that did this?'"[34] What an insightful question.

While it is difficult to make generalizations about the value and treatment of women in the Islamic faith because it spans numerous branches, sects and diverse cultures, there are some commonalities in the teaching about women. In looking at the teachings of their leaders and holy books, differences with the teachings of Christians and Jews on the value of women are apparent. For example, up to four wives at one time are acceptable though illegal in many countries[35]. Divorce is easy for a man, difficult for a woman. We are told that a man may marry outside the faith, as the children born to them are Muslim, but if a woman marries outside the faith, she becomes an infidel and guilty of adultery. Shari'a law (God's law for the Muslim, based on Qur'an and oral tradition) punishes such a crime with death.

Such was the well publicized 2014 case of Dr. Meriam Ibrahim, the young Sudanese woman who chose to follow the Orthodox Christian faith of her Ethiopian mother rather than her Muslim father, and married an American Christian man. At eight months pregnant, she was sentenced to death by hanging for her 'crime' of adultery and apostasy. Had she been willing to renounce Christianity for Islam, she would have been immediately released. Her simple response when pressured was, "How can I return when I was never a Muslim?"

It was only through pressure from the U.S. State Department, Amnesty International, and other world embassies, that her sentence was overturned. Even while leaving the country, she and her lawyers were beaten up at the airport.[36]

In civil affairs, Shari'a law sees the witness of a woman as less credible than that of a man: four women are required to one man's witness. While ancient Judaism had similar beliefs, the difference is that these have changed over time, giving women equal status and value.

Externals within Islam vary from culture to culture, but groups that are diligent in upholding Islamic teachings are prescriptive about such things as women's dress, separation of men and women in the daily life of the home, even to the point of having two kitchens and eating areas.

In their spiritual practices, men dominate and women are seen as distractions. Because women are not allowed to pray in the mosque during days of menstruation, they are said to be less likely to attain paradise.

Yes, it is still practiced today!

While we may think the practice of female genital mutilation and cutting (FGM/C) is on the decline, current studies are not bearing this out. It is defined by WHO as "all procedures that involve partial or total removal of the external female genitalia, or other injury to the female genital organs for non-medical reasons". It is recognized as an inhumane violation of human rights of women and girls, often resulting in future problems of infections and childbirth complications. In December 2012, the UN general assembly unanimously voted to work to eliminate FGM throughout the world.

"It reflects deep-rooted inequality between the sexes, and constitutes an extreme form of discrimination against women," says WHO. "It is nearly always carried out on minors and is a violation of the rights of children. The practice also violates a person's rights to health, security and physical integrity, the right to be free from torture and cruel, inhumane or degrading treatment, and the right to life when the procedure results in death."[37]

While not a teaching of Islam, FGM is still practiced and condoned in many sects and cultures where Islam predominates, and in adjacent non-Muslim areas. Some of the *hadith* (sayings attributed to Muhammad) declare that FGM is noble but not required."[38] Shite sects, for example, see it as 'noble,' while in Indonesia and Malaysia, two of the progressive countries we visit regularly, most Muslims see it as 'obligatory.'[39] Now offered as a routine medical procedure in these two countries and even part of 'birthing packages' in some hospitals, it gives the practice an air of normalcy and hides real prevalence data which could be as high as 90%.[40] Up until recently, the focus of study and advocacy has been on Africa, and little attention given to Southeast Asia where it is quietly carrying on as part of social and cultural expectations.

In 2013 UNICEF reported eight African countries where 80–98% of girls are cut: Somalia, Guinea, Djibouti, Egypt, Eritrea, Mali, Sierra Leone and Sudan.[41] The more recent surveys show the numbers dropping in many of those countries. A 2020 UNICEF report claims that more than 200 million girls and women alive today have been subjected to FGM/C in 31 countries, and 3 million girls are at risk of being cut annually.[42] We have a long way to go.

One of the worst of abusive practices against women, FGM is being fought on many fronts to see it abolished for all time. As with many cultural changes, the decision for change must come from activists and advocates within the culture.

The inequality, mistreatment and need to uphold the rights of women continue to be among the most urgent development issues of our day.

Women in Animistic Society: Fear of women's blood

After our observations of the low value of women in Nepal, we began to understand more of the practical impact of animistic beliefs on women. The fear of women's blood is one that has many implications as in many cultures it is seen to weaken or impose a curse on men. My husband relates a case of a medical evacuation of a woman in labour from a remote area in PNG. The men would not allow the helicopter to take off in the most direct route over the village, as the curse of the woman's blood might affect them! This served to frustrate the helicopter pilot, as it seemed that illogical beliefs were over-riding both safety and economic factors.

In Papua New Guinea, some of these beliefs contribute to making the rates of infant and maternal mortality some of the highest in the world. This is especially the case where women traditionally give birth in a menstrual hut outside the village, often alone. There may be superstitious taboos against cutting the cord or even touching the newborn until the placenta is delivered. If the birth occurs at night in the cold night air of the Highlands, a wet newborn might lie on the dirt floor or banana leaf for up to an hour waiting for the placenta to deliver. Hypothermia meanwhile may claim the newborn. The exhausted mother likely worked hard in the gardens right up to the time of her labour. She may have been denied the best food because of certain food taboos while pregnant, so she is not in prime condition going into the delivery in the first place. Untrained village birth attendants may be part of the process, but they too must follow the cultural taboos. The result? Only the strong survive.

In fact every year in PNG 6000 babies die, and of those up to 80% die because their fragile bodies become hypothermic.[43] This is especially true of low birth weight newborns; when they become cold their bodies burn fat-stores to stay warm, sugar and oxygen levels drop and the organs are at serious risk of damage. Recently UNICEF has introduced a pilot device called the 'Baby Cold Clock,' a tiny wrist-band that beeps and flashes to alert the mother when the temperatures drops below a safe level. She then starts 'kangaroo care' where the baby is nestled skin to skin against her chest (or the father's) with a cloth strip wrapping both of them together. The parent's body heat warms and comforts the infant to bring nurture that is also proven to enhance growth and brain development.[44]

As we travel to other places of the world we observe the same fear of women's blood, an affront against something wonderful and life giving. The sign on a high-traffic tourist beach walkway in Bali at the gate of a Hindu temple area, warns that menstruating women are not welcome inside these walls. The same sign excludes those breastfeeding, another beautiful and sustaining gift to mankind. If worship is part of our integrated lives, yet women are excluded from their own holy places for much of their life, what does that say to them about their value?

In December 2016, the world was horrified by the news of a fifteen-year-old girl's death in Nepal. The headline in the 'Washington National Post' reads, "'Impure' teen, fifteen, banished to a hut for menstruating—an outlawed practice in Nepal—perishes in cold."[45] The photo shows the friends and family of Roshani Tiruwa, interestingly only women, mourning outside the menstrual hut where she had been banished and died.

This custom known as *Chaupadi,* outlawed in Nepal in 2005, persists in many parts of Nepal as well as other countries of South Asia. Roshani was the second death in her district in a month. Some die of asphyxiation after starting a fire for warmth, others are killed from snake bites or other wild animals. An interview with a teenage girl explained the custom: "We are sent to a shed littered with hay, muck, insects and dung. The cow dung smells and the animals step on us. We don't like to live this way, but our gods won't tolerate it any other way."[46]

A year earlier *The Guardian* had done extensive interviews and research in India where girls are similarly confined to the *gaokor* hut during menstruation.[47] The condition of the huts was deplorable, especially dreaded by the girls during rainy season when water often runs in, and most lack even a proper bed. The practice has recently been brought to the attention of the National Human Rights Commission (NHRC), which is calling for the eradication of *gaokor* describing it as a "serious violation of the human rights of women."

It is strongly believed, whether in South Asia, Africa or Papua New Guinea, that breaking with traditions like this will result in crop failure, animal deaths or other illnesses. It affects schooling for girls too, as they most often will not attend during their monthly periods, even if it means missing exams. UNICEF has reported that one in ten girls in Africa miss school for several days a month, as do two thirds of girls in rural areas of India. Part of this is a poverty issue, as they are unable to purchase sanitary supplies or access bathrooms for hygiene and privacy. But the traditional stigma of being 'impure' or 'unclean' is also hard to overcome.

Menstrual Hygiene Management (MHM) is a subject of much research and is being addressed by groups such as UNICEF along with their Water, Sanitation and Hygiene (WASH) programs for schools. One group called "Days for Girls" (see www.daysforgirls.org) produces and delivers hand-sewn kits consisting of washable colourful flannel cloth sanitary liners and covers, in drawstring bags. Women all over the world are helping with this sewing project that gives the missed days back to girls, enabling their chances of remaining or doing well in school a fair chance. Some of our previous CHE trainers in Papua New Guinea have been doing the research with UNICEF to determine whether the provision of these kits will result in both increased school attendance for girls and understanding from the boys of the difficulties that girls overcome to receive the same education as boys. Preliminary results seem very positive.

These efforts again underscore the value of educating school children as well as their parents, on the importance of girls and women in society. Understanding their own bodies, as well as their unique contributions and talents, strong minds, their worth to God and society, is elevating their dignity. Change is on its way!

Multiple wives: hatred or harmony?

Another issue is polygamy, or multiple wives. One of the reasons for polygamy is the taboo against sexual intimacy during menstruation, pregnancy and breastfeeding, giving the excuse for the husband to take a second (or third!) wife. Contrary to what some believe, polygamy is most often not happy co-existence for the women, but rather a life of constant jealousy, competition, fighting or outright violence.

While Bill worked in Kainantu hospital in PNG, he was called to a gruesome scene one Sunday morning. What he found was two wives of one husband suffering virtually identical reciprocal injuries. The two had stayed home from church that day to carry on their feud with each other. Or maybe the family was tired of hearing them fight and left without them! At any rate, as anger escalated they had each brought their bush knife down on the other's skull, laying them both open to the brain. Their second blows virtually severed each other's left arm as it was brought up to protect another swipe at the head!

Miraculously, both women, who had to be separated to keep the peace in the ward during their long hospital stay, survived their potentially life-threatening identical injuries. As far as we remember, they returned home to their rivalries and jealousies, with no resolution or counselling. We wondered whether the next episode would be the end of one or both of them.

In Goroka, the capital of the PNG province where we lived, one of the volunteer roles I assumed was that of a probation officer for women being released after prison sentences. Our neighbour, Rick, was the chief Magistrate, and his wife raised awareness of many justice issues unfair to women. One of these was mandatory minimum sentencing for assault charges, in particular as they applied to women. A typical situation was assault by a jealous wife on another woman —someone with whom her husband was having an affair or had taken as an additional customary wife (the law still only allows for one legal wife). The person making the assault was seen as in the wrong, not the husband who cheated on his wife or treated one wife with disdain!

I well remember the sweet lady, with her baby born during her prison term, who was assigned to me. I soon learned her story, a very typical one. An efficient grapevine had informed her that her husband was having an affair. It was inevitable that one day she would encounter the woman on the street! The ensuing public fight began with her loud words of angry accusation. As is typical, the onlookers were amused and the crowd grew, but no one made moves to try to stop them. The yelling turned to fighting, and the young adulteress went away with the worst of the bruises—straight to the police.

At that time, likely still today, there was also a law that fined a man up to $100 for adultery! But most women didn't think of counter-charging their own husband, and besides it would not bode well for her future relationship with the husband if she sued him. So, the pregnant wife went to jail for the minimum few months, the other woman 'got the man' and moved in to take the place of the wife, and it all seemed as if it had been scripted by the husband!

I met with her weekly for several months after she was released to go home from prison on probation, always with the same sad story. She was living with an arrogant and taunting second wife, along with a callous husband, while trying to keep calm and controlled to avoid breaking her probation parole rules. To me the shame and indignity of the situation was unimaginable. Could I have lived in that household? Definitely not. At that time there was no safety net of social services for women who needed to escape an untenable home situation. Returning to her family's village was not an option because the bride price transaction had been paid. She had no ability to get a job, and all I could do was admire her courage in being able to remain in such an unhappy situation. I often wondered how things went for her after I left.

Around the same time, another good friend of mine, Naomi, was able to leave an abusive marriage with the support of her pastor and friends in Goroka and used her training as a social worker to start an organization called 'Family Voice.' A woman of courage, faith and vision, Naomi tenaciously struggled for years and developed this much-needed organization from the ground up. It has become a recognized counselling and referral service for women and youth, giving training, support and courage to women who needed to escape an abusive marriage or to work through difficult polygamous dynamics. Their staff is in the forefront of the awareness campaigns against domestic violence, gender inequality and the spread of HIV and AIDS. I am so proud of her, and the work that continues now without her.

Naomi's death from cancer in early 2016, not long after finishing a Master's degree in Australia, was a loss for the whole of Papua New Guinea, both men and women. She is remembered as a hero and a visionary, a woman who put boots on her courage. We miss her.

Gender roles: Barai of Oro Province PNG

Some of the beliefs about women or the value of boy children over girl children, are life and death issues. Others are less life threatening, but still reflect the view that men are of more value than women. We have talked about the unequal sharing of workloads as indicative of gender value, but we may not have thought much about how our own view of equal dignity between genders impacts the habits of our daily lives.

We realized how our Western cultural habits of gender roles and expectations differ from many cultures while training in the Barai people group in Oro Province of PNG, whose 'dreams and visions' we shared in the second chapter. For example, it brings shame in our culture for a man to ignore the heavy load his wife or mother is carrying while he walks empty handed. The opposite brings shame in many PNG societies!

As we struggled one day up a muddy slope, I groped at tree branches to help me climb. One of the men in our training group observed my plight and came alongside. Very counter-culturally, he offered to carry my *bilum* (string bag). I was grateful, but it was relatively short lived, as once we came within five minutes of the village he gave it back!

"I am sorry Sharon, but it would be shameful for me to be seen carrying a woman's bag," he honestly admitted as he handed it over to me. We understood the implication of losing face in an 'honour and shame culture' where one's honour is more important than a 'cause.'

Another day we came to class to find the group laughing about something. They told us some of them had been imitating "Bill following Sharon", which of course is opposite to their culture where women kept their distance behind, carrying a heavy load, while the man strode ahead carrying only an axe or bush knife.

"Okay, we want to see your charade too!" we urged. They complied with great flair, even making our gaits recognizable! "That's Bill, and that's Sharon," they explained, as the male actors started. "See, Bill is walking behind Sharon! Now they are coming to a gate, watch what happens!" They were laughing hilariously as they anticipated the action.

Over-emphasizing the movements, 'Bill' stepped forward and opened the gate, then stepped back while 'Sharon' walked through. Did we really do that so obviously? We of course laughed along with them at how ridiculous we must look to them. It felt good to be the brunt of a joke that they seemed to recognize as hitting a sore point in their own value system!

At the end of the week of training, we agreed to walk to a neighbouring village where several of the trainers resided. Most of the group was already waiting inside the house when we got there. This time Bill was ahead of me, as he had grown impatient with my frequent stops to chat with various ladies as we entered the village.

"I'm not waiting, or we'll never get there!" Bill said with annoyance. He went on ahead and climbed the typical steep three-step ladder onto the raised platform that the houses in this area were built on. Everyone grew silent, looking like something had gone wrong.

"What's the matter?" Bill asked, as he sat down, and I came up a few moments later.

"Well we had just been telling the people who live here that you would wait and that Sharon would climb the ladder ahead of you, and you might even give her a hand getting up. Now they think we were lying to them!"

We laughed and apologized for spoiling their planned teaching moment!

"We could not Survive in this Community!"

"We could never survive living here," Bill stated emphatically later that week. The group of trainers and us had stopped to rest in the shade as we walked around the Barai district for a day to visit some of the villages where the trainers lived.

"Why is that?" someone asked with a surprised and hurt expression. After all, it seemed like we really loved coming here and always told them how we enjoyed the beauty and serenity of these mountains they called home.

"Well," Bill began. "I could probably live for about two weeks, and then I would die!"

"What? Why?" They were all paying attention now!

"Because I would die of thirst!" was Bill's response. They could see he was not joking but was trying to make a serious point. The wheels were turning as they tried to wrap their minds around this new announcement. It was quiet as they waited for him to continue. They knew there was plenty of water in the river below the ridge, so why he would die of thirst?

"I would die of thirst because I would get tired of walking an hour each way to fetch buckets of water, and Sharon would refuse to do it for me!"

They were beginning to get the message: their own men were not dying of thirst, nor were they walking the hour to fetch water. That was the work of the women who had no say in the matter. If it were left up to the men to get the water, they would have built a water system long, long ago. The technology for bamboo pipes and even for pumping systems was known and easily accomplished with a little money and lots of effort. But women were their beasts of burden, an expendable commodity whose lives were meant for drudgery like that.

What did it take for European society to be liberated many generations ago from viewing half of humanity as less valuable than the other half? That saw women and girl children as good only for reproducing and doing the hard drudgery jobs? It took a worldview shift, starting with the Reformation in the sixteenth century and gradually working its way through Western Christendom—a view of equal dignity for all humanity, no matter who they are.

Now this worldview has permeated our culture. We are incensed by stories of 'untouchable' classes of people or the annual $32 billion human trafficking industry that includes children and women being exploited for labour or sexual abuse. We support the education of girls in the Middle East and Africa by addressing the complex issues that keep them away from school. Our attention is drawn toward the injustices suffered by migrant workers in the large cities of Southeast Asia.

Our children have grown up hearing stories like Dr. Seuss' elephant character, 'Horton Hears a Who', which portrays a message that all people are important--even those too small to be seen but who are clearly heard by Horton's sensitive ears! We have been taught about Jesus freeing the woman about to be stoned for adultery or calling for the children to come to Him and be blessed. We have watched with horror the movies portraying slave-trading and wondered at such inhumanity. What will it take for cultures to change that have not had these messages? Does it matter to us?

HIV and AIDS, and its toll on women

If someone tried to invent the ultimate diabolical revenge against women, they could not have come up with anything worse than HIV and AIDS! Indeed, this disease which many do not realize takes a much greater toll on women than on men, is still quietly working its devastation on a generation of reproductive age women in many parts of our world. Since the start of the epidemic, women represent over half the HIV infected, and adolescent girls (ages 10-19) are twice as likely to acquire the virus as their male counterparts.[48] The disease saps strength as it attacks the immune system, making the victim vulnerable to other killing infections such as tuberculosis and pneumonia. While there is greater availability of anti-retro viral drugs (ART's) at more affordable costs than previous decades, the health care systems of poorer countries where HIV is more prevalent are straining. The treatment is lifelong, there is no cure, no quick fix and must be monitored closely. All of this is extremely expensive.

Why is the disease taking greater toll on women? The answer is not straightforward or easily solved by education. The inequality, violence, economic poverty, inadequate schooling and lack of value that young women face in much of the world make them vulnerable to sexual exploitation. These factors cannot be addressed in isolation without going deeper. Often the whole justice system of their country is so broken that only those who can pay will be given hearings. Worldview must be changed before abuse of a young girl will seem important.

Physiology also plays a part in the vulnerability. Like the ideal soil conditions that give a higher crop yield in the farming context, the internal mucosal environment of female genitalia is more conducive than that of men for the rapid growth of any sexually transmitted disease virus. Secondly, the disease is often transmitted to teenage women, who may then be considered unfit for marriage. If they do marry and get pregnant without the diagnosis of the disease, there is a good chance of transmitting it to their baby, especially in the unhygienic village birth context. While there is much being done about the mother-to-child transmission, the risks are still great. Thirdly, the impact on the children of women either living with or dying from AIDS, is beyond measure. Often the older aunties or grandmothers bear the brunt of the care of the young orphans, and this in years when they barely have enough to feed even themselves let alone provide food and school costs for grandchildren. So three generations have been squelched, dreams of a productive and wholesome life snatched from their hands. Economies that are already ailing suffer the workforce loss of these affected women. The ripples go on and on.

Women as accused sorcerers in Papua New Guinea.

It is three or four hundred years since pre-Reformation Europe was hunting and burning so-called witches, most of them women. That blight in our own history is repeated week after week in Papua New Guinea. The natural beauty of this largely unspoiled land is being marred by the blood and cries of women in merciless killings.

It reads like the Wikipedia description of the European witch-hunts:

> *Between 40,000 and 60,000 'witches' were killed during the European witch-hunts, most of them innocent women, including 'strange old widows,' handicapped persons, simpletons, and mentally ill people. For those women who were skilled as midwives or other healers, this was often a sure claim for execution.*[49]

These same shameful atrocities are being committed on a regular basis in Papua New Guinea. Kepari Lanieta was a twenty-year-old mother accused of sorcery in February, 2013. Only after video footage of her being burned alive had gone viral did the Papua New Guinea press have the courage to tell the world about murders like this.

The story of Lanieta in magazines like *Time* and *The Guardian* sparked outbursts of anger and disgust worldwide. Still, two months later another women's leader we had known was burned alive in Bougainville. Articles like "Sorcery and Sexism in Papua New Guinea" in *The Diplomat* magazine reveal this on-going travesty to the world.[50] In May, 2015 Mifila was chopped to death by attackers after she was blamed for the death from measles of several people in her village. [51] Almost anyone in PNG can tell of the personal impact of such atrocities.

One morning two of our CHE trainers, government health workers, were driving to one of the district health centres a couple of hours from the provincial capital of Goroka. They came to a quick stop as they saw a woman in obvious pain lying beside the road. Thinking she was in labour, they got out to attend her and help her into the vehicle. To their utter horror, they saw that she was covered with second and third degree burns and in shock. They knew the scenario: a woman accused of being a sorceress, or *sanguma,* had been burned alive in her hut and somehow escaped. None of the villagers dared come to her aid.

The woman, mercifully, was successfully treated in Goroka Hospital and survived to return to her village as there was nowhere else to go. No doubt she lived in fear that she might again be blamed for the next death or disaster to befall the community. Gradually the story came out and it was even worse than imagined.

The community was one where a CHE trainer had been attempting to get a program started and initially had good response. As time went on though, she realized there were deep animosities between the clans, dynamics that make any progress impossible. She discussed it at the provincial trainers' meetings asking the others for prayer. Then word came to her that the arguments were getting worse.

It seems that when things go wrong in a culture steeped in animistic beliefs or when illness claims a life, blame is the initial response. Someone is responsible, but not the people who might really be responsible! So the fingers point, usually to women and most often the women who are vulnerable due to older age, widowhood or lack of status. Sometimes opportunistic rivals want an excuse to steal a vulnerable person's land or gardens that could be confiscated if that person were to disappear. Widows who are from other areas or those with no grown sons in the village are other targets. They are ordinary women living with the fear of being the one accused as the 'sanguma' (sorcerer) who supposedly caused the evil happening by spells or curses.

The fingers of the village this time were unable to single out one specific woman. They may have used any number of methods for 'divining' the guilty party—anything from studying a series of old bones, to each putting a *kaukau* (sweet potato) in the fire and after a certain length of time checking to see which one was uncooked—and the 'guilty one' now had a name. But on this occasion there were FIVE names!

Rather than a process of elimination among the five, they somehow decided that all were guilty, and each was tied up inside their grass hut and lit on fire. It must have been an unimaginable scene... the screams, the heat of the flames, the terror of the children, the horrific stares of the silent women who had escaped this fate for now, the blazing escape of one of the victims as she fled to the road. And then the tacit pact of silence.

Soon after the burned woman had returned home after hospital treatment, we were asked by the CHE trainer to come with the Provincial Trainer to the community, as the villagers were apparently feeling very repentant for their deed. They realized that their action had eliminated them from any further development and there were sane voices pointing that fact out to them. We agreed to all go together, but that we would not be the ones to speak.

The shame of their guilt was almost palpable as we walked the short distance from the road in to the village. The evidence had been cleaned up, as the remains of burned houses was nowhere to be seen. The people were all gathered in the centre of the village and we did not wander outside that area. The one living victim, now almost healed, sat alone and far to one side in the garb of a widow: an all-black *meri blous and laplap* (the common dress of PNG women, a full pleated top and ankle length wrap-around sarong).

The older men's faces were blank, most staring at the ground while a few younger men had haughty expressions, exuding animosity as they observed the strangers coming to visit. In most cases, in fact it is the young men who are the initial accusers. They knew why we had come—and they knew that we knew. The trainer introduced us all, made a few comments and then the Provincial Training Coordinator, known by all of us as Mama J, started in. She minced no words and we had visions of the crowd running us out at the tips of their bows and arrows! In a very culturally unorthodox approach, rather than coming at the issue indirectly with the face-saving dance usually granted even known guilty parties, she hit them square on!

"How dare you murder the mothers who gave you birth and at whose breasts you suckled?" was her almost-opening accusation. She was angry, hurt, incensed, and they knew it!

Bill and I cringed, having seen how quickly emotions can ignite, and knowing that violence is very close to the surface. But not today. Their heads just began to hang lower and lower and Mama J continued, now in full flight.

"Do you know that these women whom you have murdered were made in the image of God? Just like you. Did you realize that you were murdering the image of God?" Shock waves. No response. Remorseful faces. They had not expected her to be so direct.

There was nothing left to be said. We all felt defeated, as we knew the hope for any justice was almost non-existent. With the animistic worldview shared by the police, there is both a lack of will to enforce justice and a lack of insight into the seriousness of the crime. We wondered whether, when the incident report at the hospital was registered and reported, the police even investigated or laid charges. There was no action taken as far as we know—just another statistic of an aborted sorcery killing.

In the usual cultural reconciliation manner, we heard later that a 'sorry ceremony' had been done—pigs killed and a big feast given to say sorry (in an oblique way) to the families of the victims. Then it is considered over and done with, the deed wiped out, the women not to be spoken of again other than in hushed whispers, the trauma to the next generation unresolved.

We do know that this community has not moved forward, and that animosities and rivalries continue to surface, keeping them from working together to solve their own problems. Fear of being the next victim breeds mistrust and suspicion, the kindling in the tinderbox of tribal warfare. Next time the accusation might come from a friend who gets sick or loses a job, and someone must be blamed. Nothing will change these communities apart from deep repentance, reconciliation and spiritual healing.

While PNG is now trying to deal with this issue of atrocity within its borders, many outside observers such as Amnesty International feel the attempts are not enough. In their 2014/15 Annual Report, Amnesty International states:

> *The government took little action to address violence against women or sorcery-related violence, in spite of legal reforms providing for harsher penalties... There were further reports of women and children being subjected to violence, sometimes resulting in death, following accusations of sorcery. The UN*

Special Rapporteur on extrajudicial killings...highlighted sorcery-related killings as a concern. He was the third Special Rapporteur to report on this issue in recent years.[52]

In fact, it has been observed that as general violence worsens in a country, the violence against women increases exponentially. It seems they are the community lightning rods for frustration, the soft targets for pent up anger. The world is disgusted, even the perpetrators hate what they are doing, but who is putting real effort into stopping it?

Human Rights Watch, which does an annual World Report for each country targeting human rights issues, repeats in their 2015 report what we already surmised:

PNG is one of the most dangerous places in the world to be a woman, with an estimated 70 percent of women experiencing rape or assault in their lifetime. While such acts have long been criminalized and domestic violence was specifically proscribed under the 2013 Family Protection Act, few perpetrators are brought to justice. Lack of access to courts and police, as well as failure by many justice officials to take violence against women seriously, contribute to the extremely low arrest and conviction rates.[53]

"Where is the law?" is the obvious question we all ask.

Before its repeal in 2013[54], the controversial Sorcery Act in PNG acknowledged the accusation of sorcery as a plausible defense in murder cases. The penalty for a sorcery killing carried only two years sentence, which could be further reduced by claiming that black magic was involved. Only since the repeal of the archaic Sorcery Act are these killings now treated as murder. The old law, passed in 1971 under the Australian legislature of the day, had somehow seemed reasonable to those leaders!

Still there is the problem of reporting and finding the killers and then getting witnesses to testify. Apart from the remote locations of many of these villages, the other complication for the courts is that in most sorcery killings there is no one accused killer, but the agreement of the whole community makes them all complicit. In two such situations we have witnessed, the words, "we all agreed" were uttered.

In early 2018, in the first mass trial of ninety-seven men charged in the sorcery-related killings of seven people in 2014, all have received convictions.[55] We pray that the rule of law will break the silence. But who will be the catalysts for change that will help communities deal with such root issues? Where is the church? Where are the voices of leaders who should be speaking on behalf of women? Some of the most effective voices we hear are coming from women themselves.

Let the Women Speak

The plight of women in many societies, and the resulting health problems, emotional trauma, high infant and maternal mortality rates, calls out for action. Can the problem be solved with money? By trying to turn all women into entrepreneurs who start micro enterprises? By educating all girls? By pressuring governments to enforce existing laws dealing with rape, gender-based violence, unjust laws, marriage of minors, so-called sorcery killings?

In fact, all of these top-down actions are needed, but without addressing root belief systems, little will change. Worldview must be addressed! The will to change must come from within communities. We must give women a voice, encourage them to use it and then listen when they do. Hear the agonized voice of one of these young women who sees the issues clearly:

Emma Wakpi, Community Health Education Area Coordinator for Papua New Guinea, voices the heart cry of a modern young Papua New Guinean woman, in an essay that won first prize in a national competition. She understands the impact of belief systems and cultural blind spots on her personal wellbeing. Listen to her words:

The Haunting by Emma Wakpi[56]

It is 5:00 am and we are landing in Port Moresby. I look out the plane window and watch the wakening sun tinge the rising mist a soft gold; I am home after two weeks in Manila. As I get up and collect my gear, I remember the chivalrous gestures of strangers there; men who opened doors for me, who got up to offer me seats on public transports, male friends who grabbed shopping bags from my hands to carry them for me. The acts that seemed as natural as breathing to them made a world of difference to me, giving me a sense of worth and security and prompted me to also want to treat others with respect. The pleasure this memory evokes makes me smile and it gets broader at the feeling of belonging that is washing over me as I am surrounded by familiar imagery and faces.

Going through customs, I grin at my wantoks (tribesmen), say a good morning and make my way outside. However once outside, I lose the grin and file away the memories, for I must now contend with my reality as a woman in PNG.

The light-hearted, carefree feeling is slowly rising up out of me like the mist clearing on the tarmac, and wariness sets in. My mind and body move into auto pilot, "Careful Emma, smile briefly, keep your eyes down, walk steadily, act like you know the place – it is your territory—stride confidently but ooze humbleness. Pretend you are taking lint off your shoulder, steal a covert glance, no one is following, none look too threatening. Okay breathe; walk; smile; you are fine, you have reached your destination – you are safe…"

"Welcome home," I whisper to myself, "this is your life". I love my country, I love my people, but I am haunted; and I am weary, oh so weary.

There is a menacing overbearing presence that haunts my being every time I step away from my safe zones (home, family, friends, work); its clammy tentacles reach out and tunnel deep into my heart and mind. Sometimes it is very obscure, other times it screams its presence—it wants to possess me, infiltrate my very core and define me by its standards.

It not only haunts me, but the entire nation groans and is slowly suffocating beneath its smothering presence. This haunting seems to be rising from within the core of Papua New Guinea, surreptitiously extending its tentacles into every aspect of society and manifesting itself in various forms; whole mountains are being unceremoniously hacked to pieces, river systems defecated upon in the name of prosperity. Law and Justice are slowly being strangled by the grip of these clammy tentacles as the nation is slowly being brought to its knees.

There has to be a way to exorcise this "haunting" before it casts me forever into the abyss of despair and chokes the life out of this nation. The incessant haunting chants beliefs imprinted deep within my psyche:

"Men are of more value than women," true, true, true.

"Animistic beliefs are real," true, true, true.

"Might is right - Big Man mentality rules," true, true, true.

133

"Fatalism is a way of life, what can you change?" true, true, true.

"Promiscuity and lies are a way of life," true, true, true.

And I listen, and you listen and we allow it to possess and hypnotize us, becoming slaves who stomp rhythmically to its chants until we are jarred awake by some incident that pricks at our conscience; yet the wave of the chant carries us forward in a death grip marching us toward the precipice to throw us into the abyss of hopelessness that is the manifestation of these chants – AIDS, violence, drug abuse, political upheaval, tribal warfare, police brutality...

I realize it is futile to hack away at the manifestations that the haunting produces if I do not address the root beliefs ingrained in me since birth. I must dig deep into the recesses of my heart and mind and pry away the grip of the cursed chant – I must uproot it. I cannot let a belief system that is destroying me (and my country) dictate my life. I have to think for myself and question whether "pasin" (cultural belief), is really right.

I must sing a new song of hope and strength, of gender equality, of dignity for all, of creative minds that can forge a new future. Beliefs beget behaviours, resulting in the consequences in the society we live in.

Jarred from my death march, I fight to break free; I will not be trampled underfoot. I must fight.

As I resist and raise my war cry against the chant, I hear faint echoes of my own cry rising up from every direction. Struggling to catch a glimpse, I find understanding faces amongst the throng, and strength is garnered anew. We turn back to resume our stance and to struggle on. I will continue to raise my voice against the chant and keep forging my way. I glimpse hope...

We never heard these things before

One of the teaching modules that Medical Ambassadors International has developed for their trainers is the 'Women and Family Life' series. There is a more advanced training for CHEs who wish to specialize in Pre-Natal Support (CHEPS) for the pregnant women of the community. I trialed a few of these lessons with a group of pastor's wives in Goroka, most of whom I knew were more educated than the average women of their congregations. They were also in a good position to pass on the information to many other women. The goal of prevention education is always to teach those who can teach others so that multiplication takes place.

As we went through the discussions on hormonal issues, development of the fetus, complications of pregnancy, menopause and many other topics, they were amazed. "We have never heard these things, never talked about them before!"

I realized how the lack of empowerment of women extended even to the knowledge of their own bodies. School health education obviously did not teach it. Their mothers had not known it and what they passed on to their daughters really were the ultimate 'old wives' tales'. I was shocked when we did the menopause lesson—even the most educated of these ladies had never heard that this was a natural part of the cycle of a woman's life. They all had a story about a mother or an aunt that they now realized was going through menopause, not an illness. One said she was going to phone her mother that night and share some of the information with her!

It seemed from what the women were telling me that the cessation of monthly periods was often thought to be a symptom of an illness. Many spent money to try to be 'cured' by a local witchdoctor or by buying some unidentified cure-all medicine at the local market. They were truly feeling liberated with this new knowledge and were excited to tell their friends!

Simple understanding of how a woman's body works and how hormones affect moods, was also incorporated into a training session designed for men to attend with their wives. They were all invited to bring their husbands that day, but unfortunately only two husbands had the courage to show up! Now there is a lesson set titled 'Men Matter' where men can discuss issues important to their health, social well being and marital harmony.

The self-esteem and relationship topics that are part of the Women's curriculum have proven to be revolutionary in every country where they are taught. It is life giving for women to understand their worth, treat themselves with dignity and respect and learn to communicate in loving and respectful ways with their children and husband. Some women have shared that for the first time in their lives they are happy to have been born a woman! Many did not know that marriage can be harmonious and satisfying, in direct contrast to their cultural expectations.

Empowering Women: From Garbage Picker to Community Changer

Ita (not her real name) lived and earned her living by picking bottles from the garbage dump of a thriving Asian mega-city. Her husband had been unemployed for several years by the time the Community Education trainer met Ita and her dump site community and saw that she had leadership potential. The trainer invited her to be part of a weekly training program that would change the lifestyle and health of her family.

Listen to the summary of Ita's story, told in her own words:

> *"About three years ago when I moved to this slum area, I was desperate as my husband didn't have a job for eleven years and I must work hard to earn money for daily living. We live in a small wood hut, raised above the backup water from the overflowing gutters. I was confused how to earn income for my family and very sad about my life.*

> *One day someone invited me to send my children to CHE class, the informal school. Mrs. J with her loving care taught us mothers something new about how to develop a healthy family. We came once a week to get different kinds of lessons in health, sanitation, how to feed children and filtering water. Our children were helped in their school lessons and I felt like I had joined a different and positive community with the moral value and emotional care lessons. I enjoyed the meetings and the love of Mrs. J. She showed me how to improve my income by working harder and diligently.*

> *I got a small loan from our cooperative we had started so I could sell vegetables carried on my head, walking back and forth along the muddy lanes. At noon time I would cook the vegetables and sell various cookies and other light food. I saved enough money to buy a small cart for selling the food and also made a small shop in my house. I got encouragement and love as well as hope for a better living from the CHE program. We all were happy when my husband finally got a job at the harbour.*

Mrs. J thought I was learning well and willing to work hard, so she gave me a bigger responsibility as the volunteers' coordinator. There are both Muslim and Christian members, and Mrs. J appointed me although I am Muslim. I realized that CHE is for all religions, and for the three years I had never felt pushed to be a Christian. As a coordinator now I felt I wanted to learn more, so when Mrs. J told me there was to be a Training of Trainers course in a distant city, I decided to go. I saved my money until I was able to buy the plane ticket, as now my income had increased to almost $30 per day.

My family was so proud of me! My husband said, "See your mom is the only person in our family who has ever been able to fly on an airplane, and she bought the ticket with her own money!" I was excited and fascinated by the airplane, especially all the interesting things in the toilet.

Finally I reached the place where the course was held, three hours from the airport. My life was changed from then on, and I want to be an active CHE trainer to bless my neighbours because I have been blessed first. In fact I plan to go back to my home town to introduce the training there too."

Ita did go on to be a trainer in her community and went back to her home town and introduced the program there. No longer a garbage picker, she is an entrepreneur and a catalyst for others who want to lift themselves out of poverty. The love she described from Mrs. J is now what she shares with others.

Impact of the Oppression of Women: the whole world trembles

Sheryl WuDunne, co-author with her husband Nicholas Kristof of best-seller *Half the Sky,* is convinced there is a direct relationship between a nation's poverty and the treatment of women in the society[57]. She goes further by warning that the oppression of women is the greatest moral dilemma of our time and how we solve that will impact nations.[58] The impact is felt positively when women are in positions of responsibility and leadership. There is increased economic growth, better health and education for families, less corruption and social disparity. Facilitating the educating of girls and making micro-credit loans, financial literacy and health understanding available for women are important starts in enabling women to rise above the poverty line and into positions of influence.

The feminization of poverty is a term that has been used to indicate the disparity between the genders, specifically the disproportionate burden of poverty borne by women worldwide. This is not just in monetary wealth but in educational and job opportunities, social or cultural exclusion, property ownership, decision-making, family work responsibilities, standard of living and quality of life. Single mother households are typically at highest risk of poverty and their children more disadvantaged than their peers. The number of these households is growing worldwide which is cause for concern. Women who are impoverished or socially disadvantaged can easily become victims of other abuse by a partner or by organized crime. Human trafficking is not just a phenomenon of the developing world, but of North America and much has been written about the modern slave trade market. There are more people, most of them women, enslaved today than there were in the days of the African slave trade. The more that women are neglected and mistreated anywhere in the world, the more we will feel the ripples until the very foundations of the world are eroded.

One of the ways gender-based poverty is measured is the Gender Empowerment Measure (GEM) developed by the United Nations. It looks at the proportion of upper level jobs held by women as well as total female share of jobs and the income ratio. It includes another very objective indicator of the societal value placed on women, the number of seats of government won by women.

Results of the 2017 elections in Papua New Guinea, for example, brought no women to the one hundred eleven seats of Parliament, making it only one of five countries in the world with no female leaders in the top decision-making bodies. This is very discouraging as great efforts had been made to see women run and to train them in the issues of current debate. It is obvious that the political culture of vote buying is very detrimental, not just to the country as a whole in subverting justice, but also to women candidates who likely do not have the funds or the inclination to compete in that corrupt arena. The country will be the poorer for the loss of the decision-making voice of half their population that now sinks further into oppression.

It is not surprising then to see this lack of value of women reflected in high Maternal Mortality Ratio (MMR). This is another measure of the health standards of a country and the priority they place on women's health. It reflects maternal deaths related to pregnancy or its management, either during pregnancy, childbirth or up to forty-two days after delivery. While in PNG it is hard to get accurate numbers when many rural women die at home and are not even reported, 2013 estimates put MMR at 500 maternal deaths/100,000 live births.[59]

These may sound like mere statistics, but when translated into real human figures we get it—more than 1500 women dying annually or one every five hours in a small country of just seven million. The reasons are predictable: unhygienic and unsupervised deliveries due to remote geography that makes access to safe delivery centres impossible for many. If they do get there the centre may not have staff or supplies. Some women even hesitate to go without nice clothes for herself or the baby, and others for fear of breaking a cultural taboo (for example a male medical staff person in the room) or being roughly looked down on by health staff. The other sad result of maternal death is the orphaned baby who has a much lower chance of survival beyond the fifth birthday.

Low priority on women's health is also indicated by lack of information or access to contraception. Multiple pregnancies too close together weaken both the mother and the children, thus robbing a country of its own future. Programs that have emphasized family planning, education about nutrition during pregnancy, signs of complications to watch for, importance of a safe delivery and care of newborns, are cost-effective in nation building. By dismissing reproductive health as 'women's issues' that men find messy or mysterious, it will never change. If men on the other hand were dying at this rate from some illness...

In our own society's past, we are told that maternal mortality rates were also high, but they dropped dramatically once the education of girls became commonplace and in particular after women were enfranchised with the vote. There is a direct correlation then between the worth of girls and women and maternal survival rates.

Why, we lament, do those who willingly bear the excruciating labour pains that deliver and nurture humanity into this world also bear the heartbreaking pain of neglect, rejection, violence, overwork, inequality? Yet they do. Hearts that love the most are also most vulnerable.

This quote from Kofi Annan, former secretary general of the UN, eloquently summarizes the gains for the world as he calls on the International Community to promote gender equality and invest in women:

> Sixty years have passed since the founders of the United Nations inscribed, on the first page of our Charter, the equal rights of men and women. Since then, study after study has taught us that there is no tool for development more effective than the empowerment of women. No other policy is as likely to raise economic productivity, or to reduce infant and maternal mortality. No other policy is as sure to improve nutrition and promote health -- including the prevention of HIV/AIDS. No other policy is as powerful in increasing the chances of education for the next generation. And I would also venture that no policy is more important in preventing conflict, or in achieving reconciliation after a conflict has ended. But whatever the very real benefits of investing in women, the most important fact remains: women themselves have the right to live in dignity, in freedom from want and from fear.[60]

Discuss and Reflect:

1. Which of the stories about oppression of women touches your heart the most? Why?

2. What kinds of inequality or other issues face women disproportionately to men in your own culture?

3. Why does a simple belief like 'Imago Dei', created in God's image, have such profound impact in our treatment of others?

4. Contrast a symptomatic solution to issues of gender inequality (i.e. providing physical, economic or legislative help) vs. addressing root issues and causes (like worldview).

DEMONSTRATION

Demonstration: (noun) a practical exhibition and explanation of how something works or is performed.

--Oxford Dictionary

Much more is learned through seeing and hearing than through hearing alone. Demonstration includes both exhibition and explanation, both positive and negative, successes and failures. We need the demonstrations to learn how to duplicate successes and minimize failures. While this is a vital step in the process, knowing how to scale up from the demonstration is often the greater dilemma.

CHAPTER 6

People and Place: The importance of belonging

Everyone will sit under their own vine
and under their own fig tree,
and no one will make them afraid.

Micah 4:4

A Place to thrive, not just survive

"To be rooted is perhaps the most important and least recognized need of the human soul."

So wrote Simone Weil, a French philosopher living in the first half of the last century, words that have been often quoted but less often lived out by most of our world.

In pondering this idea in the context of the many places of the world we have known, we have realized that being connected with a place and the community in that place is central to being a secure and confident person. 'A place to belong' is in the core of our being.

Garbage Pickers of the Manila Landfill Sites: "I like my little home!"

The focus for our Community Health Education 2012 Regional Consultation was Urban CHE strategies. We decided it would be appropriate to hold it in Manila and to take the group right to the hub of urban poverty, the Manila dump sites. As well, women who were being trained as CHEs from those sites were invited to participate in our meetings. It made our topic real.

We all prepared for the afternoon we were to spend in the garbage picker communities by equipping ourselves with rubber boots and facemasks from the local hardware! We were told that if it rained the open sewers and run-off from Manila suburbs coursed their way right through these sites, and the improvised walkways and drains would not keep our feet above the water. We were glad for those boots!

But nothing prepared us for the smell! The thought of raising a family in such an unhygienic environment was beyond my comprehension, even after spending so much time in the very basic rural communities of PNG. In spite of the relentless stench and smoke from burning garbage, children played happily with their improvised games as in any more normal neighbourhood. They were not bothered by the smell or by having to dodge bags of filthy refuse as they skipped and ran. Kick the can was a favourite soccer-substitute game, as was hopscotch and marbles like anywhere else in the world. Child health of course was a question we raised, as we knew that the diseases spread by flies and contaminated water must all be prevalent here.

The residents of the community, especially the mothers and children, earned a mere survival income from picking through the garbage as it was dumped by the city garbage collection trucks, and collecting all the recyclable plastics. These plastics were washed in a dirty drain, packed into sacks and sold to buyers, earning them about a dollar per day. World Bank now defines abject poverty as less than $1.90 per day.

Our guides and informants were the CHE volunteers who lived there and shared with their peers the weekly lessons they were learning from their trainers about health and caring for their families. One of these volunteers took me to her small home built from the 'found' materials from the dump site: fences made from old bedsprings, walls of plywood chunks mixed with the iconic rusty corrugated roof iron sheets and a few wooden planks, a roof of plywood layered with plastic tarps. Yet somehow the inside seemed tidy and cozy! Small pots of flowers and herbs hung from the outside walls where each could catch a few rays of sunlight.

"I like my little home—we made it all with material we found here," she proudly stated. "It did not cost us anything."

We had discussed the art of Appreciative Inquiry with the conference participants that week, so I asked what she liked about her community. The current best practices in development show us that focusing on our assets and resources, what we like rather than dislike about our lives, is much more motivating than a needs focus. So, I wondered, would there be anything at all positive she would point to about living in this community?

"Oh, I enjoy many things here," she began with a smile on her face. "For one thing we don't have to go anywhere to work, our work is right here. Previously my husband worked in a construction job, but by the time he travelled to the job site and bought lunch there, he makes the same amount by working right here." I marvelled at her attitude, knowing that the work was tedious, smelly and competitive.

She had more. "Another thing is that the pastor who lives here has shown us how to start raising pigs for extra income. He doesn't have to buy any feed at all except some starter feed for the newly weaned piglets. We know which trucks come with restaurant waste, and the food that is not good for our own consumption is perfect feed for the pigs. Pigs grow fast and are easy to sell for a good amount of money, as Filipinos do love their pork!"

We later met this pastor and his wife, who further supported their work with a small store selling basic essentials for the residents. They had been there for years, moving with the people when the dumpsites were full and the land ready to be reclaimed. Their four children had done well, the older two in university. Their dedication gives meaning to the term 'incarnational.'

This was first hand learning for all of us. We concluded that everyone, whatever their circumstance, wants a place to call their own where they can raise their children with love and take pride in the work of their own hands. I walked away that afternoon with new appreciation, even admiration, for the resilience of the underprivileged of the world. If they are motivated to create their own space and work, to find beauty in the midst of poverty, not much seems to stand in their way. They will advance. We can all be creative beings when released from a mindset that binds us to the poverty of the here and now, or that tells us that we are not good enough to ever live differently.

Egma's Story: The Worldwide Plight of Urban Squatter Settlements

Egma is one of the most fearless and effective urban trainers in Community Health Education (CHE) that we know. We have been amazed by her stories of changed lives in Port Moresby slums, some of the most difficult and unhygienic squatter settlements to be found anywhere in the world, which she fearlessly frequents. The hard-core criminal elements of the city inhabit these areas too, but they have learned to know her and protect her.

We have known this diminutive but determined Papua New Guinean woman since the 2006 CHE Training of Trainers workshop she was part of in Port Moresby, the capital city. She immediately picked up the concepts and was asked by her church to implement the program in the nearby squatter settlements.

Egma rose to the challenge with no funding, just a strong sense of calling and a lasting commitment that has not given up. Fortunately her dedication and perseverance does not depend on money or recognition. The church has given token acknowledgment to her work from time to time. For example, last year they gave her five minutes for several consecutive Sunday services to talk about the causes and symptoms of tuberculosis, which is rampant in the surrounding communities. We applaud the church that recognizes the need for training about such issues.

As she trains community ladies in basic lessons such as hygiene, nutrition, identifying and treating tuberculosis, malaria and HIV/AIDS, she sees change. Even in hard places like the homes built on stilts right over the ocean shore, simple changes make a difference. One of the young mothers told her that because her kids are healthier, she no longer has to spend hours in hospital queues with them every week, so she can be more productive at home. She is now able to contribute to the family nutrition by growing a garden. Other women have come up with ideas for income generation, such as selling simple homemade foods to other settlement dwellers.

Egma has shown the women that even small spaces between their shanty homes can be utilized for container gardens in discarded items like old tires, plastic bottles hung from the sides of buildings or old broken canoes.

The CHE volunteers she has trained have become the tuberculosis peer educator treatment partners in the TB DOTS (Directly Observed Treatment, Short-course) program, run out of the local clinic. World Health Organization recommends this six to eight-month treatment program, with a peer directly observing patients taking the medication, as the most cost-effective way to stop the spread of TB. Volunteers such as those Egma trained can identify potential TB patients and take them to the health centre for treatment. A similar program implemented in the CHE project areas of the Philippines demonstrated that their volunteers found even more than the predicted number of cases, thus being commended as greater than one hundred per cent successful! These are crucial programs for eradicating a disease like TB, which is rife in overcrowded areas like squatter settlements. Consistent treatment in turn prevents the rise of drug resistant strains, which will have global impact for all of us.

One of the early CHE trainings Egma did was in a renowned, crime-ridden settlement where the group was responsive and enthusiastic. She had no idea that one of the lady participants was the local witch doctor until the week was almost over. That day one of the participants told her that she had a bad headache, and that she had gone for help to the witchdoctor. This witch doctor told her that since being in this training she realized that her power was nothing compared to the power of Jesus, and that she had decided to renounce her magic practices!

Later an amazing story showed the impact of this decision. One night after a death in the settlement, a group of people took burning bamboo torches and headed to the cemetery for a customary sorcery ceremony where they supposedly would hear from the dead person as to who was responsible for this death. In their minds this would indicate to them the real cause of death. However, on this night they could not make the burning bamboo stay lit. They would go a short distance and the torches would go out, only to be re-lit and extinguished again.

Then the witch doctor lady called out, "Your lights will not be able to burn any further than the place where you are now, because a stronger light now resides here." She was telling them that their dark practices were now subject to a Light far brighter than their feeble bamboo torches.

This former witch doctor now lives in that Light, and is employed as a caretaker at the church that sent Egma into her community.

One reason for her effectiveness is that Egma is herself a mother of four and part of a squatter settlement, making her vulnerable to the same problems as the mothers she trains. Sure enough, she found herself facing the biggest challenge of all—legal notice that her family was to be evicted and the settlement bulldozed down!

This is a hardship not unfamiliar in today's urban world—forced eviction and re-development of slum communities. Egma represents millions of people living today in squatter settlements, on land belonging to others or to the state. Houses spring up overnight on city landfill sites, built with materials discarded as waste by others, or on undeveloped public land. After some years the state sells the land to a developer, or the city decides to clean up the area.

It is hard to imagine the feeling of being told that a bulldozer will arrive the next day to eliminate your community! This is the plight of urban poor the world over, especially when a city hurries to clean up because they have been chosen to host a big regional or international sports event, such as was happening in Port Moresby at the time. Even though the squatters have illegally built dwellings on the land and expect one day to have to move, the rudeness and sometimes brutality of the evictors when that day comes brings added distress to the settlers.

"What can we salvage from our home to rebuild?" they ask themselves.

"What can we carry with us, and where will we go?" become the obvious questions.

Egma and the 3000 Paga Hill residents, whose homes dotted a steep mountain slope overlooking Papua New Guinea's capital city and the ocean, became victims in 2014 to urban development. Some of them had resided there for four generations! Without consultation, their prime downtown sea view mountain slope, before considered worthless, had been leased to a developer and was destined to become a "world class planned luxury estate."

Destruction began. Egma, as one of the more educated home owners, stood outside her home resisting the orders to leave, and the bulldozer driver stopped short of her home and abandoned his wrecking. Egma became an advocate in the battle for the rights of the people. They began court proceedings to register some of the waterfront land as reclaimed from the sea, which gave them traditional ownership rights. The court agreed with them and issued a restraining order to prevent further demolition of homes until land ownership was determined.

In spite of the court order, the bulldozers again appeared on July 22, 2014, along with the police. They destroyed an historic church, a preschool and even irreplaceable WWII artifacts! These seemed to represent the last vestiges of hope for the people, and then the final one hundred seventy homes, including Egma's, were demolished, burned and buried.[61]

The result: justice perverted and more homeless people, including Egma's family with four children. Some of the people agreed to be relocated to the outskirts of the city, with some land for gardens, but the promised water, electricity and toilet blocks have still not been completed.

Egma's house and belongings, with the exception of a few suitcases of books and clothing that they could hurriedly rescue, were gone. Even the building materials they had been collecting for the day when they would have to build in another place were destroyed. What should they do? She and her husband could have afforded to rebuild. Instead they chose to identify for several months with the people—Egma spending her days on the street, finding shelter wherever possible at night, which when raining was at her husband's workplace.

The swift demolition soon came to the notice of a British human rights centre, International State Crimes Initiative. Dr. Kristian Lasslett made a poignant observation. "The case of Paga Hill is emblematic of a broader trend, where local communities are facing forced evictions, implemented through violence, by actors who have often obtained the land through land transactions with a question mark over them." [62] He also commended the Paga Hill settlers, who have not chosen to retaliate despite their treatment, but rather to respect the laws of the country.

The destruction had clearly been contempt of court by the police and the Australian development company, so again Egma and other residents prepared their case. Patiently they waited, as one court date after another was postponed! They knew that just treatment would mean that the state should compensate them somewhat for their lost dwellings, enabling them to build again elsewhere. They are still waiting, still hopeful! Meanwhile Egma and her husband built another temporary home also on land designated for development, then re-built on some land given them by a friend. It is quite near her church and the other settlements where her CHE mothers live. She sees this as God's provision and faithfulness to them, although whether they will ever gain title to their small block they do not know. In a recent letter, she reports that the CHE work goes on in spite of so many odds against them.

While an unsung hero in the eyes of the world, Egma is very much a hero to her community. By taking an advocacy role in her stride with the same determination she has shown for teaching physical and spiritual wholeness, she has demonstrated that God is concerned for all needs and that His call for justice for the poor is to be taken seriously. We ourselves have been impacted by her unrelenting passion to see lives and communities transformed. Her strength comes from a deep belief within her in the power of God whose love for justice and righteousness are His very essence. Because of that, Egma is one who rises above her circumstances.

Belonging is good for our Health!

Material wealth is not an indicator of well-being! However connection with those around us brings improvement to mental and physical health, increased order and safety, decreased addictions, less juvenile misconduct and even correlates to longer life spans.

Now termed the 'Blue Zones,' research on longevity has described the lifestyles and environments of the world's most long-living people, found in five specific locations. [63] The term first appeared in a November 2005 'National Geographic Magazine' article by researcher Dan Buettner, who has since written a book entitled *The Blue Zones: Lessons for Living Longer from the People Who've Lived the Longest.*[64] The five places? Sardinia in Italy, where one village in the decade up to 2016 boasted twenty centenarians; Okinawa islands of Japan; Loma Linda, California where Seventh-day Adventists predominate; Nicoya Peninsula, Costa Rica; Icaria, Greece where one out of three people make it to their ninety's and almost no dementia.

It is interesting to note the commonalities among these places, in addition to the diet and physical activity factors. These are socio-spiritual dynamics: putting family ahead of other concerns, social engagement with people of all ages in the community, active spiritual or religious involvement, having purpose in life. The importance of being rooted in the social and spiritual fabric of our place is evidently now proven to be what will bring both longer life and satisfaction along the way. It seems that it is not access to outside resources or wealth, or even medical services that are determinants of health. Rather, human flourishing is sustained by interconnectedness with the people in one's place through the relationships, social and physical activities that have developed over a lifetime, and a sense of purpose and faith.

Buettner authored a similar *'National Geographic Magazine'* article in November 2017 on research into happiness and how that is derived[65]. As with health and longevity, the link between happiness and place is strong, as the country itself must provide for security in health care, safety, education and economic opportunity for citizens to enjoy wellbeing. The three countries that emerge highest, for different reasons, on the 'happiness index' are Denmark, Costa Rica and Singapore. It would seem that the key is finding balance between meaningful work and time for socialization, faith and volunteer activities in a secure environment that minimizes stress.

We all need our 'tribe' and our place to belong where people love us and are proud of our accomplishments. Connected families and lifelong friends keep us grounded and secure, accountable for our actions, motivated to live well. I grew up on a family farm with grandparents living only minutes away. During the years when my parents were working their hardest, our grandparents had the time to include my sisters and me in their lives. I talked endlessly with Grandpa on almost any topic or question, borrowed his musical instruments one by one and practiced the lessons he gave me. I valued his advice and wisdom and even today can recall conversations. I watched Grandma bake cookies, sew quilts and talk about raising kids. The delicious smell of her kitchen was somehow intertwined with growing up. I belonged.

Abundant Communities start at home

The Abundant Community Initiative that we have been part of in the context of our own Alberta communities points out the need for connectedness even in the so-called middle class.[66] The name is derived from the book by the same title written in 2012 by John McKnight and Peter Block.[67] They have done years of research and sociology studies on community development, in particular pioneering the concept of Asset Based Community Development (ABCD) now used all over the world and which we will describe in more detail in Chapter 8. Abundant Community is neighbours connecting with neighbours to support and enjoy one another, network skills and interests, provide safe environments for children and to plan possible improvements in their community.

In our cities, even hamlets, we may not know our next-door neighbours. The isolation and loneliness that we have created by our busy and individualistic lifestyles is working against us. Isolation leads to increased addictions and crime as people do not know each other or care what is happening to each other's children. We are surviving, but not thriving in community togetherness as we witness in many of the rural villages in other parts of the world. We have much to learn from the strengths of our global neighbours.

Dr. Sasa: a grounded Chin village boy sets his sights high

It was December 2012 and we were in Aizawl, the stunning ridge-top capital city of Mizoram, a small north east state of India. Flying in from the heat of Calcutta, we were quick to realize that we would need to purchase some warm blankets as soon as we had gone through our clearance protocol at the Tourist Affairs office. We would be heading out to Chapi with Dr. Sasa early in the morning and would need those blankets and the jackets we had with us. At this time of year and at 3500 feet elevation, night and early morning temperatures dip to almost freezing.

We had been warned that the trip from Aizawl to the south-eastern India-Myanmar border would be arduous. Of course, the twenty-two-hour nonstop bus journey was spectacularly beautiful, even though the last six hours were cramped and cold in the back of a large lorry truck. The ribbon of narrow road wound through the lower slopes of the Himalayas, in seeming endless layers of rugged green mountains with villages between. The adaptability and architectural ability of the hardy mountain people to build on such steep slopes amazed us. Every village was post-card beautiful. The street side of the houses made them appear as one storey, however each of them was supported on the other side by posts with at least three floors jutting precariously over the steep drop below. There was absolutely no level ground on which to build except for the ridges along the sides of the highway on which we were traveling. We observed that each village in this predominately (87%) Christian state had a stately white church as its main feature, and melodious singing could sometimes be heard wafting through the air.

The scenery before the blanket of darkness had fallen was spectacular, but as we continued on through the night we experienced more awe-inspiring surprises. The high elevation and crisp air made the bright stars jump out of the sky, seeming light years closer than they appear at home. We had not known what to expect from this journey, but we certainly were not disappointed.

We were traveling with Canadians Dave and Ann, who had retired early from their jobs in Newfoundland and spent most of each year as Community Health Education promoters in South and South-East Asia. We had met them the previous year at our annual CHE consultation in Chiang Mai, Thailand. Being new at that time to CHE, they had asked if we would accompany them to introduce the strategy to Dr. Sasa and the Health and Hope Society that he had founded for the training of Community Health Workers in his native Chin State of Myanmar, formerly known as Burma. We became good friends through the shared experience, and we worked together well. Dave helped us to laugh about what we might otherwise have taken too seriously, and Ann as a nurse took to the lesson materials with great enthusiasm.

Having been several times to Myanmar, we also knew of the desperate situation of the minority ethnic groups, living mostly in states along country borders, and experiencing lack of access to health and education from decades of cruel harassment by the military. Military abuse and government neglect made Chin State the least developed in Myanmar with the highest poverty rate. There were no health centres, no telephones or electricity and minimal education. Just about the time we visited in December 2012, a cease-fire was signed between the Myanmar Army and the Chin State National Front. While this and the 2015 multi-party general election, the first since 1990, opened the way for addressing the issues in the over-looked border state, deep-seated poverty takes a long time to erase.

Even with the oppression they suffered, we observed that the solid faith of these people was characterized by hope, which surely contributed to their survival. Like many other animistic ethnic groups such as the Karen, Wa, Naga, Lisu and Rawong, the Chin had responded readily to the Christian missionaries who came in the late 1800's during the time of British rule. The fact that they were almost all Christian brought further alienation from the dominant Buddhist government.

The Rideouts had connected to Dr. Sasa through a Canadian couple in Armenia who knew him as a medical student there. He told them of the need for relief food for the Chin State due to an invasion of rats that were eating the food crops. The rats flourish and multiply when the bamboo in the forest bears flowers, a phenomenon that occurs every fifty years.[68] Sasa, in his final year, gained permission to return to help with relief supplies during the famine time. Observing how desperate their health need was, he vowed to return after graduating.

Two years later when we arrived, he was a fully qualified doctor living in Chapi on the Indian side of the river than forms the Myanmar-Mizoram border. Because of the winding course of the river, Chapi is in fact surrounded on three sides by Myanmar. The arbitrary river border chosen by the British many years back separates the large Mara language group from family members on either side. The training centre that Sasa's team had built was high up on the Lushai mountains, locally known as the 'Chin Hills', where it seemed we were looking down on the clouds rather than up at them. As we sat each morning before breakfast on the narrow deck outside the small rooms where we slept, the clouds appeared to us like white lakes surrounded by dark green forests. As the sun rose higher and its heat dissipated the clouds, the lakes disappeared and the contour of the land became visible, with forests and terraced gardens giving way to small homesteads identified by wisps of smoke from numerous cooking fires.

Chapi village is home to around two hundred households that somehow manage to terrace the slopes for gardens and rice farming and to graze some livestock on these inhospitable mountain ridges. Their Mara language is spoken in about forty villages in Mizoram on the India side of the border, and possibly fourteen hundred villages in Myanmar. Though not illegal for Mara people to cross the river here, there was a specific short distance they were allowed to go inside the other country. Sasa himself had breached that law a number of years ago when he walked out to attend university in Shilong, India without permission from Myanmar authorities. He later repeated the affront when he made his way to medical school in Armenia. At the time of our visit, he would have been arrested if he had tried to re-enter Myanmar. Fortunately, he has now regained his citizenship as well as the respect he deserves. We would piece together more of his incredible story of hardship and determination over the next twelve days.

Our invitation was to assess how the CHE model would fit with his Community Health Worker training for Myanmar Chin State villages, which have no other medical personnel or facilities. We had expected time to assess or talk about their programs, but instead they had brought us thirty or more of their coordinators and trainees, all prepared for training. They asked that we immediately proceed with twelve straight days of training, with only Christmas Day off! After all, they explained, it had been easier for us to travel there than most of the group who had walked up to five days. Even though we felt somewhat unprepared we were happy to have this opportunity to spend time teaching and interacting with such a dedicated and enthusiastic group. Our respect for Sasa had already grown and his determination was unquestionable.

Growing up in a Chin village, Sasa witnessed many of his friends die of preventable illnesses, or mothers lose infants in childbirth because the nearest hospital was many day's walk away. He had helped carry people through the jungle trails in a futile effort to get them to hospital before their life ebbed away. Sasa knew poverty first hand. Village schooling finished at grade ten, but Sasa was determined to get an education and help his people. His parents encouraged him and are models of the kindness and generosity we now see in him. His father, whom we named the "Apostle Paul of Burma," had walked through all fourteen hundred forty-one villages of the Mara language group, planted seven hundred churches, been shot at and imprisoned several times by the Burmese military and still strode tall and strong. His mother was illiterate and tiny in stature but had memorized so much of the Bible that she was often asked to speak at women's conferences. She told us of seeing the Burmese army camped above their village ready to rape and pillage, but she felt compelled to take them some produce from her garden. The captain was totally nonplussed by this tiny lady who walked bravely into their camp with vegetables in the basket hanging by a strap from her head, and her simple statement, "I think your men need some fresh vegetables." They left the next morning!

Supported by these stalwart parents, young Sasa, who spoke only his Mara native tongue, made his way to an uncle's home in the national capital, Yangon, for high school. He did not know how to ride a bus, so just jumped when he saw the landmark identifying his uncle's house, breaking an arm as he did so. His 'funny' clothing, felted wool shoes and strange speech made him the object of ridicule by his peers. One day, overwhelmed by the rejection, homesickness and the temptation to give up and return home, he remembers sitting under a big tree and praying that it would fall on him and end his life right there. Instead, the tree spoke to him!

"All you have to do is learn to speak Burmese," it seemed to say. "Now what could be so hard about that?" Stunned into a new determination, he managed to learn Burmese and graduate from grade twelve. University in India was next.

Carrying only one live chicken in a native basket hanging from his head and the encouragement of his parents and village, he walked several days out of Burma into India. He made friends along the way as he asked directions to Shilong, India and received help from the friendly Mizoram folk who could see that this polite young boy was poor but determined in his goal. He soon realized that he would need more than a chicken to fund his education, and paused for over a year at a rock quarry to earn his tuition, experiencing the backbreaking toil of a labourer. He was too embarrassed to tell his parents about this as he worked his way through university in Shilong. He knew the village was praying for him, proud of him and counting on him to finish, so he would do it no matter what. He belonged to them, after all.

Medical college was his next dream. Seeing a newspaper advertisement on a bulletin board for medical school in Armenia, he decided this was his chance. The village people again backed him, selling chickens or pigs or cows to buy him a ticket from India to Armenia, and he was launched into his dream. It was obvious that he was extremely disadvantaged and none of his friends at home had realized the cost of living in a city or the extent of tuition fees. Fortunately a Canadian mission couple soon connected with him and they became his family there.

Somewhere along the way he was introduced to Baroness Carolyn Cox of the British House of Lords and the HART Foundation, which looks for promising young people in conflict areas to help through university. Sasa became one of her 'family' as well, and she supports his work and connects him with influential people right to this day. When he founded Health and Hope Society, Prince Charles became their patron. Sasa continues the tradition of finding intelligent young people from Burma and sending them out to universities in India, China and Philippines with the help of his British friends. These educated men and women will indeed be influential in the change we know will come to Myanmar. Sasa's own brother went to medical college in China and graduated with top honours even though he had to learn Chinese to study medicine.

So now Sasa was home, a full-fledged doctor with a vision to train others to become community health workers, not just to treat but to prevent illness. This is a vision close to our hearts, so we felt privileged to participate with him. Up to the point of this writing, he has trained over 834 of these health volunteers in his six-month program, a good start in his goal of two per village.

In the two weeks we spent in Chapi, there were several groups of Chin villagers who walked across the river border to Chapi centre. One group, about a dozen high school principals from around the

State, had walked for days to receive the laptop computers that Sasa had been given to pass on to them from a donor. Solar panels for charging them were included, along with a few brief instructions on how to use them! Their English was quite good, and in our time of sharing with them that evening, one stood and said, "I am sixty-two years old, and I thought that I would die without ever seeing a white person! I am so happy to meet you all."

We were surprised, but then realized just how intentionally isolated the government had kept these people in the far west of the country. It took a special permit for a foreigner to travel to Chin State, and it was only good for four days. This meant that it would be physically impossible to get as far off the beaten track as their communities were located. Bill was quick with his reply. "Well we assure you that there are better looking specimens than the four of us!" They all chuckled, knowing that we were even older than they.

These were the educated men of their communities, responsible for the young people, but also the ones who held the government two-way radios. This obligated them to report any unauthorized visitors or activities. They were dignified in their demeanour, yet their economic poverty appeared obvious from their gaunt frames and tattered clothing. We realized that poverty is only in the mindset of those who either give or wear that label—it had not occurred to these men, whose status in their community put them as respected leaders, to think of themselves as poor. They were rich in relationships. They were grateful for the camaraderie of each other's company, for the hospitality they were receiving here and for meeting the unexpected strangers they had encountered this night. They were secure in their inner beings, rooted in their communities, at peace with God and the world. Their peace was not dependent on possessions or technology or threatened by the war being waged against them. We were learning again that having a place to belong is of far greater significance than having possessions to put in that place.

These oppressed villagers were confirming that having a place to belong is of far greater significance than having possessions to put in that place.

Another delegation that came, ninety-two of them, were from Sasa's own village of Lailenpi about three day's walk away. Some were his benefactors who had sold their last chickens to pay his trip to medical school and had not seen him for thirteen years. They were about to defy the army that oppresses and brutalizes them, as they came with an illegal mission in mind—to carry back building supplies from India that Sasa had accumulated for them to build a health post and training centre in Lailenpi. They sent a messenger ahead of them to tell Sasa they were coming, but it was too late to warn them that the military had just been to Chapi to 'interview' the four of us and would be staying around in the area for a few days. We had not seen the usually upbeat Sasa this worried, as he knew the danger for them if they were detected. Then it started to pour rain, the first and only time we had seen rain while there, and Sasa smiled. "The military are the first to run for cover in heavy rain like this. They will all be hanging out in their tents."

Sure enough. The group of villagers slipped across the border, wet but unobserved by both Indian and Burmese armies that the rumour mill told us were camped on the hills above us having a consultation. Drenched clothes hung on the rail-thin bodies of the tired villagers but their spirits were strong. There were no hints of complaint or requests for help from us, again the first white people that most had met, only warm open smiles and firm confident handshakes.

They dried out by the fires, ate a hearty meal and all came together for the evening to talk and share their stories. We were amazed that their tales were not of hardship or pain as we expected, but of God's sustaining grace and the great love they experience from the One they said never leaves or forsakes them! How humbling for us to learn firsthand how this message, coming to them in 1907, really works in the hardest times of suffering a people group could face. Praying the Lord's Prayer together at the end of the evening was a moving statement of solidarity among Christians who will never meet again on this earth but who share a hope of eternity together. This was not a moment to forget.

Bill felt compelled to get up at 5:00 the next morning to once more shake the hands of these dear Mara people as they slipped into the darkness of the thick morning fog and disappeared with their heavy loads of building materials. They would do their part in bringing the vision of a training centre and clinic in their village to reality.

Christmas in Chapi

Christmas 2012 in Chapi was unforgettable. More realistically it was Christmas week, as the communal feasting and singing seemed to go on for days. Each year three families volunteer for the privilege of hosting Christmas the following year, which involves raising a number of poultry, pigs and cows specifically for that purpose. It also means taking down the partition walls in their homes to have an 'open house' for the events of the week. We would find out why.

Village life revolves around the three churches. Even though all of them are the same as there is only one denomination in the language group, one would not be large enough for everyone. Each evening all through the Christmas week there were services, with singing accompanied only by the beat of a large traditional drum, and guest speakers from other churches. After each service, everyone was invited to one of the 'open houses' for more singing and dancing. Now it became interesting! Following the lead of the drummer, the singing turned into action—first marching then jogging to the beat in concentric circles in the middle of the house-turned-one-room! It seemed the whole house started moving as people one by one joined the circles like a great rotating mosh pit, moving faster and faster as the beat of the drums dictated. This continued for hours! All the youth looked forward to coming home from colleges for Christmas as village life for them was far more vibrant than the city—no wonder!

Outside Christmas guests in the village were a novelty, so we were invited to all three churches on Christmas day. We had taught our group of trainees, at Sasa's request, the first verse of 'Joy to the World' in English, and they quickly were dubbed the Canadian Choir and invited to perform at each of the churches. As they knew only one verse, we sang it once through and then in rounds about three more times! No matter, it was the special Christmas entertainment from the outsiders that they seemed to appreciate. Before and after the services we were invited to several homes where we enjoyed the hospitality of these generous people. We knew that they ate like this only once a year, but they truly enjoyed it and knew what it meant to celebrate as an entire community. Later when I showed some pictures to a grade two class in Alberta, one observant young child remarked that it would sure be fun to celebrate Christmas with so many people together rather than every family alone inside their own home! Even a child recognized the beauty of a connected community where belonging was better than stuff!

Dr. Sasa is naturally gifted with leadership ability. His sense of presence in settings far outside his own comfort zone, such as the British royalty and House of Lords, and his ability to make totally spontaneous articulate speeches in English-as-a-third language, leave us in awe. He accompanied us back to Aizawl after our time in Chapi as Baroness Carolyn Cox and four of her HART Foundation Board members were coming to pay a visit. Here again our lives would unexpectedly intersect with someone we now know to be one of the heroes of our world.

Soon after arriving at our hotel from the long journey back to Aizawl, we were briefly introduced to Baroness Cox and her team and informed that we would accompany them for dinner at the home of one of the Ministers of Mizoram Parliament. I panicked! Unlike Sasa who had a formal black suit stored here for such occasions, I only had my jeans and warm jacket. I noticed that the UK delegates were all attired in formal suits. I had been gifted a lovely handwoven shawl by Sasa's mother, one of my treasures still, which I knew I could wear. I just hoped that the local market would provide me a long wrap skirt like the ladies wore in Chapi.

I found Khai Aye, one of the young women who worked with Sasa, and explained my dilemma. "Khai Aye, could you find us a taxi and take me to a market—fast! We have to be at the Minister's home in fifteen minutes."

Sure enough, within minutes I found a black handwoven cloth with a bit of embroidery on it that would go well with my shawl, wrapped it over my jeans and we were on our way. When we entered the home of the Minister and his wife, they were overjoyed to see me in their traditional clothing and made a huge fuss, much to my embarrassment as I felt that the British guests looked slightly disapproving at my lack of formality. Oh well, Canadians might be forgiven for being ignorant of class protocols and propriety! If the locals were pleased, I was more than pleased.

I remember little about the dinner, except the way that Baroness Cox interacted with the Minister's family like old friends, which it appeared they were as she had brought appropriate gifts for each of them including the children. Her kind attentiveness was impressive, and I was making mental notes. She must have taken lessons from Queen Elizabeth, I mused! We were grateful and amazed for the totally unplanned privilege of being brought together in this little-known part of the world with such a woman of stature. Her contagious zeal for the broken and ignored outside the margins impressed upon our lives the desire to emulate her selfless compassion. The next day as she recounted to us some of her stories, we sensed her heart and fearless passion for justice for the neglected and mistreated of the world, particularly in sensitive conflict areas. Not only does she believe in the vital importance of education, she is doing something about it by identifying and finding scholarships for youth in these countries.

How amazing in a little-known part of the world to encounter a famous woman whose contagious zeal for the broken and ignored of this world impressed upon our lives the desire to emulate her selfless compassion.

All of this is motivated by her stalwart Christian faith in a God who inspires her to fight for a just society and for the fundamental freedoms which will allow the next generations to thrive. In her mid-seventies at the time we met her, she was still traveling to restricted areas, mostly the contested border areas where displaced and stateless people congregate, and the most unjust situations are seen. Danger or discomfort seemed never a consideration to her. As we listened to her, we could not help but admire her tenacity and bravery as she was determined to interview victims of injustice and bring the real stories back to her peers in the House of Lords. The biography of her life, written by Lela Gilbert, is fittingly titled *Baroness Cox, Eyewitness to a broken world.*[69] Her influence, eloquence and abilities are respected worldwide, but those she personally attends to most are not the rich or the famous or the literates who will read her book. They are the broken and the hidden ones throughout the world from Sudan to Burma, the lost and ignored who need her eyes in order to be found.

Beyond that valley live our enemies: Papua New Guinea 2007

Sometimes our deeply ingrained sense of place can carry with it the negative baggage of past generations. Such was the case in Mina's village in PNG. Mina, the trainer who had invited us to come see the changes in her community this particular day, had been one of the most unlikely participants in our first Training of Trainers workshop in Goroka. Later we found out that she had not completed even her primary schooling, but what she lacked in other qualifications she certainly made up for in determination. It was unusual for village men to listen to a woman, but it seemed the women recognized her leadership and the men were gradually convinced.

So began the village transformation from an unhealthy environment with smoke-filled huts and open defecation to the clean-swept courtyards and tidy hedges outlining the homes that we saw today. Over a few years their community became a pleasant and healthy place to live, with windows ventilating their homes, a separate outside cook house, animals fenced outside the village, each home with its own pit latrine and tidy kitchen garden for some quick vegetables. All this was done with their own efforts and the encouraging motivation of one of their own mothers who had taken the initiative to go out to the town to receive training. Mina had memorized everything she had been taught, as most oral learners do, unlike us literate learners who rely on reading skills. She was functionally illiterate. This is common in many PNG villages where almost no adult women and very few men are able to read and write even though they may have attended three or more years of school as children. This did not deter Mina. The simple picture booklets we had distributed, illustrating the cause and prevention of the most common illnesses had very few words, and she was able to impress the others with her new life-giving knowledge as she showed them the booklets.

As we walked up and down the steep ridge on which the village was built, we could not help but admire the phenomenal views in every direction. "How far does your clan's land extend?" we asked. She pointed into the distance about a two-hour walk in each direction.

"That is where our gardens are," she pointed, and explained that she walked almost daily a couple of hours to the garden sites. They are still practicing the primitive slash-and-burn method of agriculture, where the charred soil from the burned trees and underbrush provides fertilizer and eliminates weeds. Cultivation is all by hand with shovels. The gardens are moved every two or three years to restore the soil. It is labour intensive, not to mention the two hours to carry their produce back home in heavy *bilums,* the string bags hanging down their backs from straps on their foreheads. It is little wonder that back pain plagues the older women who have done this all their lives. The men usually help with the garden site preparation as their contribution.

"And then over on that mountain," she pointed, "that is where our enemies live." Startled by the statement, I looked to see if she was serious. She was.

"Birua b'long yupela?" (Your enemies?) I questioned, to make sure I had heard correctly.

"Oh, it has been years since we have fought them," she was quick to explain. She knew we had taught that harmonious relationships with each other, ourselves, the environment and with God were foundational to a healthy community.

"So why do you still call them enemies?" I asked, puzzled. She shrugged in a noncommittal way. I probed again, "What is the name of that place?" The village name she mentioned was a familiar one to me. I could not imagine these two communities calling each other enemies but apparently that was the case.

As we drove over the steep winding road on our return to Goroka, I pondered what it must be like to drive past an 'enemy village' on the way to town, or for the children to make a wide berth to avoid walking over 'enemy land' on their way to school. How does that feel? Is this the way much of the rest of the world has grown up, always looking over towards the enemy lurking on the next mountain? What does that do to one's psyche as the concept of 'us against them' is instilled from the time a child can communicate? How can that word be erased from a child's vocabulary if the adults still use it years after the last conflict?

I was imagining how the security of the child's home and place is impacted by knowing that conflict could erupt at any moment, or by overhearing adults recount the battle exploits of the last war. The startling reality is that border conflict and religious wars seem to almost spontaneously spring up around the world, ignited with what to us seems barely a spark of provocation. I had a new insight that day into how that could happen.

Children of Conflict: Finding Place in a refugee camp, Albania 1999

It was our thirtieth wedding anniversary, and we wrote to tell our friends at home that we were spending it by the Adriatic Sea. Oh yes, in a refugee camp where we were volunteering for a few months with Samaritan's Purse who were overseeing a camp of twenty-five hundred families. These were families from Kosovo, who at great peril had fled across the mountainous border into Albania. Some came with tractors or in the backs of trucks with some possessions, but most came on foot with barely an extra change of clothing. Samaritan's Purse had been granted a large flat piece of ground by the seaside for a tent city, next another of the same size run by a Norwegian agency, and then an Italian camp.

We were initially asked to help set up medical care for the camp, including the organization of the occupants into groups for training in health and hygiene using the Community Health Education format. I was to work with those implementing formal education for the expected five thousand or so children who would need such normal routines and friendship to assist with the post-trauma stress that most were suffering from. Informal recreation for the children was another part of this. It was wonderful to see the kids being able to laugh and head off together to the sea, which most had never seen before, and to sit in peer groups in the tents designated for classrooms. We realize that most of the refugee camps of the world today are grossly over-crowded and often unsafe places for children, having become progressively worse as the years pass and the numbers of refugees in the world increases. Still it is the children who suffer the most both during the conflict and later with emotional wounds of the trauma.

One of the family units we spent time with consisted of two widows who were caring for ten children. Two of the children were the niece and nephew of one of the women, and as I recall they were eight and three years of age. Their father was fighting in Kosovo with the Kosovo Liberation Army (KLA) and they had witnessed their mother shot right before their eyes. This auntie, the sister of the murdered woman, had caught a glimpse of the body of a victim on television news and recognized it as her sister. This occurred early enough in the conflict that there was still news coverage happening. She realized that her sister's two children would be alone. So she bravely made her way the several hours to where they lived, and escaped with them along with her own children across the mountains to Albania. The little boy seemed young enough to be well adjusted in the secure care of his aunt, but the girl was obviously severely traumatized, staring soberly into nothing most of the day and experiencing nightmares and flashbacks. We went out and bought a small doll for her, which elicited a momentary smile and gave her something to constantly carry and hug. Even though there were experts in Post-Traumatic Stress Disorder (PTSD) who had quickly been deployed to the camps and we referred her for their special attention, we know she will carry the invisible emotional wounds for her lifetime. She remains in my mind as the face of the war.

There were training classes needed for teachers, both for their camp classroom concerns and to prepare them for their return home to Kosovo when the war ended. I had to learn some of the lessons first before passing them on to the teachers. For example, both Bill and I went through the workshop on landmines and unexploded ordnances (called UXO's). NATO joint forces had learned from the Bosnia war all the types and ways the mines were probably being employed. We knew this was important training for teachers to pass on to the children of the camp in preparation for their return home. While I have long since forgotten most of the landmine training, the teachers no doubt had to keep it firmly in their minds for several years, reinforced by the people they knew who sacrificed a limb, an eye or their lives for even momentarily neglecting this important knowledge.

The teachers encouraged the children to express their emotions through art. One of the drawings I saw depicted a village invasion by the Yugoslavian army—there were planes in the sky, dead bodies in a row as though lined up and shot, fire burning through the roofs of several houses, guns firing from tanks, soldiers standing guard with guns pointed at the people in the centre of the village whose hands were in the air, a mother carrying a bleeding child—way too detailed and graphic to have been just imagination. It was hoped that when expressed through art, the children would have their feelings validated by sympathetic adults and know that the horrors they had witnessed were terribly wrong. The healing process would not be a quick one.

Forgiveness is a process

Bill and I learned much from these refugees: about dedication to family and place, about determination and loyalty, about the resilience of the human spirit, about making even a tent into a home where they could continue to be hospitable. But one important lesson we learned from a group of ten- to twelve-year olds.

We were in one of the tent-classrooms of some lively refugee children, grades five and six. The teacher asked if we could explain what Samaritan's Purse meant, as they all knew they were in the camp run by this organization and that the English words meant something. So we offered to organize an impromptu skit that would explain the name, the story of the Good Samaritan as told by Jesus.[70] The kids really got into the action of the story, as we told each of the actors what role they would play. The bandits were vicious; the two callous passers-by turned their noses up at the injured man's need. Two children played the donkey, which the Samaritan actor helped the injured victim to ride. Arriving at the inn, he got out his purse and generously paid for all the medical care needed before going on his way. We explained that purse was what inspired the name of the organization, Samaritan's Purse. They understood the meaning after seeing the skit.

"So which of the three people who encountered the injured man was a real neighbour?" we asked, as Jesus had after telling the story. They all knew the answer. The Samaritan man of course, and he was the one they all admired and wanted to emulate. They appreciated the fact that we as strangers would come all the way to Albania to help them in their distress and open the 'purse' to provide for them.

Next, we explained the cultural relationships in the story: the traveler attacked by the bandits was Jewish, and the dynamic between them and the Samaritan people in the next country was one of enmity and jealousy. They right away saw the similarity between this story and their own conflict with the Serbian people.

"So, what would you do if you saw a Serbian man injured by the roadside when you came along?" was our next question, thinking maybe there was some thoughtful processing going on, that some of them might see the futility of trying to annihilate one's neighbours.

Their faces suddenly became pictures of rage, and their dark eyes flashed. In an instant those innocent ten-year olds became vicious animals. "We would stab him, kill him, chop him up..." Their fists were punching the air, and all of them were talking at once. Even the teacher was nodding, a knowing smile on her face.

"Hmm," we could not help but nod too, observing the rage that the kind of pain they had experienced had generated. This was a generation of war-traumatized children many of whom would be suffering flashbacks, nightmares, fears, anxiety attacks and depression for years or for their whole lives. They did not have the maturity to see a bigger picture or to know the long-term effect on their own health and wellbeing that these desires for revenge would precipitate. Forgiveness was not a concept that would be introduced easily or soon. Healing of these hurts would take time and the patience of understanding adults who we could only hope would be there for them. We would pray that they might one day be introduced to the total forgiveness that God offers to each of us, which gives a basis for forgiving others. Children of conflict: a special demographic that must receive special attention for the survival of their nations.

We understand now how truly evil it is to uproot children from their place, to rob them of that security and even worse, to re-program them to become fighters where their impressionable spirits can easily be taught to hate. The cruelty of child-soldiers is well documented.

We also are slow now to talk about forgiveness when hurts are fresh and deep. The children taught us that. It is one thing to say the words, but it is a miracle to feel released from the pain—time and God alone can do that once they are again rooted in place.

At Home they are Heroes

The parents of these children represent millions of refugees worldwide. They were people of significance, of accomplishment, maybe even heroes in their community or family—before. Now they are living in transient camps bordering the home countries they have fled. All of their roots have been displaced, their individual identity neutralized into anonymity, their faces masking the pain they hold inside for the sake of their families. They long for home. We long for home for them, for a place they will be secure and again become community stalwarts.

We are fortunate to come across alternative stories all over the globe where a strong sense of place has formed strong individuals. They are beautiful but unsung heroes of their worlds, of our world. They are the glue that holds together the families and the communities where they live. They are so significant that the foundations of the earth would not hold up without them remaining rooted in their place. Go ahead, look for them in your own community, they are there and you can name them! They can be counted on, trusted, the helpers in times of need, the keepers of the keys to a healthy and well-functioning place. We have noted that these reluctant champions do not have wealth or notoriety and are found in the most unlikely places.

Emma comes immediately to mind. We first noticed her because she seemed to be smiling all the time. As we got to know Emma in Goroka, that sunny smile revealed a somewhat shy but brilliant and competent young Papua New Guinean woman who had just returned from Australia after completing her Bachelors' degree in Business. In her job interview with the administrator of the mission where she worked when we met, she offered to do any financial or administrative work as long as it did not involve answering the telephone or talking to people! He knew that would change with time, so they agreed to hire her. We encouraged her to take the CHE training and it became obvious that she had a natural communication gift and leadership potential under that shy exterior. Soon that gift became recognized both in her workplace, in the communities where she taught CHE lessons and at the wider level of Christian Health Services in the country. Her influence and passionate concern to see communities transform will continue spread as in 2018 she completed a Master's degree in Health Policy and Leadership from Perth, Australia.

Another was Nick, the village chief of a remote island in the Solomon Islands. Bright, educated and desirous of progress, he and Bill hit it off immediately and were soon conversing like old school chums. He knew that the divisions existing in the community would not foster development, so he attended the training the CHE coordinator from Honiara had organized for us to facilitate. Nick began somewhat reluctantly, but then as he soaked it all in he saw how these ideas would impact his fractured community. Immediately afterwards, he got the factions together for mediation and was ready to lead the people with renewed vision. That is a true servant of the people.

Sam had been seen as a troublemaker, a bit of a rogue in his Papua New Guinea village. People can change, and he did—the energy that he used for mischief was now directed towards bringing help and services to his neglected place that was far off the government grid. He relentlessly came to the door where the CHE coordinator had his office, telling him again and again that the people were ready and waiting for training, until finally it was agreed to give them a chance. Sam organized the people to build a road, complete with a small bridge so they were accessible to vehicles. They decided they would build a community centre and instead of any traditional building, they built it in the shape of a helicopter with a wooden propeller that they could rotate! When asked what they were thinking, their reply surprised and amused us. "We realized we would never ride in a helicopter or see a real one land in our village, so we decided to just go ahead and build one!"

Linda lived in the Eastern Highlands of PNG and knew how to motivate others. One day a woman came to her with a baby she had adopted from a destitute clan member. She asked Linda if she would commit to helping her with finances to raise the orphan and pay school fees when the time came for school. Linda took a handful of peanut seeds from her bag and placed them in the woman's hand. "Take these and plant them, and each year save what you harvest from them. When the child is old enough for school, the seeds will have multiplied into a large crop that will provide the money you need." The following year the woman came back to show her a much bigger bag of seeds, which was the first year's harvest. She was well on her way!

William was an ordinary but hard-working Marigot farmer in Dominica in the West Indies. As a faithful leader in his Methodist church, he understood that a disciplined life working his small banana plantation would allow him to send all his children to post-secondary school. They became teachers and a bank manager, the solid citizens that every nation needs. We had developed a good friendship during our three-month stay at the hospital there, and he took over leading the inter-church group we started. A number of years later, after a particularly devastating hurricane had felled most of the trees in the area, he saw the opportunity to mill lumber with a chainsaw, rather than wasting the trees. While many others became depressed by the calamity or waited for handouts, he got to work.

Joyce, an unassuming Papua New Guinea woman, always has a smile to pass on to anyone she meets. Even with a bedridden son who needs to be fed and turned every two hours, she taught a preschool program at the Catholic church, and initiated a music band for youth with only videos as lessons. She was in the first group of CHE trainers in the church and took the healthy home concept as a core topic with both children and youth. The whole group of multi-church trainers was inspired when she wrote a "Healthy Home" song, which the children memorized and sang until it had embedded itself into the heart of every family in the church. The four verses addressed physical, social, mental and spiritual aspects of health, while the chorus inspired mindset change, "With God's help we can change the way we live…"

Known to us only as Peter's Mama, she was the intelligent but uneducated mother who made sure that her son went to school at a time in Papua New Guinea's development where schools were few and far between. Peter lived in mountainous Chimbu province and the steep slopes and rivers he negotiated from seven years of age onward to get to school were part of life that he did not question. He told us that his mother rose at 3:00 am to cook sweet potato for him to carry to school and she obviously instilled in him the importance of school in spite of the two-hour hike to get there. He would eat one of those sweet potatoes on the way to school, hide one in a tree for the journey home, and consume the third at school—very methodical, coached well by his mentor-mother who innately knew that school would be important for his future. His positive influence for good development in his region and province now bears witness to that mother. Every successful and educated Papua New Guinean can point to a mother who encouraged them to go beyond the norm. I have watched those mothers, my heart crying for their hard and thankless work to grow their family's food, cook over an open fire on the ground, carry wood and water. They do it without grumbling, they laugh easily at the slightest amusement, they cry when someone leaves the village for an extended period and again when they return, they love all the village children. Their hands are never idle as they walk from place to place or sit in the market selling vegetables and working on the intricate and colourful design of their latest string *bilum*.

Their names are simply Mama; they are found everywhere in the world.

The Making of a Survivor—finding the 'Positive Deviants'

The people described above are what some development experts have defined as 'positive deviants.' The term was first applied in Vietnam in the work of Jerry and Monique Sternin working with Save the Children on a nutritional program in the 1990's, after noticing that there were a few people in the communities who had well-nourished children.[71] Using nutritious food that was grown locally but usually not given to children and feeding them more often than the usual two meals a day, without knowing it they were providing models that could be used to teach others. The principles of using local resources and local experts, which focuses on the strengths, not the weakness of the community, have proved effective and sustainable everywhere. When combined with community organization to solve specific problems, the solutions are appropriate for the cultural context and not dependent on outside expertise that bring outside 'best practices.' The 'positive deviants' within the community provide living proof to their peers that changes can produce the improved lives everyone desires by taking their ideas to a larger scale. It takes time to find these champions in each community, but eminently worthwhile as often they hold the keys to moving forward

Place and the physical environment—"God so loved the Cosmos"

Every culture in this world has been shaped in large part by its physical environment. Even a place with harsh climate or geography, is called home by its inhabitants and everyone loves home. The call of the sea or the desert, the prairies or the mountains, pulses through the veins of those born and raised there. They see the beauty that others miss, sights beyond the eyes of those who shiver or sweat or puff their way up a steep rocky slope and wonder how people could choose to live there.

There are many other reasons to love the natural world and care for the land that sustains life. For some it is animistic fears that lead to respect and pantheistic deification of nature, for others the preservation of the world is for further consumption in years to come. Others want to fulfill a stewardship mandate given by God since the beginning of time. The interdependency of land and people dictates how a people lives, what they grow, the kind of development that makes sense, the emotional and physical security of the children. The more that outside forces change and exploit the land and its goodness with uncaring thought for the people who have lived there for generations, the more we will see whole civilizations drift into chaos or oblivion. We have seen it happen in Africa, in Southeast Asia, in South America.

People of faith should be at the forefront of environmental care, the greatest lovers of the natural world, the clearest voices speaking against the injustices of land abuse and people exploitation. Why? Because God loves the world, all of the world, and not just the people in it. It is said unmistakably clearly in an often-quoted verse, John 3:16: "For God so loved the world (Greek *kosmos*) that He sent His only son..." The cosmos extends from the stars to the atoms, the macro to the micro and everything in between. The grace of a lovingly attentive God is big enough to reach them all and He loves the diversity in people, culture, land, flora and fauna. We would love to hear a confident choir of voices reflecting the kind of passion for the whole of life and the environment that surely God feels.

People and place are intertwined. Cultures are born out of their environments. But without tending or restoring the environmental piece of the picture, the survival of the people in that place will be in jeopardy. The longing everyone seems to have for even a small space to call their own, to see it flourish and to connect with others in that space, must not be taken for granted. The island nations of the Pacific are some of the most strongly connected to their land that we have witnessed, where 'land and people' are almost synonymous. We learned much about that in a visit to Kiribati.

Intertwining People and Place: Kiribati 2003

The sliver of land became smaller and smaller until it was just a dark line on the curve of the horizon before disappearing into the blue Pacific Ocean. Like a dream that you know is absolutely real, only part of me understood the danger of being out in the vast ocean for three hours in a twenty-foot open dinghy powered by one small forty horsepower engine. Bill and I revelled in the beauty of the unfamiliar ocean, awed by the dolphins and flying fish that kept us company for much of the trip, and tried to relax into the wooden bench seat through the bouncing waves as though riding a horse at a full gallop. While I drank in the serenity of the open ocean and the nation that is the first to see the sun rise each new morning, I reviewed the events of the past week that had brought us into this predicament.

A few months earlier we had not even known where the nation of Kiribati (pronounced kir'-i-bas) was. When Dr. Park, World Health Organization country manager there, had contacted us about coming to these far away islands to teach the Community Health Education program to health and church leaders, we agreed before studying much about the place. We did learn that Kiribati was a series of thirty-three atolls in the crosshairs of the Equator and the International dateline, flung wildly over 3.5 million square kilometers of the central Pacific Ocean. None of the atolls have an elevation over one meter! Christmas Island, near Hawaii, is the most known and visited of the atolls, but from there it is a three-hour flight to get to their capital, Tarawa, where most of the population lives. We glibly booked our flight from Fiji to Tarawa.

While the tiny island nation of Kiribati is insignificant on the map of the world, even flying over it one can barely spot the small atolls stretching across vast distances of ocean. The thought of landing an airplane on one of those dots of land was daunting enough, only to learn that Dr. Park had arranged a flight on a small inter-island plane to one of the 'outer islands' for our second week. We learned he had a threefold plan for us: after presenting the CHE concept to the Protestant church and Tangintebu Theological College leaders in Tarawa, he wanted us to test out the strategy to see if a real community on one of the islands would accept it, and finally in the third week we would conduct training with the Ministry of Health department heads.

We were about to be treated to a cultural immersion unlike any other in just three short weeks among a people reported to be the friendliest on the planet! We not only enjoyed their friendliness but found Kiribati to be the most culturally structured and unique place we have visited, a fact we attributed to the isolation and fierce independence of a people who recognize the deep connection with each other and the sea for survival. Its history tells us that Christianity was brought from Hawaii and Samoa in the mid-1800's, and now is claimed by up to ninety-six per cent of the population. As in other Pacific Islands, the church encouraged the people's natural ability to sing and dance, and from an early age, choirs and choir competitions are a huge part of their social lives. We got in on one of these competitions while in Tarawa, where groups mixed with kids from four years to college age belted out their own compositions in four-part harmony and choreography fit for a New York stage. We went to be polite but stayed for hours!

After the thirty-minute flight from Tarawa the second week, our arrival in Marakei began with a drive around the whole island. We learned that this two-hour journey was obligatory for all visitors in order to stop and be introduced at their 'spirit sites.' Ours though was a somewhat unconventional trip, as was replayed in detail later that evening to the gathering of the whole community by their chief who had accompanied us. Nothing was private in this place!

"This couple," he told them, "instead of giving the customary offerings of tobacco or money to the spirits, offered prayers to God for the safety and peace of each village and gave some small picture books

SHARON BIEBER

to the children. They say this is a Christian way." Everyone looked thoughtful but did not say anything. Well, we thought, after all they were Christians too, albeit layered over an animistic worldview.

This was not the last of our cultural blunders, which they seemed quite interested and open to discuss. It was hard not to step on the toes of high-risk behaviour when it came to talking about HIV/AIDS. Awareness of this virus was new to most of them, and we realized posed a great threat to the survival of their culture because of the Chinese fishing boats that were illegally fishing close to their islands and sending men ashore to seek out the local young girls. Because their culture placed hospitality over almost every other value, they saw offering their daughters to these men as a cultural obligation (in exchange of course for televisions or other goods). The same we learned was true if other visitors or relatives from neighbouring islands came. Our training that week focused on discussions of such practices that might be threatening to the health and future of their way of life, and as always, the solutions came from them and not from us. By simply bringing these things into the open, practices that they had taken for granted began to be questioned. They told us that if outside enemies came to invade their island, the men were prepared to fight to the death to defend their families. Yet as they began to realize there were other enemies just as real that were quietly invading without them being recognizing as enemies, they began serious discussions that we knew needed time to resolve.

Defecation on the ocean shore was another eye-opening topic. They admitted that the beach was not a nice place to sit and enjoy the view because of the human waste and garbage, a fact that we had discovered already. Fortunately, we were housed in the Community Rest House which boasted the only toilet on the island! That was about to change.

After a week of feeling constantly amazed with what we were learning and becoming quite attached to this friendly place with their simple diet and lifestyle, our time was over. Everyone knew us, as the intensive days of health education training merged into communal evenings filled with eating and dancing together in their traditional community meeting house. Called a *maneaba,* it is a huge rectangular thatched roof that comes almost to the ground and is entered by bowing low under the open sides. Taught from childhood to be very respectful, if a meeting is in progress, everyone walks by in silence and even motorbikes must be turned off and pushed quietly until the meeting house is passed. We have never encountered such an organized society, where everyone has a role and at gatherings both men and women wear colour-coded skirts that identifies that role. They sit in a specific place on the floor in the community house in order of importance to recognize and respect those roles, with the chief and his leaders in the innermost circle. So on the last night when the head chief of the island announced that there were going to be changes coming, we all knew that his word would be law. But what he said surprised us and reinforced our sense of their connectedness to this island, their land.

"We are going to implement some changes here," he said, "and not because the health authorities are telling us to do this, it is from our own conclusions after our discussions. God has created us in His image and put us in this beautiful place that we all love. But look at this place. He intended us to look after the world we live in, not to use the beach like a toilet or to throw garbage anywhere! Marakei is our 'garden of Eden' and we are going to begin to treat it like that—starting now!" Nobody looked surprised.

He went on, "We don't need a five-year plan either (as we had discussed in the discovery-dream-design-deliver planning cycle). We know what we need to do, and we are going to start building toilets and garbage pits now!" We were amazed as we listened, because we try to be very low key in our seminars, presenting some ideas, mostly asking questions, letting them discuss things in their own language and often not even getting the full translation of their conclusions. This same chief had made comments on a topic about domestic violence, declaring that women had been created of lesser importance than men and that it was culturally acceptable to punish women who stepped out of line! We noticed that the discussion that followed that comment went on for a long time...and hope it continues to be questioned!

This being our last evening with the community, the speeches went on for some time, and then I was requested to start the dancing along with the chief. Others joined in according to their rank and file. Then the games of charades, a popular entertainment that had the children rolling in laughter, went on and on, acted with gusto against the heavy beat of the music from their boom box in the background. It was about this time that someone slipped under the low hanging roof and made their way to where we were sitting on the floor in our assigned place beside the nurse and volunteer health workers. They whispered the news that they had just heard on the local radio—the plane that was supposed to come to Marakei the next morning to pick us up was down for repairs.

"Oh no, how long will that take?" we asked, assuming a few hours.

"Maybe a few days, maybe a week or more depending on parts," was the nonchalant reply. This was obviously a common occurrence, which they had neglected to mention to us before we came. Now I can read on the internet about the unreliability of flights to the outer islands, and the even more rare ferries, but at that time we just assumed that the schedule was the schedule!

"What about boats?" we questioned, this time with a bit more worry. Our most important seminar, the one with the health department heads, was scheduled to start on Monday and this was Saturday. We did not want to lose the opportunity for that training which Dr. Park was so keen for us to do. Again, they shrugged and said they rarely saw a boat except their own fishing canoes, most of which did not have motors.

"My husband has a motor for his boat," the nurse offered, "but it is broken down right now. Maybe we will ask if he can get the mechanic to work on it tonight. Otherwise no need to worry, we are happy for you to stay as long as you need to. We so seldom have visitors here." We knew she meant it, after all, they saw this as the Garden of Eden! We could have happily stayed.

They worked on that motor most of the night, and by morning they were ready to go. The mechanic offered to come along for reassurance. Bill called Dr. Park on a VHF radio to inform him what was happening. "Well," he said, "you can do it if you feel ok, but World Health Organization would never authorize any of their staff to go out on a small motor boat in the ocean for three hours! Are you sure Sharon is fine with it?" he added. And then as a final question, "Have you prayed about this?" Bill was somewhat noncommittal in his answers to the questions, as we had barely taken time to consider the danger, only realizing that the option was available and we had better take it. Besides, by now we felt that we were among trusted friends and had heard many stories of their prowess at sea.

So without further ado we loaded our bags into the boat, waved goodbye to our new friends, and were at the mercy of the young man on the rudder, the mechanic and the nurse's husband who was the skipper sitting on the prow watching the water ahead as the land behind grew slimmer and melted into ocean.

The boat operator asked, "Which way?" The skipper looked carefully at the waves as though reading a map, then silently pointed his hand in the direction we were to head. That direction, with no instruments or navigational tools, no landmarks and not even the stars to guide them, took us in exactly three hours to the back door of the house where Dr. Park lived!

As a postscript, the nation of Kiribati and the resilient people who have survived in harmony with these waters for about two thousand years are now feeling a new danger. Rising ocean levels are worrying them enough to warrant the pre-emptive purchase of land two thousand kilometers away in Fiji.[72] President Anote Tong initiated this twenty-hectare purchase in 2014, stating that while it would be difficult for the current 110,000 population to all settle there, it would not be impossible. In the meantime, they are using the new land to grow food crops to supplement their own food security. They are the first of the small nations most at risk by climate change to take this step, making them leaders in thinking ahead to avoid future humanitarian dispersal of their people. People and place, they believe, must survive together.

Discuss and Reflect:

1. Where did you grow up, and how well do you know the roots or history of that place? How does that place hold a special influence in your sense of security and belonging?

2. Did any of the stories of belonging or being removed from a place remind you of an experience of your own?

3. How does war, migration and family separation affect our world as a whole?

4. What steps might we all take to love our own place and to sustain it for the next generation?

CHAPTER 7

Work as a Gift: Meaningless drudgery as enslavement

"There is nothing better for people than to be happy and to do good while they live. That each may eat and drink and find satisfaction in all their labour—this is the gift of God."

-- 'The Teacher': Ecclesiastes 3:12,13

Mara Volunteers, not counting the cost: Chin State, Myanmar

We watched with quiet admiration that pre-dawn morning as the Mara men and women helped each other pick up the heavy loads they were about to carry for three days. For us it is beyond comprehension to imagine carrying building supplies over leach-infested trails without pay, when surely a helicopter could drop them on location so easily! But then we have never been in a situation where it would be illegal to bring materials from across a border, even though these materials would not be otherwise available. Nor have we ever valued a health training centre and clinic so desperately that any amount of work would be considered insignificant to make it happen. Such was the attitude of the thin, poorly clad, rag tag group of ninety-two villagers from Lailenpi that disappeared into the foggy morning to cross the Indian border back home into Myanmar. We carried on with our training as they walked away with the long rolls of metal sheeting, nails, tools, and of course the food supplies that would sustain them on the journey. Dr. Sasa breathed a huge sigh of relief when they were across the river and no shots had been fired, indicating that the army camped in the hills above had not spotted them. Our quiet prayers that they would be 'invisible' to the eyes of the army were answered!

Their hard work seemed to be pure joy, a gift they wanted to contribute. The training centre was built, used for a couple of years—then completely destroyed in 2017 by Cyclone Mora! Not dissuaded, they built again, this time with bricks and cyclone resistant construction. Their goal of having two health volunteers for each of the villages of Chin State and then into neighbouring states will not be thwarted. Now most amazingly, they have the promise of an airstrip! Yes, in 2016 Missionary Aviation Fellowship was able to establish a presence in Myanmar, and Lailenpi got onto their radar as one of the first airstrips to be built. This effectively will open their world for the first time. It will enable medical supplies to reach the entire half of Chin State that can otherwise be accessed only by walking, motorcycle or heavy four wheel driving over tracks that cannot be called roads. All because a group of passionate people were willing to believe their lives could change if they worked for it together, no matter what the cost.

Work as fulfillment; overwork as meaningless drudgery

Half a world away, we watched similarly underfed and overworked women hoist baskets of gravel and rocks onto each other's backs, suspended by wide straps over their heads. These women were a road construction crew in Nepal, and there was no apparent joy in this labour. Only drudgery, counting down the hours of toil that they must endure until the day was finished and they could collect enough pay to feed their family another meal. No self-respecting human being should be asked to endure the work they were undertaking. I cried helpless tears of anger for the injustice towards these poor women. Inhumane was the only word I had to describe what I was witnessing.

Hard work is a gift, even pleasure when it ends with fulfillment or accomplishment; if every day is just more meaningless toil then at best it is called drudgery.

We observed a similar sight more recently a few continents away from Nepal where another barefoot old Indonesian lady slipped past our group like a shadow. She staggered a bit under the too-heavy load of firewood on her back. Her spine was bent almost perpendicular to the rest of her body, evidence of years of such backbreaking toil. Thirty of us were getting out of a bus for an outing to a museum for a break in our conference when she walked past unnoticed by most of the group, just part of the landscape. Likely she walked past this museum every day as she made her contribution to the family cook fire, with no concept of what was inside that fancy building. It contained her own heritage, her own cultural objects and history but they were not for her to know. They were for the outsiders who could pay to see them. Our hearts broke again, knowing that she represented women too numerous to contemplate, with no voice and no advocate.

This idea of a 'shadow person' so moved us that it inspired the theme of our next conference where the migrant workers of Southeast Asia were to be the focus. Many of them also are shadows, even invisible, yet doing the backbreaking or unpleasant jobs that the rest of society is unwilling to do. Buildings magically are being built, toilets somehow auto-cleaned, children raised without parenting—or are they? Are there real human hands doing this work? Do they have feelings just like us? Or are they mere shadows of humanity in endless poverty, ignored by those enjoying the benefits?

The plight of migrant workers in Southeast Asia

Like the millions of refugees mentioned in the last chapter, displaced from their homeland by war or persecution, millions more have left homelands to work. Either by their own choice or by a deceptive agent's promise of work in another country to enable them to send money back home, these displaced people are simply known as migrant workers or overseas foreign workers. Their living conditions have become public knowledge from their social media posts. Most are young men, single or with a young wife back home, and strong enough to cope with this hard work. Others are women who are officially domestic workers but locally referred to as maids. They too put in long hours, yet unlike the male construction workers they often have to live in the home of the employer with no respite in an abusive situation.

They came to Singapore, Hong Kong, Kuala Lumpur, Dubai or one of the other big cities of Southeast Asia or the Middle East to find work. Instead they lost their social network, sometimes even their identity, and found they had been misled or lied to about the job that awaited them. This is modern day slavery and by definition these kinds of conditions of exploitation and servitude constitute trafficking in persons. From Philippines alone, statistics for 2016 recorded 2.24 million nationals working overseas, with over half in the Middle East.[73]

Singapore, one of the world's most developed cities, claims well over a million migrant workers just in the construction industry. We have watched them being transported to the job sites early in the morning in the back of large trucks, and returned late afternoon to their high-rise living quarters, which some call 'vertical slums'. They check in through a turnstile and go back to their rooms where up to forty men in multiple bunk beds occupy a one-bedroom apartment with one toilet. They wait their turn to cook a meal on the single stovetop. This is not a place to call home!

In Hong Kong there are 350,000 foreign domestic workers, mostly women from Indonesia and Philippines. They are some of the better treated as in Hong Kong there are labour laws that mandate one day off per week. However, they must by law reside with their employer and here is where it often breaks down, as there is no escape from long hours of work, lack of proper food or other mistreatment. The headline in a May 17, 2017 TIME World reads: "In the World's Most Expensive City, one in ten Maids Sleeps in a Kitchen, Toilet, or Corner of the Living Room." [74] Documented stories from 'maids' in Hong Kong are appalling and hark back to stories of slavery hundreds of years ago.

Such is the reality of millions of people who leave their homes and families in India, Bangladesh, Nepal, Myanmar, China, Philippines or Indonesia in search of higher wages. They pay a large sum, often

US$5,000-$10,000 to a recruiter who passes them on to a contractor or agency. The men work largely in the construction industry or as cleaners, the women as domestic helpers or in restaurants; sadly, many end up in the commercial sex trade. The latter have little hope of escape, and the former are held captive by the large sum that they need to pay back for the recruitment and costs of getting the job. By the time they pay for their debt, accommodation and food, there is little to send back home which had been their motivation for going in the first place. Without health benefits, or any other basic human rights of the citizens, they are at the mercy of their employers who most often hold their passports so they cannot buy a return plane ticket and leave.

A bright teenager from Bangladesh was told he had received a scholarship to finish high school in Malaysia. Instead when he got there his passport was taken and he was put to work in construction. When that proved too physically demanding for a youth, he was given a place cleaning halls and toilets in a big modern mall. In the interview that told his story, he explained that he and the other cleaners live in the storage closets in the mall parking lots and sleep in shifts as there are more cleaners than space. Meanwhile the busy shoppers have no concept of the 'miraculous' way the building is kept clean by this invisible group of migrant slaves. In this case his contract finished, but he was too embarrassed to go home and go back to school years behind all his peers. He felt his life had been ruined. So he will likely stay, his future unclear but certainly without the roots of home and family which will fade into a wistful memory.

Some migrant workers whose contracts were legitimate may return home after four or more years. When injuries come it is a different story, as health issues are dealt with haphazardly or not at all, and often become debilitating. The injured worker is then of no use to the employer and is shipped home, a failure in the eyes of his or her family and less employable than when they left. Such was the story of Rose...

I have nobody I can talk to

We had settled into our seats on Air Asia, bound for the Philippines from Malaysia. I was in the middle seat and as the tiny Filipino lady slipped in next to the window I smiled and greeted her. I do not usually attempt to work on the computer on these flights as most are short and the seats very small and cramped. But today I needed to complete the planning for an upcoming training, and the four-hour flight would give enough time.

As I worked, I was conscious of her eyes staring at my computer and found it a bit annoying, but I ignored it and tried to keep my focus. Finally, in a timid voice she spoke, "I am sorry to bother you, but do you do some kind of health work?"

I answered her briefly but kindly with a short explanation of the kind of Training of Trainers I was preparing for. I carried on until the next question, again very softly spoken. "Sorry to ask, but what kinds of health lessons do you teach?"

I knew from the tone of the questions and her hesitancy that she had something more on her mind, something important enough that it emboldened her to talk to a stranger whose body language indicated a desire to be left alone. I knew that she was likely an overseas foreign worker coming home from Malaysia on leave. It was not that I did not know or understand some of the issues she was likely facing, as we had just finished our Regional Conference in Malaysia where the focus had been on migrant workers! My heart won over my mind, and somewhat reluctantly I closed my computer and gave her my full attention, beginning by asking her about herself. It was as if the floodgates had opened.

Rose was a domestic worker for a family in Malaysia who gave her little rest from the hard work they expected of her. A day off was a rare occurrence and often she worked late into the night after the family was asleep. She was going home for medical reasons. When I asked if she was being mistreated, she only said, "It is very complicated."

She finally revealed the reason for her health concerns, as she hesitantly pulled her hands out from the sleeves of the hoodie that she had pulled over them and exposed first the top and then the underside of her hands. They were red and swollen, cracked and hard like wax. I had never seen anything like this and quickly nudged Bill from his reading beside me. The doctor that the employer had sent her to in Malaysia had simply given her cream and said the hands were dry, but she knew there was something seriously wrong as the fingers became more bent and hard to straighten. As Bill checked his suspected diagnosis on his computer medical app, she talked more about her life back home, her parents, her sisters. She wondered if this sickness was somehow related to the "dark secrets she kept inside." By now she was shedding tears and I was holding mine back!

"I have nobody I can talk to in Malaysia," she confided. For two years she had not had a sympathetic ear or a kind smile to encourage her to share her struggles. I asked if she prayed, and she said that God was her only comfort and yes, she prayed. But having been brought up in an old-school Catholic home, her father taught her that if she read the Bible her mind would go crazy! So even that source of encouragement had not been available to her.

My attitude must have conveyed that she could talk, that she was free to say whatever she wanted to an impartial stranger, because I did not consciously encourage her to share her deep secrets, but share she did! My tears began to join hers as I clutched those deformed hands and we were simply sisters in the painful struggles of a sad life. I felt that she was representative of hundreds of thousands of these domestic near-slaves and I cried for all of them who were alone with no sympathetic ear to hear or eyes to shed tears with them.

It was more than coincidence that in the city to which we both were headed that day we have a good friend who is a psychiatrist, so Bill wrote her a note with his observations. We were relieved to be able to send Rose to her for counsel and referral to an appropriate specialist for treatment of the serious illness Bill suspected she had. She thanked us again and again with genuine appreciation. We heard that she made an appointment the very next day, and later was under the care of a specialist.

We last glimpsed her going through the customs line accompanied by an older lady, possibly her agent who was seeing her home, and once recovered would make sure Rose returned to fulfill her financial obligations to her. Rose turned and her eyes sought us out. She gave a big smile and a wave and went on ahead to collect her baggage.

Serving Migrants in Singapore

One of our good friends in Singapore, Dr. Goh, founded HealthServe, a non-profit organization that cares for overseas foreign workers who have no rights to medical care within Singapore. Situated near the high-rise dormitories, the clinics enlist shifts of volunteer doctors, medical students and other helpers mostly from Singapore church connections. While providing medical care, counselling, social assistance and other support services, they hear the stories of abuse or neglect and try to advocate with the employer on behalf of the worker. Most injured workers are left to sit all day in their rooms and become quite depressed. The clinic with its understanding volunteers who treat them as peers is the only bright spot for them.

On one of the occasions when we visited the clinic with Dr. Goh, we met an exceptional young Bangladeshi man, Mukul. He has a Bachelors' degree in Social Sciences and had published a novel and a book of poetry before coming to work in the construction sector in Singapore eight years previously. He befriended some of the clinic staff while coming for treatment, and shared with them how many long nights were spent in writing, as his love for writing poetry gave hope to an otherwise bleak life. When he wrote about his life at home and his mother's smile, they became alive again to him.

At the encouragement of his new friends at HealthServe, he collected some of his poems and Dr. Goh had them translated to English and then edited into verse by an acclaimed Singaporean poet. He loved what he read! The poems were written with honest emotion born out of the pain of isolation and the longing for loved ones. They give tremendous insight into the life and dreams of a migrant worker. At the time we met him, his poems were being printed into a booklet, titled *'Me Migrant'*, which was ready by our next visit. The HealthServe staff also arranged for media coverage, resulting in the filming of a short documentary of his life. The film crew took him back to his place in Bangladesh, then followed the process of his coming to Singapore and the construction work he did there.

As a mother, I am especially touched by his wistful poems to his own mother and home:

> Can I have a cup of tea, mother
> Mixed with ginger and a piece of lemon
> Stirred to behold the redness of fresh tea leaves
> A cup of hot tea

But then the realization that it is only a dream, a passing fancy before reality sets in...

> How happy I was
> Like I was in heaven till the phone alarm
> Rang suddenly
> And I am lying across a shelf bed
> Unable to hold back tears...

> I remember you too much, mother.[75]

Canada is no exception

Back home in Canada, we were picking up a latte at a fast food café as we embarked on a road trip. It was early morning but the young Filipino woman who served us had a bright smile on her face. I thanked her for the friendly greeting and beautiful smile so early in the morning. Then Bill asked her what part of the Philippines she was from and told her we were soon going there. "Oh, could you bring back my daughter?" she jokingly asked. "Or put me in your suitcase?"

"You have a daughter back home; that must be hard." I responded. "How old is she?"

"Only six," she said, now with her lovely brown eyes holding back tears.

I could feel the aching heart of a devoted mother. "How often do you see her?"

"It has been almost two years, but I talk to her on skype every night as she goes to bed and tell her how much I love her." Now the tears began to overflow, and she was getting embarrassed. Her co-workers patted her shoulder; we saw they cared about her plight. We felt badly to have caused her this emotional pain while at work, so as we left with our coffee, we told her we were very sorry and hoped they could be united again as a family soon.

We know this story from both sides of the ocean. Dreams of a higher income and a better life for one's family, dreams that displace mothers or fathers out of the reach of family for two or even twenty years at a time—is money worth that kind of sacrifice? Is the acquisition of goods or a better house an all-pervasive lie working to the detriment of the whole world? Might this kind of consumerism eventually destroy us all?

Our questions cannot help but continue. Would it not be better to stimulate opportunities that would keep these dedicated and hard-working people in their own families as contributing members of the growth of their own countries?

Why don't you just return home?

In a village like the one our latte server may have come from, a Filipino community health trainer introduced us to a project where she had connected the women with Heifer International. The participants, all CHE volunteers, had been given a bred heifer or goat and were trained to care for it and to pass on the first offspring to another family. These in turn would pass on their first offspring to yet another family.

Reaching the village in late afternoon, we saw numerous cows and goats being brought home from their pasturelands for the night. The women were chatting and laughing, and then as they gathered in a large circle to talk with us we heard excited and happy stories. Some had received the 'fourth generation' offspring, which meant that now the original dozen or so recipients had multiplied by at least four times. Their household economy was improving and they could stay home with their families instead of going away as Overseas Foreign Workers.

We could not help but notice one woman who seemed out of place in the joyful circle. Her sad face and lack of conversation or laughter was in direct contrast with the rest of the lively group. I quietly pointed her out to Lotlot, the trainer and translator, and she learned the story. This mother of four had taken a job as a domestic helper in Dubai and was home on a short leave midway through her four-year contract. She would go back the next day. Her youngest, about three years old, was clinging to her and crying as she sat with the other women. I took the opportunity afterwards to visit and listen to some details of her life as a domestic helper.

The story was growing familiar to me. Her contract had not been honoured, as the pay was much less and the hours longer than promised, in fact 24-7 would not be exaggerating much. The wealthy family she served entertained a lot, and she was expected to be up early caring for the family and preparing for guests, and to stay up at night until everything had been cleaned up. As a devout Catholic, she would have loved the opportunity to attend a mass once in a while, but even that short time off was not allowed. Her brief skype calls home just made everyone miss each other more. I asked why she was returning to Dubai, why she did not simply break her contract and stay home to join the other women in raising some livestock? Her noncommittal reply told me that her husband was demanding this life of her, as she had barely paid back the recruiting fees to the agent by this point. These obligations seemed to be the 'hook' that often brings the workers back the second time, and after that it becomes easier to stay even longer to send more money home. First a television, then a better house, then kids' college fees…never enough for the allure of money seems the way to gain status. But who speaks for the children?

In this small microcosm of a community, we sensed answers emerging to our question: when does the joy of work change to the burden of drudgery? While most of the women were finding pleasure in working hard to care for animals that were helping to sustain them in their own homes, for this woman the elusiveness of a promised dream of riches brought meaningless toil that was tearing a family apart. She had not considered that there were entrepreneurial and pleasant options to make life at home better, especially for the needs of her children.

Hard work done together produces joy, PNG 2016

Tears came to our eyes as we watched the video documenting the journey of Papua New Guinean villagers bringing water supply materials to six communities high on the Raicoast mountains. This time they were tears of amazement and wonder. Determination and strength shone from the faces of men and women as they carried huge rolls of plastic pipe and the other supplies that would bring water to hundreds of households tucked out of sight from the world. The laughter of the children who accompanied them, the heart-stopping bamboo hanging bridges that carried them over ravines where swift water flowed a hundred feet below, and the slippery steep slopes where they pulled and pushed the loads held us in awe.

Like the Mara villagers in Myanmar, it seemed that no amount of work was too much when the end result would be so fulfilling. Indeed, it would spell liberation from toil for the women and children who had to carry water every day of their lives from streams far from their homes. The fact that they brought the materials in by themselves, without the helicopter drop that some groups would have waited endlessly to see, would make that water even sweeter! The excitement of the celebration that the video captured came through loud and clear—"we have done it, we have together accomplished our goal!"

What had given them the confidence and determination to work together to see a project like this to completion? Josiah, a humble health worker from their local Health Centre, had taken the CHE training and then began incorporating health education into his normal work and patrols to the dozen or so villages on this remote plateau. For almost ten years he had worked on changing the mindset of poverty and helplessness to one of determined strength. They established health committees and appointed volunteers and addressed their issues.

Two trainers from Goroka, Freda and Koyu made the arduous journey several times to assist in training the volunteers. During the filming of the documentary, these two quiet heroes who had introduced the CHE program in these mountains through great personal effort and sacrifice remained in the background taking no credit. Though bursting with pride for the community, they stole none of the honour, none of the limelight as the videographers panned the faces and filmed the speeches. Again, we laud the unsung heroes who made it happen and then stepped aside.

No amount of hard work is too much when it is done together to accomplish a common goal

When coffee is more than coffee

In the Highlands of Papua New Guinea, almost every family with a small amount of traditional land has a few coffee trees in what they call a 'coffee garden.' Coffee that is grown a mile high in good soil watered with mountain-pure rain has the potential for being the best there is. Lack of proper handling and storage is a problem though, if it is to retain prime quality from the farmer to the coffee shops of the world. A second problem is a mindset that informs the people, 'if there is enough for today it is enough.' For some, coffee is a 'social crop'—when bride price or a funeral costs are needed there are coffee trees to fall back on. Others call coffee season 'beer season' for obvious reasons. During election year or other occasions when there are politicians handing out cash, the coffee gardens are neglected as people follow the campaign trails.

In order for farmers to see their coffee as a real business that produces a family income, a change in mindset must come first. We have seen some of the communities impacted by CHE begin to take care of their trees and then to prioritize the coffee income for family needs such as education or improving their houses. After financial literacy classes, some start savings accounts, which we know is another step towards resilience when hard times hit.

In seeking progress towards improving quality control, we invited a coffee expert from Hong Kong to come as an adviser to the coffee industry of the Highlands. Quality control means getting the coffee from the cherry stage to a high-grade bean landed in the buyer countries. Sam is a former Laos refugee to Canada who has returned to Southeast Asia to bring his expertise to farmers who do not have the advantages he was blessed with in Canada. He has taught us that in the typical village pulping and haphazard drying process, the coffee beans are vulnerable to carcinogenic mould, called aflatoxin, and the water from the washing and fermenting process becomes a pollutant to the ground water. New methods of milling, drying and storage avoid all these issues and keep the quality high right from the get-go.

So right now, we are working with the CHE Area Coordinator to upgrade her family coffee factory in order to improve the quality and the price, and to use the extra profit to support the CHE work throughout the region. Defining it as a Social Enterprise, her goals are People-Planet-Profit or the 'triple bottom line,' a term coined by John Elkington of SustainAbility in 1994.[76] She has added Prosperity, which completes the circle to see abundance in all areas of life for the communities. Importing to another Social Enterprise in Canada under the brand *Amamas,* meaning to enjoy or be joyful, will be the next step towards single origin, pure process, mile high specialty coffee with a compelling back-story. Our hope is to see our western coffee infatuation truly give back to those who produce the crop.

From the coffee cherry to the cup, we want the chain shortened and the profits returned to PNG while at the same time considering all environmental factors. Support for farmers and their community development, for the Area Coordinator and other trainers who need travel funds to keep visiting their communities, for training them in natural farming methods…all this is possible because we coffee drinkers want our daily grind to count for something bigger. We believe it can all happen with God's help and for His intentions of human flourishing.

Hard work has meaning when generosity is the end result

Winston Churchill is credited with saying, *"We make a living by what we get, but we make a life by what we give."* From our observations of life, the real infusion of satisfaction into work is that it enables generosity. We conclude from this that generosity is the ultimate end goal of work; everyone is capable of it in some way however small or big that might be. Stories such as the ones we have told bear witness to the fact that hard work is life giving when we know that it will sustain others in some way. Giving brings joy. If work means having just enough to feed, clothe and educate one's own family and extend some generosity to others, there is joy. When we are able to use our abilities and our efforts to accomplish visible change in the lives of those we value, we feel pleasure. Status, respect and gratitude from the community bring further fulfillment.

Unrecognized generosity may be even more rewarding, having been done without selfish motives. Doctors, nurses, social or development workers who give days or even years of their lives to serve the less fortunate most often do it not for the acclaim of the beneficiaries but for the pleasure of simply knowing it is the right thing to do. Those villagers we have described who work hard to improve the lives of others in the community do it for the satisfaction of knowing that the next generation will not bear the same pain and losses that they have.

But why do so many go through this life with only toil and so little reward and little means for generosity? What is the reward for the millions of overburdened and under-appreciated women of much of the world who struggle to raise children without proper nutrition or shelter? It pains us that we have no answer, no straightforward solution. Just a little bit of knowledge could make a huge difference for them, the kind of knowledge our great-grandmothers knew. We are humbled to think that the 'accident of birth' that placed us in our country and families of origin also brought so many opportunities that rewarded us with health, security and fulfillment.

Giving to others releases both the rich and poor from debilitating self-centeredness. It breaks the addiction to consumerism, transcends social norms and sets people free from the grasping and hoarding that leads to shrivelled hearts. Giving and receiving—we must develop both with joyfulness, humility and without paternalism. We were designed to be interdependent beings, co-benefiting from each other in order to become fully human. Living this out brings simple joy, uncomplicated pleasure.

The measure of generosity is not what is given but what is left behind. Generosity breaks the poverty mindset that cripples both rich and poor.

Generosity demonstrated by the poor is especially significant because it represents their heart, a self-sacrifice that cost something. Someone defined generosity as not what is given away but what is left behind…it is easy to give when there is a lot more where that came from. The poverty mindset that binds the poor to the trap of believing they cannot change is broken by acts of kindness that dare them to give to others. Simple gifts of time, of listening and empathy for another do not require money but enlarge the capacity to believe in one's own abilities.

In his compelling book, *Terrify No More,* the founder of International Justice Mission, Gary Haugen, makes an interesting observation about our Western society. While we seem so rich to most of the world, we remain powerless to spread the wealth. Quoting an old saying, "all that is necessary for the triumph of evil is that good men do nothing," he questions why, if this is true, do good people seem paralyzed to act? We suffer, he believes, from our own kind of poverty which keeps us crippled on the sidelines, watching as evil seems to triumph over good.

What is this poverty? We are debilitated, says Haugen by three deficiencies: a poverty of compassion, a poverty of purpose and a poverty of hope. We underestimate the value of a single life and we underestimate God's determination to rescue us from a trivial existence, free up our hands and hearts from unworthy distractions and apply them to what will make a difference in someone else's life.[77] Compassion, purpose, hope—if we possessed these in generous doses, could it really bring dignity to countless men, women and children in the sea of humanity around us? Could those 'good men and women' instead of doing nothing become unstoppable in their determination to change the world?

Has a poverty mindset stifled the kindness of those viewed as rich? At the same time, is there a 'generosity key' we have missed in working with the so-called poor? If we could unleash a spirit of generosity on the world around us, what a legacy that would leave.

Meanwhile, let us stop blaming the 'rich' for their callousness, and the 'poor' for the crippling value systems that keep them poor. Rather we can all point inward to our own poverty of mind and heart and ask what we need to change.

DISCUSS AND REFLECT:

1. How much satisfaction do you feel in your own work? What could make it more fulfilling for you?

2. What have you learned about the reward or lack of reward of work in the stories told here?

3. How does generosity span economic, social or cultural boundaries? How does it destroy the poverty mindset?

4. Might you suffer from poverty of compassion, purpose or hope? Do you have talents, abilities or tangible resources that you could use to benefit others? What reward might come from that?

CHAPTER 8

Give a Person a Fish:
Or teach an entrepreneur?

The prophet replied to the widow, "How can I help you? Tell me, what do you have in your house?" 2 Kings 4:2

Assets versus needs assessment

The widow in the story from the above quote had two sons and large debts bequeathed to her by her deceased husband. She had no way to repay and now the creditors were demanding her two sons as bonded servants. This is a story from ancient Middle East and the prophet was Elisha, but it has a hauntingly modern ring to it. Any number of countries in South or Southeast Asia might be the setting for this same scenario. Vast numbers of young sons and daughters are sent away, many outside their countries to work in near slavery with hopes of releasing their family from debt. We have told some of these stories in the previous chapter.

The ancient widow-prophet interaction, however, has a very enlightening twist to it. Instead of providing money or even a job, neither of which he had, Elisha asked her to identify her resources: "What do you have in your house?" Only after she looked at her own resources, meagre as they were, did he offer a solution.

For years conventional wisdom for development workers was to begin the process of community engagement with a needs assessment. Later evolving into community participatory learning activities, the goal was to help them discover their 'felt needs' and set priorities for action. We have finally come to the realization that by focusing on needs we may imply or reinforce a sense of poverty and helplessness. It does not take much understanding of human nature to know that if we are told things are looking bad, they suddenly look even worse!

The same cup can be seen as half full or half empty, just by choosing our focus. There are of course times when the cup really is almost empty and short-term relief is necessary in order to ensure survival. This is the reality in situations of war or physical disasters. The hardest part of relief is to know when is enough or when it becomes a hindrance to future development. Numerous stories of when the good intentions and kindness of the helpers have become detrimental have been very appropriately told in Corbett and Fikkert's book, "When Helping Hurts: How to Alleviate Poverty without Hurting the Poor...and Yourself." [78]

The widow in the ancient Middle East story did not have to sell or send away her two sons. By discovering that she did have something in her own house, a jar of oil, the poverty cycle was broken. With a willingness to risk following the prophet's absurd instructions, she borrowed jars and then started pouring oil. A miracle happened; the oil jar was bottomless! She lived among neighbours who were willing to help her and buy from her, turning her from a victim to an entrepreneur. Taking a person who feels hopeless and helpless and changing the poverty mentality that is crippling their mind, frees them to notice the abundance around them. This is miraculous. It is as liberating as setting a captive free. We have seen when this happens—and when it does not.

But where are the fences?

Our experience in Fiji is limited to a few short visits for envisioning seminars with local groups or church leaders, so we do not claim to understand much of the ethnic Fijian mindset. However, we do see many similarities with the other Pacific Islanders and with Papua New Guinea in particular. There is a deep faith in God, but underlying these beliefs are many superstitions and a fatalism that sometimes holds them back.

This was very obvious on one occasion when we were visiting a rural inland community where the hills and vegetation gave ample opportunity for animal husbandry and agricultural crops. The most common cash crop was kava, the root of which is crushed and mixed with water in a large communal bowl to be used in a social setting. This has been tradition in the Pacific for centuries, either as a ceremonial ritual or as a mild drug with effects similar to alcohol. The bowl is typically passed from person to person in the group, with each one taking a drink in turn from a large ladle. We noted that even some church board meetings started with kava! Maybe the resulting mood elevation, anxiety reduction and sociability results in harmonious and relaxed meetings, but the over-use leads to addiction, liver disease, impaired driving and lethargy. Its popularity of course makes kava a cash crop that has a ready local market and that can easily be harvested and sold when money is needed.

This particular community seemed content with their traditional crop. Their homes were simple but comfortable enough, their lifestyle relaxed with social connections strong. As they began pointing out to us the boundaries of the land owned by their clan, they noticed on the distant hills a few cattle. "Oh, those are our cows wandering way over there. Sometimes they come home," they casually remarked. Being rural people ourselves, we were curious about these wandering cows that only occasionally came home.

"Don't you use fences to keep them in the pastures you want them in?" we asked.

"Oh no, we usually do not build fences," was their off-handed reply. "The cows know their owners and eventually return."

"But what prevents someone else from claiming them if they wander into their land?" It seemed to us quite odd, and certainly unlike Papua New Guinea where everyone knew that if a stray pig started digging in a neighbour's garden it could precipitate a clan war! This 'don't fence me in' idea seemed quite intriguing, and certainly would cut down the workload of any rancher we knew!

"Yes, that does sometimes happen," they admitted with a shrug.

Then they told us the story of the cattle project that had been initiated by an Australian organization, which the community had readily accepted. It seemed that someone from outside had done a survey and noted that the land was suitable for cattle. The local residents had some experience and enjoyment of raising cattle but did not have the capacity to run a larger scale business undertaking. So, in typical relief model, a benefactor organization was found and building proceeded. Some very nice corrals, a calving barn, workshop and fences were built, and cattle were purchased. The project was off and running well. The local men liked riding horses and the cowboy role, while the Australian manager organized the activities of the ranch. That is, until his contract was finished. It was time for him to leave and there was no replacement for him since his sponsors expected that by this time it would be locally run.

The Australian tried to hand over to one of the local men, and for a time it continued. Then unexpected repairs were needed, finances were not accounted for, cows began wandering and everyone became discouraged. The cattle project ended and so did the benefits they had enjoyed from the profits. The buildings and corrals were all still there, and even many of the cows that were wandering freely over the hills.

"Are you doing anything to revive the project, to get it going again yourselves?" we wondered aloud. Their answer left us wondering even more.

"Yes, we go to the project buildings once a month and have an all-night prayer meeting."

"That's a nice idea," we responded, "and so you pray about how to go about organizing yourselves to run it again?"

"Oh no, nothing like that!" was their quick response. "We pray for another Australian to come and run it for us like before."

Maybe their answer was just for our benefit, appearing serious for us gullible outsiders...

Stranded on the Island

The River Crossing role-play has been used almost universally for decades as the eye-opening introduction to the perils of relief and the superiority of development approaches. We do not know where it originated but it is an effective discussion tool as communities act it out with their impromptu interpretation. One version goes something like this:

Two people have walked to town for the day and return late afternoon expecting to cross the same river they had walked across with ease that morning, only to find it in flood. They walk back and forth discussing options, fearful because neither are good swimmers, and talking about the worry their family will be feeling if they are not home by dark. Along comes a staff person of a large NGO, possibly an expatriate (Bill sometimes plays this role much to everyone's delight!) who asks about their problem, boasts a bit then offers a solution, "Climb on my back and I will carry each of you across." However, his back is not as strong as he had thought and the river is indeed deeper than expected, so he finds a convenient place to leave the first traveller on a small island mid-river. The so-called helper then leaves, complaining of a sore back.

Now the two friends are separated and even more worried until a local village lady comes along and asks, "What is the problem?" She has grown up in the area and knows that under the surface of the water are submerged rocks where the locals cross easily. The traveler on shore follows her step by step to the other side, then is reassured that he knows the way now and can go back and get his friend who is still stranded on the island.

As the role-play discussion turns into application to their own setting, many examples of how they have been left 'stranded in the river' begin to emerge. The need not to have outsiders do the work for them is obvious and long-term sustainability is easy for them to visualize.

We remember one of the first times we facilitated this role-play in a small hamlet in Nepal. The discussion seemed to go on and on with the translator completely engrossed in the conversation and unable to keep up a running translation commentary for us. It appeared to us that the women and men were on different sides of an argument about why a certain project had failed and what should have been done! It was late in the evening, and we finally slipped out and went to bed, leaving them to carry on into the night. We had witnessed the power of a visual story contextualized into their setting to capture their interest in solving their own problems.

Moving from relief to long-term development

We have seen dependency-inducing projects from the inside too—the excited medical personnel looking forward to serving the poor, the boxes of North American pharmaceutical donations ready to take along, young medical or nursing students eager to try out the skills they are learning. Along with our two teenage children, we were part of one such organized trip with about twenty other medical practitioners and their families. After the thrill of the experience wore off, discomfort with the whole process told us we could not do this again.

We could see that by treating patients and dispensing medicine without cost, we were unwittingly undermining the local health care facilities and workers. Our early experience in PNG should have taught us that. Not only were the medications free, they were often not available in the host country. So how would a local doctor continue the prescription? And did our translators understand enough to adequately explain to the patients when and how to take the medicines? Did the treatments prescribed meet local protocol? Did the Canadian and US doctors who had spent years in other specialties really understand the tropical diseases they were treating? Was our well-intentioned help really helping at all, or were we hurting their long-term health? Their need for better health care and living conditions was obvious. But did our one-week foray into curative medicine in this rural area do anything to better their future community or family health status? Perhaps it was simply a great experience for our kids as an enthusiastic team incorporated them into the program by letting them weigh babies and take blood pressures. But at what expense, if there was damage control needed after we went home or if we had somehow tarnished the confidence of the people in their own healthcare system?

In the excellent book, *When Healthcare Hurts*[79], Greg Seager has thoroughly researched the complications of such short-term medical missions. The four intertwining categories of best practices Seager outlines are:

- patient safety
- integration and collaboration with the national healthcare system
- facilitating health development
- community empowerment.

He starts with similar questions that we had asked ourselves after reflecting on our trip. He concludes that short-term healthcare workers could bring improvements to healthcare quality and empower communities to help themselves by working alongside the government system and providers who would like to upgrade to international standards. Knowing how to do that, taking time to research the local government systems as well as international initiatives, and then making connections with the appropriate authorities is essential.

Fitting in with the country's health objectives rather than our own agendas is the first step in dropping the paternalism that usually characterizes our efforts. We seem naturally much better at relief than development. We are also typically sceptical of systems that are different from what we are used to, every country assuming its own is best!

The eight Millennium Development Goals set forth by the United Nations were laudable, but their 2015 targets were next to impossible to reach for less developed countries. Building on these Goals, now there are seventeen Sustainable Development Goals[80] to attain by 2030.

The best laid plans fall apart when natural disaster sets a country back and all the priorities become focused on survival. Outside teams are an essential part of recovery but they often leave with the agony of knowing that they may be instilling a dependency mentality into the people.

We can articulate the problems well—relief done long-term creates dependency and poverty mentality. Aid is an industry where the organizations may benefit more than the recipients. Corruption and crime are fuelled by international aid money, while inappropriate or unequal development often creates disparity and disunity in communities. The list is long and discouraging. Whole countries have gone backward rather than forward after natural disasters.

Shia is a Southeast Asian colleague experienced in the CHE methods, a woman whose understanding of the issues has fuelled her determination to look for better solutions. She has seen the devastation of tsunamis and earthquakes and has lived among the people who have suffered through more than one disaster. While many of us do our small part and walk away, she stays and brainstorms using the asset-based approach. What remaining resources are there after the disaster, she asks, and what is needed to restore the healthy home concept? Is there still space for some domestic animals or fish and kitchen gardens? What about including in the re-building some common spaces and play areas for the children? This is called place making, capitalizing on the local assets, ideas and possibilities to create good public spaces, a new place that promotes the common good.

Shia masterfully takes the community from being victims of the disaster to overcomers, learning to produce their own building materials and build their own homes, using their own concrete pillars, sun dried bricks and bamboo. After bringing in architectural experts to conduct place-based building workshops in which the community members can brainstorm and decide what is culturally, structurally and materially appropriate for them, amazing designs emerge. Builders gain skill and experience by helping themselves and their neighbours re-build homes, and then launch their own construction business. Now they have moved from victims to entrepreneurs as they learn to market their skills to other communities and run their own businesses. Even the school children in one place got involved in helping to build their own schools! Finally community common spaces such as a business centre, a healthy life training centre, leisure and sports areas and even an evacuation building emerged.

This same process can apply to crafts, agriculture, food products, clothing production or any small-scale, home-based businesses that could sustain a family. Key to all of this seems the creation of common spaces for people to meet naturally, talk and discuss their progress. Along with business training, Shia also includes classes in moral values such as integrity, truthfulness, consideration, family harmony, inclusiveness and other relevant topics that ensure calm and happy communities. This approach will go a long way towards peacefulness in communities where other elements seek to put wedges of intolerance between them. Peacemaking is taking place at the same time as place making.

We saw the contrast to Shia's model in another city where hundreds were left homeless from a tsunami, but where the government insisted that their workers would do all the work. They decided where to relocate the displaced without consulting them, then built housing for them with hired builders while the unemployed homeless sat and watched!

The old cliché, 'Give a man a fish and he will eat for a day; teach a man to fish and he will eat for a lifetime' must be modified! It is quite evident that just learning how to fish will not ensure that a person eats for a lifetime, as myriads of things could go wrong to prevent fishing. What that fisherman needs to learn is how to care for reefs and practice conservation, to repair his own fishing gear and even produce new gear to market to others. Only then can he continue to work through the storms or the downturn in the fish market or the seasonal movements of fish. Value-added products or diversification of some kind is the next level for the man who wants to continue eating fish!

Asset Based Community Development

Now well known in community-building circles, Asset Based Community Development or (ABCD), was first described in 1993 by John McKnight and John Kretzman in *Building Communities from the Inside Out: A Path Towards Finding and Mobilizing a Community's Assets*[81]. They later founded the Asset-Based Community Development Institute (ABCD) as part of the Community Development Program of Northwestern University in Illinois based on their years of study and experience. McKnight and Peter Block more recently wrote *Abundant Community: Awakening the Power of Families and Neighborhoods.*[82] They describe the deficit-driven approach to responding to community needs, which begins from the assumption that disadvantaged communities and neighbourhoods are troubled places characterized by long lists of unmet needs. Social services buy into this approach, leaving the communities to see their value and well-being as simply clients whose needs must be met by outsiders. This deepens dependency and stifles community leadership. Often service providers seem to benefit more than the residents, as needs are placed in measurable categories with systems and professions to solve them. These systematized solutions often have little to do with the people who live there, but more to do with the professional outsiders who come to 'help'—and now we recognize that the whole aid industry worldwide has bought into these ideas of how to solve problems!

McKnight and Kretzman employ an asset-based approach to community that begins with a very different understanding of what community might be—a place full of untapped assets. They identify three categories of assets:

- Individual Assets: Recognizing that every individual is gifted in some way, the gifts, capabilities, skills and talents of individual citizens may be identified and mobilized. This must also include the elderly, youth, unemployed and new immigrants. These are people who would traditionally be marginalized.

- Citizens' Associations: These are the formal or informal associations that operate within a community (including places of worship, service clubs, cultural or craft groups, sports teams). Even if loosely organized, these are key connections and are community assets.

- Formal Institutions: Businesses, schools, libraries, educational institutions, hospitals, parks; service providers such as these also need to be engaged in the community development process.

In workshop settings when we have given opportunity for participants to identify the first level, their individual giftedness, we all come away amazed at the variety and extent of skills, knowledge and passions represented in the room. We normally use three colours of post-it notes for each person to identify what they love to do with their hands (skills), their head (knowledge and educational skills), and their heart (the things they are passionate about). When these are stuck onto the wall, a huge 'wall of wonder' emerges. Imagine the feeling of strength that could emerge if an entire community listed their hand–head–heart skills?

Abundant Community Initiative, Edmonton Alberta

These activities are not just community building exercises that apply to developing countries or disadvantaged communities. The problems in Canada may be different but are just as real and as needful of interdependent solutions. Our own Alberta capital city has demonstrated this in their city council-supported Abundant Community Edmonton (ACE).[83] Started formally by Howard Lawrence in 2013, they describe

ACE as a neighbourhood engagement and community organizing approach to build a culture of care and connection at the city block level.

Based on the Knight and Block approach described above, they are taking it to a new level of organization that is providing a working model for all of North American cities. By fostering a culture of "turning strangers into neighbours", the community has renewed pride, new visions to develop, care for the environment and increased safety in their area has reduced the social isolation and loneliness so prevalent in our modern individualistic cities.

In CHE-like structure, Neighbourhood Connectors are hired to recruit and organize Block Connectors who in turn get to know the twenty or more households on their own block. They collate the vision, priorities and interest groups that result from their home visiting. Lawrence started this informally on his own block by introducing himself at each home, asking them about their vision for their neighbourhood, their hobbies and interests, skills and passions and enabling connections to take place. The concept caught on, and he began enlisting willing persons on each block to become the block connectors. The enthusiastic response prompted the city council to endorse and fund Lawrence as a full-time facilitator to take the concept systematically through any community that asked for it. Currently of the two hundred or so city community associations (they call them leagues), over a quarter are actively involved in the initiative and dozens more have started. It is taking over the city for good!

The benefits of such neighbourhood organization are worth the effort—inclusion for isolated groups at the margins like the disabled, seniors or minorities, reduced crime rates, safer places for children to play and to join organized activities, improved mental and physical health, systems in place for disaster response, new vision to improve the community—everyone benefits because we all respond to caring attention.

Complementing rather than Competing

Jeffrey is a CHE practitioner in a southern region of Philippines. Working with a group of fisher-folk he realized that the labour intensive single person fishing businesses were barely at the subsistence level. Their families were still below the poverty line. He had learned from a CHE workshop on Asset Based Community Development the importance of associations in bringing people of similar skills or interests together for economy of scale. By setting up legally recognized associations, the fisher-folk were able to get better market prices, buy supplies at cheaper costs and lobby for rights and against infringements of their fishing territories. In their weekly meetings, the group learned honest business practices and budgeting, as well as life skills such as how to improve family dynamics by resolving conflicts without violence. Communication skills and general cooperation grew within their group; trust grows in this context even between those who before have been competitors.

While these associations are less structured than farming cooperatives that share profits, they can be an important building block of community. Family income increases. People of different faith groups begin to work together. Neighbours are seen as having assets to contribute and add to each other's individual abilities. Often better equipment can be purchased and shared by association members. People begin to trust each other and to know whom to count on in times of personal difficulty or natural disaster. Networks like this produce healthy development towards a peaceful society.

Historically in western culture self-employed tradespeople and artisans grouped together in guilds for support, material supplies and protection in their town or area. Master craftsmen passed on their skills to apprentices who eventually set up shop on their own. Other professional groups such as medical and dental practitioners started associations to ensure uniform and ethical standards of their practitioners. Within the theatre arts and media there are guilds that exert influence on their membership, as do trade unions.

With the resurgence of interest in traditional arts and crafts, artisan guilds are once again common. My personal experience has been membership for over thirty years in a weaving guild, the Sheep Creek Weavers, which has an active membership of more than seventy-five fibre artists from our area. We meet for monthly meetings and for workshops where skills are taught and at the same time lives are shared.

This is part of the social connectedness that I consider an important network in my life. For others it may be more informal, a seasonal music group, a book club, a hiking or sports association, a prayer group or a choir. These informal associations also give structure and connections to our society and form the bonds that keep our communities resilient at times of adversity. Having a network of friends that can be called on with no hesitation is a better asset than money in the bank when tough times come. Some have said that we all need at least three close friends nearby that we can call on for anything at any time of the day or night. In an age where isolation in our culture is considered a contributing factor to physical and mental illness, we doubt that many could name those three people. Men in our society are even less likely than women to have that close cadre of friendships, indicating that we have something important to learn from groups like those fisher-folk in the Philippines.

Building social capital as nation-building

The term 'social capital' is often misunderstood because we equate capital with money or financial resources. Social capital is simply who we know, the networks in which we interact; but assumed in that is the reciprocal value that comes from who we know. Small networks, from family and clan ties to informal interest groups or clubs, to associations of individuals in one livelihood or profession, all make up social capital. The groups or networks or faith communities we are part of are seldom seen as a resource, part of our net worth, when in fact these may be the most important measures of our assets and indeed of the strength of a society. Rarely are questions about our social networks asked in a job interview or included on a resume. However, many careers or businesses succeed or fail based on the strength of the social network of the individuals in the company, the types of social resources and knowledge that are in those networks and the closeness of these ties. The old quip, 'not what you know but who you know' was right after all!

Social capital of course may be misused by elite who ply their powerful connections to the exclusion or detriment of the poor. For example, those who have access to information about government programs or ability to secure funds are often the ones who benefit from resources that were meant for betterment of the total society. Disadvantaged groups need advocates; governing bodies need accountability. The trainers in our CHE approach can often be that link. Not only do they teach communities to act by analyzing and solving their own problems, they link them to other agencies or government programs that are available but unknown to many living in hardship. Instead poverty, violence and injustice erodes social networks, disrupts relationships and makes it easy to fall victim to unscrupulous loan sharks.

A strong community and eventually a strong nation is one where trust between individual citizens has been well developed. This comes when there are opportunities for free involvement in groups, churches or volunteer activities where diverse opinions and contributions are valued. Barriers of social or ethnic intolerance can be broken. This starts early and continues all through life.

In our country, children and youth develop personal and leadership skills through the training of clubs, sports teams, summer camps or youth groups. Without such opportunities none of us would have learned to voice dissenting opinions, to cooperate with others who are different from ourselves or to take a position we feel unqualified for but which our friends have trusted us to do.

We contrast this with many of the less developed countries where we have lived, and while the smaller family ties are tight, the lack of wider associations available for either youth or adults to participate in is apparent. Urban youth experience boredom while rural youth live with daily toil. Informal sports are often their only outlet unless they are fortunate enough to be part of a strong faith community where youth activities are available. While their close friendships and family ties are stronger than ours, they are centred largely in their home community without the larger social capital networks resulting from post-secondary education or work connections outside the community. Nation building requires these broader networks, where diversity in abilities and philosophy is valued and where individual giftedness is recognized. Without this, a tribal or homogeneous society may look on outside institutions or government rather than themselves as the glue to hold them together and develop their resources.

The Community Health Education strategy leads very naturally to the development of social capital. In recognizing individual and community resources and talents and building upon these, the knowledge and skill base is increased. Training of Trainers workshops identify potential leaders and community motivators, who in turn do training in the community, commonly resulting in various groups forming. CHE volunteer peer educators, mothers' clubs, farming or bee-keeping or coffee-grower associations, children's clubs, saving and loan or micro-enterprise groups are examples. Relationship building yields trust building, which means increased social capital and linkages with wider networks for training or government services that were previously unknown or unavailable. What begins as horizontal social networks now has vertical elements as the small local networks have connection to higher-level institutions and finances.

This concept is termed the 'ring of power'. Building from the inside out, the ring begins with individual gifts and talents at the centre, moving out to a circle of associations of similar groups and then the outer ring of government or business institutions and other funding organizations. This produces a strong and resilient community as contrasted to one where outside organizations and institutions move to the centre to take primary responsibility for developing communities, instead reducing them to dependency.

What makes a community resilient?

After the worst typhoon in history, Yolanda, struck Tacloban in the Philippines in 2013, the topic of community resilience became for them the buzz word. The Philippines government recognized resilient communities as the important link between each phase of their Disaster Cycle. This Cycle is universally standard, but the idea of every activity pointing inward to resilient communities was unique and captured our attention.

The Disaster Cycle is as follows:
- Response: relief for immediate life preservation by providing basic needs in the form of food, water, shelter and medical aid to ensure survival during and after a natural disaster

- Rehabilitation and Recovery: rebuilding or restoring of homes, businesses, institutions and livelihoods to regain normal or improve function in affected communities
- Prevention and Mitigation: recognizing and correcting vulnerable areas, such as building sea walls and dikes, reforestation and improved warning systems
- Preparedness: Educating populations on the risks of their area, strengthening their capacity to anticipate and secure their homes or livelihood against future emergencies

All four of these components keep the big picture in view: adding future resilience to the affected communities. Relief must have a finish plan right from the start before it becomes addictive, and results in dependency of recipients and co-dependency by relief organizations. Rehabilitation needs to include and empower the affected communities as they learn new hands-on skills or agricultural methods for future livelihood. It also provides for counselling and emotional support. Prevention and mitigation ensure less damage or death in future events. Preparedness aims for resilience at the personal and family level by strengthening physical, social and spiritual ties, giving communities the ability to recover and develop further.

In defining resilience we use the illustration of a green branch and a dry branch. The one bends and bends, then returns to its original shape, whereas the other snaps under pressure. The study of which communities are going to snap and which bounce back is fascinating and quite predictable. Those that survive well have the kinds of social connection assets we have described. They know who lives in every house, who needs help with mobility or other frailties, the resources of each family and how they can help each other.

We witnessed this when several months after Typhoon Yolanda, we were invited by a Cebu church group to accompany them to the island of Comotes that had been on the storm's path and had borne significant damage. They had collected food aid and other supplies to deliver. When our ferry arrived that evening, the people were gathered and waiting at the church. We will not forget how they described their ordeal.

Most of the community had fled to the church when the gale became serious, as they knew it to be a strong building, and they sustained each other with prayer and singing while comforting the terrified children. Presence together with the assurance of God's presence held them as the winds wailed in human-sounding screams and moans, and as flying roofs and other debris banged against the building. They described these horrific sounds and how they clung to each other for hours while the fury of the storm raged. The spiritual strength and close community bonds were obvious. The emotional capacity they drew from each other was a sustaining asset and a big part of the resilience we observed in the Filipino people.

Another event of that evening stands out—the skilful performance by the children and youth of a song with a dance they had choreographed. They had obviously experienced what they were singing and their fledgling faith was evident in the passion of their voices and bodies:

> *When the oceans rise and thunders roar,*
> *I will soar with you above the storm.*
> *Father You are king over all the earth.*
> *I will be still and know You are God.*
> *I will be still and know You are God.*

Tears misted every eye as the force of the words struck us and the sincerity on their young faces told a story that will hold them for a lifetime. Like an anchor in a stormy sea, their faith will continue to make them resilient for tough times ahead.

Economic reserve also defines a resilient community. A family that has been taught to do a budget that includes some saving will be better able to recover from adversity. Diversifying of crops rather than single cropping is another strategy for disaster proofing. We saw vast areas of coconut tree trunks snapped off like match sticks while some banana trees still stood. Rice crops were beginning to yield again as they were quicker to replant. Business often flourishes after disasters, as people rush to buy materials to repair homes. What does not help is when materials that are available locally are brought in from outside, or when bales of free used clothing put the local seamstresses out of business. We saw a social service office with a room full of used clothing still tied in bales, as they told us they were embarrassed to offer the out-of-style or inappropriate cold climate clothing that would not be well appreciated here!

Structural resilience of buildings is obviously important. Disaster has greater impact on the squatter's settlements on seaside or public lands, with flimsy dwellings built with whatever materials are available. These are the vulnerable ones that government authorities try to relocate, most often unsuccessfully as the residents depend on the sea or the inner city for their meagre income. After a disaster they may move to the temporary shelters or even permanent public housing but within a few years the slums are rising again. As their relocation projects were built without any consultation or labour from the displaced, small wonder they have little sense of vested interest in their new communities.

A discussion of environmental resilience can result in a long list of practices that need to be changed and others that should be instigated. In some places the cutting down of forests for (often illegal) logging, firewood or primitive slash-and-burn agricultural methods is an obvious devastation to specific areas and to our planet. Forest conservation, alternative crops, water catchment and storage, better agricultural methods, dikes or drainage ditches or sea walls, can all be taken on as projects by a community that has been empowered to look at their own issues and take action together.

As an exercise in determining their resilience, we have given community groups or leaders the task of listing their assets and vulnerabilities in physical, environmental, social, spiritual and emotional areas. The lists become long but revealing, as they realize that the community has more assets than they thought but also many areas of vulnerability that need attention and work.

In fact, we should all be doing this kind of basic preparation within our own homes and families, checking from time to time how we score in our physical, social, spiritual, emotional and economic resilience. Putting together a simple family plan might be a good rainy day activity with the kids that could pay off in the future.

DISCUSS AND REFLECT:

1. Do a quick inventory of personal 'assets' that you could contribute to others:
   Head: What three (or more) areas of knowledge do you have interest or training in? E.G. Languages, accounting, computer…

   Heart: What three things are you passionate about doing or learning? E.G. a sport, working with kids…

   Hands: What three skills do you do with your hands? E.G. wood working, musical instrument, baking…

2. Have you ever felt "left alone on the island" by someone who has offered to help you and did not follow through or wanted to do it for you rather than teach you? Describe that. Or have you ever done this to another?

3. Have you ever been involved in dependency-producing work or relationships that may be more about building yourself up than the other? How could you become intentional about shifting into interdependent/entrepreneurial/leadership development for the others involved?

4. How 'real-time' socially connected are you in groups or networks of people? List the face-to-face associations or groups where you get to know diverse people that you can truly count on. Do you invest time in three or more close friendships?

MULTIPLICATION

Sometimes called 'scaling up', good ideas need to spread. What works in one area can be used or adapted in another area. Experience and resources must be shared to have meaning; eventually their spread means the potential to impact whole societies.

CHAPTER 9

Use What You Have Been Given:
Build on what has gone before

"We cannot all do great things—but we can do small things with great love."

--attributed to Mother Teresa

You have more than you think you do

My husband, known then as Billy, was in grade five and had recently moved to Calgary from small town Brooks. His class appointed him to carry the funds they had raised for Red Cross to their head office two bus rides away in the centre of the city. With the two nickels they had provided him for the return bus journey safely tucked into his pocket, he bravely set out into the unfamiliar territory.

The bus trip went well, the money handed over. It was not until he went to catch the bus home that he discovered his pocket was empty, and realized the mistake he had made—he was supposed to have taken a transfer ticket when he changed buses rather than using the second nickel! Now he had nothing for his return journey. Today many ten year olds carry a cell phone and would simply call their mother to come and pick them up. But this was 1953 and cell phones were not even a dream.

Billy stayed calm and remembered the tactical action he had been taught by his parents: when in difficulty, pray. The short SOS prayer done, an idea came to try his pocket again. He felt it! A coin was there after all. Just one. To his dismay, when he pulled it out he found it was only a penny! Then again the compulsion, "check your pocket." He felt it! Another coin, but only one, and again it was a penny. With the uncomplicated faith of a child, he expectantly kept repeating the procedure. Five times he reached into that pocket to find a single coin, each time a penny--and then the pocket provided no more. It was enough. God had listened. The lesson that God would provide just enough and just in time had been embedded into the heart of an impressionable child.

Fast-forward twenty-eight years to a dilapidated hospital in Kainantu, Papua New Guinea where now Dr. Bill was in charge. His passion for excellence had taught him that lack of resources was no excuse for lack of action. When the Provincial Health Office told him there were no funds allotted for facility maintenance for Kainantu *haus sik* (hospital), that their coffers were empty, he looked in his own hospital budget and found there was enough for a few cans of paint. Some fresh paint in a couple of the wards, plus lots of soap and water, would make a start. One penny's worth of change as it were.

So the transformation of Kainantu hospital began. We heard there was a Rotary Club in the town, which surely would like a small project like this. And yes, they did! They had some money for more paint. The large Wycliffe Bible Translators centre a few miles away would surely have some people who would love to volunteer to help paint. And yes, they did! The wards were already perking up, and the staff morale had taken a huge upward turn as they saw this kind of community support. They got busy scrubbing and polishing, a contribution they could easily make.

Curtains on the windows, I decided, would really add to the comfort for patients and liven the ambience. I went to the provincial capital, Goroka, and picked out several large bolts of cotton polyester printed in a colourful Pacific Islands pattern. During the previous weeks I had taught some basic hand sewing to the mothers of severely malnourished children in the hospital nutrition ward. These mothers had to stay there with their children for several weeks while they gained strength. Sewing, along with some teaching on nutrition and cooking, was their only relief from the boredom of the long days of waiting. With a few borrowed sewing machines, their instruction accelerated and soon the simple curtains were churning out. They did a good job, because those curtains stayed on the windows for twenty years!

Word spread to the provincial capital that things were looking up in Kainantu, and the Provincial Health Officer, Dr. Christie, came for a look along with the Works and Supply officer responsible for government facility maintenance. They walked around the freshly painted wards, then looked underneath at the rotting support posts and the peeling outside paint. The proverbial pencil sharpening began, and they suddenly found some budget to help with these issues. Not only that, they miraculously found money to build an entire new obstetrics ward!

The construction and renovation phase now began in earnest. How exciting for the staff who had never known this kind of pleasant working environment. The next surprise was when our good friend Dr. Jim Decker, the dentist from the neighbouring mission, came and offered funds from his family foundation to renovate a building for a dental unit. It would accommodate two dental chairs and Dr. Jim would train a dental therapist to do the basic dental procedures. They would also build two staff houses on the hospital grounds. Even the mothers in the nutrition ward had something to look forward to as we planned a new building in the style and materials of their own traditional round homes with a customary open fire in the middle for their cooking classes, but with the addition of a chimney to keep it smoke-free.

The next year's provincial health budget included a whole new Intensive Care Unit, complete with piped in oxygen, which was only found in a few other large centres in the country at the time. That opened in October 1982.

The fully upgraded hospital, which started with a few cans of paint and the belief that if we use what we already have the rest will follow, had become reality. This has become a life principle that we teach widely to communities throughout the developing world. Many of them have been waiting for years in hopes that government service 'handouts' would come their way. Meanwhile, governments and other outside organizations are waiting to see initiative from the inside before they are willing to put forward limited resources they do not want to see wasted.

The final outcome for us came with a surprise phone call from Dr. Christie a year later asking that we move to Goroka and replace him. Bill responded, "But why me when you have lots of better qualified doctors right there in Goroka?"

"Because I want you to do for this province what you have done in Kainantu!" was the response. Apparently, the attitude of simply using what you have in your pocket with wisdom and enthusiasm is not common to everyone. Most of us hyper-analyze and decide to wait until all the needed resources show up.

> *Simply use what you have with wisdom and enthusiasm and trust that the other resources will show up. We all have far more than we imagine.*

Like the boy who gave his meagre lunch basket to Jesus and got to witness the amazing multiplication of his five loaves and two fish, the lesson is best learned through the simple eyes and heart of a child. We all have more to give than we ever imagined.

"Everything we do builds on our past and connects with our future."

We don't remember who first challenged us with these words, but it has continued to echo in our ears from the time we began our work careers. Now it is much easier to look back and see the connections.

Maybe the idea came from my late sister Linda, who used to say, "God does not waste experiences, so we shouldn't either." She saw her whole life as one building block after another and could draw positive learning from even the seeming negative experiences. This attitude encouraged education of all kinds, as she knew the collective wisdom of life would benefit either herself or someone else at some point.

Opportunities for learning, she claimed, should never be turned down. Linda had numerous and varied work and volunteer experiences, each one of which she saw as connected with something she had done or learned before. Her accomplishments ranged from being a public school teacher, to starting a pre-school, to teaching in a Teacher's College in Umtata, South Africa, to editing and writing materials for an African

Bible College, to completing a Master's degree in Applied Linguistics in order to write a Xhosa language Bible Concordance. Not to mention all the experiences and people's lives that she touched along the way. No experience and no small act done in kindness was ever wasted.

From the jungles to Calgary streets, 1986

When we returned to Calgary from Papua New Guinea in 1986, we wanted our experiences of working in a developing country to inform our work decisions as we integrated into life back home. Bill contemplated doing a Master's degree in Community Medicine in Calgary. The dean of Community Health in Calgary, along with other faculty who interviewed him concluded, "Why do a Master's? You should be teaching our students since you have already done the things that we hope to train our graduates for!"

As he worked at a walk-in clinic for income, we kept asking these university colleagues and other friends, "But where is the Third World of Calgary?"

The inner city though, seemed overloaded with homeless people, indigents and addicts. Many had mental illnesses and layer upon layer of other health and social issues. Unable to pay even the small healthcare premiums which our province charged at that time (now it is free), they did not know how to jump through the hurdles of application forms and bureaucracy in order to get their health insurance cards. It seemed a hassle and they were seen as a bother to the emergency departments and medical clinics when they showed up. They were truly falling through the cracks of the good care that the rest of our citizens were accessing.

Our good friends, Dr. Marilyn and John Kish, were drawn into the enthusiasm of starting something new, as they too had recently returned from six years in Papua New Guinea. John had worked in administration for a private company and then as a university lecturer in economics, while Marilyn worked first in a hospital and later for the university student health. John's skill in administration and economics, and his wise people skills, translated well into setting up and administering a clinic. So John helped set up a small family practice clinic in South Calgary as the financial base for the four of us to start a volunteer-run clinic in the inner city.

About the same time, the leadership of Central United Church in downtown Calgary felt burdened by the needs they saw around them and the many who daily came to their back door for help. They invited other downtown churches to discuss ways to coordinate ministry to the homeless and addicts in their area. It was beyond coincidence that at this point our paths connected, and the vision for a facility dedicated to the needs of the destitute was birthed.

It was mid-1988. The funds from a parishioner's endowment purchased a lovely old sandstone brick building owned by the Canadian Bible Society, ideally located in front of a downtown LRT (Light Rail Transit) stop. The renovations soon transformed the former bookstore into an inviting place for the group we were targeting—the marginalized who needed to have a free shower, see a doctor, be given counsel and referrals for social or housing concerns.

The working group arrived at consensus for a suitable name, CUPS. Chosen to reflect the intention of Mark 9:41, giving a cup of water in Christ's name, the full name under which it was registered in the Societies Act of Alberta is Calgary Urban Project Society (CUPS). Churches from a dozen denominations as well as social agencies, shelters, medical groups and individuals came forward with offers of support.

John Kish was a quiet motivator who gave people the impression that his ideas and numbers could be trusted. Kind-hearted to the core, we never heard a mean-spirited comment come from his lips. I was astounded by the magic of those spreadsheets that were churned out from his computer, as he was the first person I had seen using an Excel spreadsheet to make projections of expenses, income and the details in between. His eyes and voice would be alive as he explained them to us. "If this happens then, look—these will be the results, and here is the bottom line!" These were the kinds of numbers we all needed, and apparently the bank did as well since they were willing to take a gamble on a loan for the renovations and several initial months of rent.

John knew exactly how much revenue we could expect per patient from the government and how long it would take to be paid. He had the administrative systems in place to track patient records and bill the government health care system on a fee-for-service basis even though these patients still had to be registered for formal health insurance.

This was a cumbersome process, but he knew that payment eventually would come for medical services rendered. His projections were correct, enabling the rent and bank loan to be paid, and to our knowledge always on time.

We all miss John since his death from cancer in 2009. He and Bill were especially close, having worked together in setting up not one but three clinics. Bill as a visionary needed John's practical administrative wisdom, and John seemed to get excited by Bill's challenges. Theirs was the kind of friendship that many men want but never find. John could always be counted on to listen with attentiveness and then give well-thought-out and practical counsel, not just on business decisions, but on all aspects of life. He loved God with his whole heart and sought counsel from above—and it showed.

The CUPS doors were open initially for evening clinic hours in the fall of 1988, with one paid nurse to give consistency and to supervise the volunteer staff. The evening hours were temporary, in order to utilize volunteer family doctors and office staff on a regular rotating basis when their own offices hours were finished. Once payments started coming from Alberta Health, an Executive Director, Carol, was hired and helped to train volunteers to address other physical, emotional, spiritual and social concerns of those that entered the doors. These amazing volunteers were highly competent and dedicated. The healing that they sought to bring on all levels to the neglected, the 'very least of these' in the eyes of society, in fact brought healing to everyone involved and beyond. Such is the unexpected result of human kindness.

Bill, as the first Medical Director, looked forward to each of the evenings he was there and came home with enthusiasm for the fulfilling work of having some small part in touching the lives of the incredible people he met. He also enjoyed frequenting the pawnshop next door—so much that the owner started saving things he knew Bill might like. He still wears the cowboy boots he bought there, the most comfortable he has ever owned!

By March 1989 the clinic and referral centre were open from noon to 8:00 pm daily except Sunday. My role was to approach the family doctors (and later dentists as well) that we knew or had connections with through the Christian Medical and Dental Society and get commitments for them to work one or more shifts weekly, bi-weekly or even monthly. The list of volunteers was heartening, with thirteen regulars and another dozen or so as back-up relief. It did not seem difficult to find volunteers, as it appeared it was fun to work at CUPS— not that the problems were fun, but the relaxed atmosphere, lack of pressure and sense of shared purpose made it enjoyable. All of the clients had heart-rending stories. All presented challenges, often multiple layers of health and social issues that needed to be peeled back one by one before the real needs were exposed. The deep caring of the medical professionals was evident to me. As volunteer medical coordinator, it made me so proud to know these men and women who had the capacity to treat everyone with dignity and equality. The team of volunteers in the counselling and referral centre were likewise the cream of the faith communities of Calgary. Everyone was there to serve, and how much better could it get than that?

After several months of operation, average numbers were calculated and projected on John's magic spreadsheets, the data needed to propose ongoing funding to the Alberta Health Services. They agreed to John's proposal for funding on a capitation or projected volume basis, rather than the tedious work of registering each patient in the system and collecting the fees much later. This was our province's first such experiment in capitation funding rather than fee-for-service.

The response of the government health care office had been heartening: "The last thing we want to be accused of is not looking after the most vulnerable in our society." With the capitation funding in place, we felt assured that the clinic was viable, a consistent budget could be planned for, a full-time medical director paid and the clinic open longer hours.

Over the years many doctors with cross-cultural experience found their way here, like Dr. James Watt, who had served in Zimbabwe and had expertise in HIV and AIDS which was only beginning to be recognized as a problem in Canada at the time. Dr. Don Curry had worked for years in rural Pakistan. Dr. Rita Dahlke, with years of experience in the Northwest Territories, served as Medical Director for ten years. These doctors had been prepared for this raw and real kind of service and were calm, accepting and caring, even though the problems were different in this setting. Dr. Wayne Elford, a Professor Emeritus retired from the Calgary Department of Family Medicine, dedicated his academic and international experience from Nepal and Africa. Many young medical students and residents have honed their skills of compassion and have learned to listen beyond the surface problems through their electives at the CUPS clinic. Still they come, and these elective spots fill up quickly.

Homelessness was already becoming an issue in cities all over the country, and affluent Calgary was no exception. Most found their way to CUPS fairly quickly. A young architect friend of ours who was concerned with homelessness, Stacy, had started Connection Housing in 1987 and soon fit into the referral mix at CUPS. This became the hub of a group of volunteers who found rental units and approached landlords to negotiate on the security deposit, which is a major deterrent for a person coming off the street. After appropriately placing those needing housing, they continued to support them with encouragement and with monitoring their accommodation and landlord issues. It would be ten more years until a local philanthropist established the Calgary Homeless Foundation, bringing together all groups with similar goals. With both Provincial and National financial backing, they are now well on their way to their goal of eradicating homelessness in Calgary.

Some of the saddest situations the CUPS staff encountered were with women, many of them abused by partners or pimps or in hiding to escape abusive relationships. At this time the move towards women's shelters and homeless shelters was just at the beginning stages as well, so the challenge of protecting these women required connections with social services that often the women did not realize existed for them. We worked closely with Servants Anonymous Society, also formed in 1989 to address the issue of women involved in sexual exploitation that wanted to escape and learn new life skills. Such collaborations are essential, as any one group cannot address all aspects of need.

Children of single mothers and sex workers were also falling through the cracks, with mothering skills lacking and daycare unaffordable. A young social work student from the University of Calgary did a project at CUPS with single mothers that turned into a career for her—and the One World Child Development program was born. It obviously touched a real need, as both she and the program are there to this day and are acclaimed for the quality counselling, parenting classes and early intervention for pre-school to kindergarten age kids. The Nurturing Parenting program provides support, education and training to parents.

Being right in the middle of the drug dealing area of the city, CUPS became the fixed site for a needle exchange program until later when a van was provided as a mobile site. Gordon and Ivy were employed as street outreach workers, with nurses on site carrying out the actual needle exchange. Oh, the stories—I hope their books will be forthcoming one day!

After a number of years, knowing that the CUPS clinic was running well, receiving Alberta Health Funding and serving the needs that it was meant to serve, our involvement ended. New boards and directors came and went. The numbers outgrew the building and they moved to a larger facility, then again to another even larger. Then in 2008 Bill decided to go back and check in on it again and offer to do summer locums while we were home from our overseas assignments. This seemed to us to integrate the amazing parallels between what we were involved with in other countries with our own home inner city needs, as well as opportunity for Bill to keep his hand in medicine.

One summer day Bill was ready to do his morning shift and arrived before the doors were open. Not being regular staff, he did not have keys to the back door used by staff, so waited with the patients who were lined up at the front door. A very kind-looking, older man in the queue saw Bill's look of confusion and asked if he was here hoping to see the doctor. "Would you believe that I am the doctor?" Bill replied.

The man gave a knowing nod and smile of pity and had the grace not to prod or ask any more questions. Once the doors were open and the patients came through his examining room one by one, of course this man eventually appeared. Very surprised and somewhat embarrassed he blurted, "Oh no, you really ARE the doctor!"

Bill was impressed at the many small kindnesses that street people like this man most often show to each other. It was not that way though on another morning when again he had to wait for the door to open. This time he thought he would wait very near the door, which meant 'queue jumping' and some annoyed looks. The woman who had been camped in her sleeping bag nearest the door in order to get in first, gruffly ordered, "Get to the back of the line! Some of us have been here a long time and you can't just jump in at the front."

Obediently he walked to the back of the line. You already know who the first patient was when he opened the examining room door! "Oh no! I am so sorry, I am so sorry," she apologized. "I didn't know you were the doctor!"

Maybe we all need to be more aware of whom we might be talking to—one of these so-called 'down-and-outers' could be an angel unawares! Or a former university professor, or a corporate lawyer or a concert pianist. Or a sky diving instructor, as one of the doctors who led a hepatitis C support group at CUPS discovered one day. She had been part of an urban CHE workshop we were conducting, and as a practical assignment we had challenged each participant to talk to some neighbours and identify the 'assets' or individual giftedness of a few of these people around them. She related to the rest of us the next week her surprise when she went around the support group to ask the three questions—what were their practical skills, their knowledge and their passions? The unique skills and knowledge possessed by these men in various stages of recovery helped her to view them in a totally different light. In fact, who has not experienced this levelling of the playing field as we begin to really get to know and appreciate people for who they are? Often their life circumstances and yes, foolish mistakes too, have left them without the options that most of us have. Poverty can in some cases be generational, but in our society it is most often a series of difficult blows that the person did not have the emotional, spiritual or life skills to surmount. "There but for the grace of God go I," as quipped an anonymously wise person long ago, may likewise be our own best first response.

Today the health and associated social needs of the marginalized in Calgary inner city are still big issues and CUPS continues to have an important role in serving these people. New programs evolve to meet those needs, reflecting the innovative attitudes that are part of CUPS' culture. It now includes a Women's Health Clinic, a Shared Care Mental Health program, Pre- and Post-Natal programs, Pediatric care, Hepatitis C treatment and support groups, a Diabetes program,

Dental and Vision Care, visiting medical specialists, outreach medical services to seven shelters and detox centres, and numerous collaborative programs with other partner agencies.

I write about CUPS, not that it be seen as something unusual or unique, but as an example of the process by which many such humanitarian not-for-profit efforts are birthed. There will be a few people in place as the 'midwives' of the idea, and many others who work tireless for years to bring it to pass—medical personnel, social workers, counsellors, administrators, volunteers.

We could recount similar histories of many other organizations started by Calgarians who took the risks and began with what they had. Here are a few examples:

Pat Nixon, in 1984 took the Burning Bush Coffeehouse and planted The Mustard Seed that now feeds and shelters nearly 400 otherwise homeless men and women. Stacy McGhee and Connection Housing as we mentioned already, in 1987 began bringing willing landlords together with the working poor. Also in 1987, Pastor Bob Purdie and a small group at St. Stephen's Anglican Church, began Inn From the Cold to address child and family homelessness by giving shelter, sanctuary and eventual healing. Many other churches joined them. Carl DeLine and Marilyn Dyck founded The Back Door in 1988 (Doorways since 2001), where about one hundred street youths each year learn to set goals that lead to legal work and housing. Dominique of Servants Anonymous Foundation went from helping women exit the streets in Calgary in 1988 to an international initiative along with our friend Naomi, to rescue women vulnerable to trafficking in Nepal and several Eastern European countries. Pastor Don Delaney of Victory Foundation started with an inner city Street Church in 1990 and now has multiple houses for people in recovery or otherwise homeless. In 1998 the late Arthur Smith founded The Calgary Homeless Foundation with a vision to gather all the agencies and collectively pursue with a systems' approach an end to homelessness. Jim Moore is a visionary and founding director of a group that in 2003 transformed an old hotel into Calgary Dream Centre. Men in recovery find mental, social, physical and spiritual support to restore dignity and renew dreams to function again in families and society. Now owning more than thirty houses for follow-up support of the graduates, two Dream Centre houses for women in recovery have been added.

I could go on, but the astounding list would include over fifty such programs or groups started in Calgary. Notice how many of them were forming at about the same time as CUPS? We might conclude it was a '*kairos*' point in time when social concern for the growing homeless population and others falling outside the social safety net was coming to the collective conscience of the city. Has it made a difference? As in the story of the little boy throwing beached starfish back into the water, "It may not make a big difference, but it made a difference for that one!" And with all of us together, it has made a big difference. Even with a growing population and economic downturn in Calgary, in 2016 homelessness had decreased by twenty-six per cent. That is simply a number, but the back-stories of thousands of people are represented by that number, each one of them with parents, siblings, friends, children—our community. May we in our sophistication never out-grow compassion.

A truly humbling surprise came to us in June 2017 when the Governor General of Canada conferred a very prestigious award, the Meritorious Service Medal, to ourselves, Marilyn Kish (and John posthumously) and the two main pastors involved in the founding of the CUPS clinic. We accepted this recognition on behalf of the numerous other medical directors, executive officers and faithful staff and volunteers who have followed and made it the successful place of compassionate care that it is today. Thank you, Canada, for the recognition and for being the kind of nation that encourages altruism!

The message from all these stories? If you feel the nudging to do something, just start with what you have. Very likely others will come alongside, and who knows how it will multiply?

Connecting in Post-war Kosovo: June 1999

After being home for several years, founding another multi-disciplinary clinic called Health Plus and seeing our kids into university, Bill and I were again called upon to build on the skills and experience we had gained in other contexts. This time it was with Samaritan's Purse, in a war zone! Amazingly, the life skills we could draw upon were now deeply ingrained.

It was early 1999 and the whole world knew that the Balkan state of Kosovo in Yugoslavia was under siege from neighbouring Serbia. News channels documented hundreds of thousands of Kosovo people fleeing their country in the biggest wave of refugees since WWII. The Yugoslavia conflict that began with Bosnia in 1992 had again erupted. Ethnic diversity had held tentatively together under President Tito, but after his death the country began to fracture along religious fault lines: Catholic republics of Slovenia, Montenegro and Croatia declared independence, but when mainly Muslim Bosnia tried to secede they came up against Orthodox Serbians and Croatians. We heard the term ethnic cleansing, meaning ethnically targeted expulsion from one's country. Genocide shocked the world as 100,000 Bosnians lost their lives, and 2.2 million fled the country.[84]

Then Albanian-speaking Kosovo, primarily Muslim, bid for independence, something the Serbian population would not endorse. War again broke out with Serbian armed forces moving into Kosovo and NATO intervening much more quickly to try to prevent another Bosnia.

By June 1999 the war was officially over, and NATO had successfully restored peace and a semblance of order, although Serbia continued to claim Kosovo as part of its territory until the Brussels Agreement of 2013. Though the fighting was over, oh the mess that remained! We had started out in the Samaritan's Purse refugee camp in Albania, which housed twenty-five hundred families. This tent-city began to empty as soon as news of the peace accord came. Bill and I were among the staff selected to be part of the logistics team that would follow the refugees back to Kosovo. Bill was assigned to the medical needs assessment and I, the educational needs. We were to look at the structural and equipment damage to the hospitals and schools, and what community health clinics were salvageable. The area that SP chose to focus on was near the borders with Albania and Macedonia that had been most hard hit in the war. Our team decided to settle in Gjakove, one of the larger north-eastern towns, as a base for medical, educational and housing rehabilitation of the surrounding farm communities.

Having never seen a post-war zone before, our senses were shocked with the lingering smell and sight of scorched houses and shops, shelled and burned schools and health centres, heaps of rubble left as tile roofs caved in on burning buildings. Walking through the town of Gjakove, I remember stopping to look at the charred and twisted tables of a coffee bar surrounded by fallen concrete and tiles. I could not even fathom how this mess would ever be cleaned up. It was early July, and farmers had returned hoping to get some crops or gardens growing. Instead they found their farms full of land mines. Since thousands of men were dead or missing, it left those remaining without much hope of getting field work done.

An excerpt from a letter I sent to friends at home the week after we arrived still brings tears of emotional memories to my eyes:

"We did not realize when we returned to Albania in mid-June that the refugees would be anxious to get back immediately to Kosovo and that Samaritan's Purse would be following them back within days. What it meant was that we were some of the first outsiders to enter the country after the war, and what a tremendous privilege that is.

On July 2, seventeen of us set off with four Samaritan's Purse vehicles on the ten-hour drive over the mountains from Albania to Kosovo. It was broken by the long wait at the border as loaded trucks, tractors pulling trailers like covered wagons, and every other imaginable vehicle filled with returning refugees made their way through. Every border in the country had similar lines, as over 800,000 refugees were returning home! This does not include those who chose to be repatriated in the countries they had fled to.

Immediately inside Kosovo, we saw taped off areas denoting mine danger, and the evidence of devastation all along as we drove through the countryside. The further north we drove, the more damage we saw with some houses still burning. The first sight in entering Gjakove was the huge three-story police station, which had been bombed by a NATO cruise missile and then burned by the Serbs themselves to destroy the evidence of atrocities as their Serb army headquarters. The downtown section of the town of sixty thousand population was almost completely burned. The amazing thing that we all felt almost immediately though, was a sense of calm, safety and relief, reflecting the feelings of the local population who had stayed in hiding during the three month siege and could finally relax and walk around openly.

The streets were full of people walking and enjoying meeting friends again. It took just a few short days until the looted and burned out shops were selling goods again in front of the rubble, and sidewalk vendors were offering much needed merchandise.

It has not taken us long to get to know people, as everyone we meet these days wants to tell the tragic stories of their escape—and of their loved ones who didn't escape. Many people recognize us from the refugee camp, and it is like meeting old friends who have shared dangers together. Many have invited us to walk with them through their burned homes and we feel the sadness with them. What an incredible privilege to be here at such a critical time, just days after the war has finished, and to be the first outsiders to share their burdens. Even though we are helpless in the face of such pain, somehow it gives them hope to know that their plight had not gone unnoticed by the rest of the world.

We have seen how the many people who remained here during the war survived and heard their tales of horror over endless cups of Turkish coffee. We have talked with teachers and medical people about how they are coping with the little they have. Just to be present here with them as we offer some comfort and hope of restoration of their devastated society has been one of the most moving experiences of our lives. We feel no doubt in our minds that it was the Lord who brought us here for this moment of time."

My letter went on to state that according to UN reports, of the 1.5 million inhabitants of Kosovo, ninety percent had been displaced during the war period and up to forty percent of homes were destroyed or damaged. In the face of such suffering, the simple gift of our concerned presence, our listening ears and tears, though so inadequate was the most important thing and the only thing we had to give. What had happened could not be undone. We had to let go of our desire to solve their problems and simply trust with them for better days ahead.

We also saw that prayer was a universal connector: even though we were Christians and they were Muslim, our offer to pray with a family after hearing their story was never turned down. Somehow it seems that the human heart knows and longs for connection with a God who sees and cares about suffering and who uses ordinary people like us as his instruments for healing.

> We cannot underestimate the gift of our presence, our listening ear or our tears. Often that is the most important thing and the only thing we can give

The stories became even more real as we became friends with some of the people who lived in tents in the back yards of their uninhabitable homes, with relatives whose homes were intact, or even in the corner of their barns. Our kind-hearted neighbours, Bessie and Helman, teachers with two teenage sons, were one family whose house had been spared. However, the large almost-new home of his brother Njazi and wife Atafeti, who had an optometry practice in town, was now in ruins. They had four beautiful young children, who in spite of their plight always seemed immaculately dressed. The smell of 'burned everything,' pervaded the space as we walked into the remains of their once beautiful home.

I cried with Atafeti as she took me into their bedroom and picked up some charred lace from a treasured crocheted bedspread, a special wedding gift for which the Kosovar ladies are famous. I took a piece of it home to Canada and framed it behind glass to return to her so she would have some tangible piece of it as a memorial. Some of the rich blue tile in the bathroom was intact, but with ugly brown streaks of whatever chemical had melted from the ceiling and dripped over the tiles and the half-melted toilet. Likewise, the kitchen was a twisted mess of burned appliances and cupboards. The senseless waste of a beautiful home, not from an uncontrollable wildfire as we have seen in places like Fort McMurray in northern Alberta or Australia's bush fires, but from a malicious army throwing incendiary bombs into random homes on a street, was overwhelmingly sad. I could not imagine how long it would take or if ever it could be restored.

Yet I was extremely privileged to be able to see the newly renovated home eighteen months later. It had taken hard work, savings, loans and possibly gifts from relatives, but the results were beautiful. The concrete and steel wall and roof structures had been intact and room by room it was re-built—a beautiful bedroom suite now in their master bedroom, the modern bathroom fixtures and tiled walls, a lovely kitchen built to European standards.

In a letter at the time I had written,

> "It was almost as hard not to burst into tears seeing the lovely new kitchen yesterday as it was when we first walked in and saw the burned ruins in July 1999. To see both chapters of their history, and the new life and hope arising from the ashes, reminded me that I had quoted to them a year ago that there would be 'a crown of beauty instead of ashes, the oil of joy instead of mourning.'[85] The tears now are for the joy of remembering what it was before and has now become."

It had been a surprise for us to see how well developed the Kosovar homes, lifestyle and infrastructure had been before the war, very similar to much of Western Europe. After having spent the few weeks in Albania with the refugee camp over the spring and summer, we could not help but compare the comfortable pre-war life of Kosovo to their ethnic Albanian cousins across the border in Albania.

Across that line of mountains Enver Hoxha's strict Stalin-influenced dictatorship had suppressed Albania and kept them in isolation from

World War II until the 1990's. The Albanians told us that they were made to think that every other country in the world was their enemy ready to invade, and the mushroom-shaped concrete bunkers that dotted the whole countryside were proof they really believed it was so. On our first visit to Albania in 1995, riding by train we postulated all kinds of reasons for these structures, with an average of 5.7 of them per square kilometer, but never did we imagine they were bunkers!

It seemed that the country's funds had been wasted in building bunkers rather than in developing schools, hospitals and roads! We saw that the people were steeped in poverty and a mind-set unable to see options for rising above it. Even though majority Albanian-speaking Kosovo had struggled under the moderate communist government of Yugoslavian Marshall Tito, the relative freedom they had to develop and prosper while Tito was alive was light years ahead of Albania. It was amusing to see the surprise of the Albanians who came to Kosovo to help out after the war. They had no idea of the disparity that existed between their two side-by-side countries of similar ethnic origins, so obviously an issue of politics and leaders.

One of the memories that will never be erased was our first Sunday in Kosovo. We had heard that there were only seven fledgling Protestant Churches in the country, with congregations of fifteen to thirty people each. It took some questions and searching for us to find the Gjakove group that morning, but we persevered and after walking down several wrong alleys found the narrow stone stairway leading to the damp, somewhat dark basement meeting room. They showed the two of us to a simple wooden bench at the back of the room where about twenty very weary-looking people were gathered. We found out that this was their first meeting since the expulsion order had sent most of the population fleeing across the border and rest into hiding. Some of these people, including Pastor Nick were among the few who had remained in the city, moving from house to house for three months to avoid being caught.

Pastor Nick immediately motioned a young man to come and sit behind us to translate. I almost wished I had not had the privilege of understanding the sermon, as my face was wet with tears for the entire time, such palpable anguish was being expressed. I was embarrassed by my emotion, being complete strangers and the only outsiders present, but both Bill and I were amazed and touched by the honesty of that sermon. Pastor Nick confessed with deep conviction his own questioning of God's silence during their ordeal and the weakness of his faith. He read the Bible passage about Peter's denial of Jesus and the first meeting afterwards where Jesus asked him, "Peter, do you love me?" Then he encouraged his small and wavering flock to confess their failure and reaffirm their love, as Christ was asking them the same question he had asked Peter. His grace would be granted just as it had been to Peter, and whatever they had done to survive or however they had denied Christ would be forgiven. I had never felt such lack of judgment, such identification by the clergy with the sinner.

We went to the Pastor's house for tea after the service, beginning a good friendship with the family, which included a baby boy born right as the war was starting, right up to a daughter finishing high school and two sons in their early twenties who had together started a church in Pristina, the capital city. We learned that Pastor Nick was among the first Protestant Christians in the country, having been converted while in the army in Croatia. After returning, he started a small church, and then in 1985 officially inaugurated the Kosovo Protestant Evangelical Church (KPEC) which today has forty-two churches and around fifteen thousand followers. Its President is now his eldest son Driton, and the large church in Pristina is still pastored by son Artur. Over the time that we were coming and going from Kosovo, we saw the Gjakove church increase and we helped them get one of the large refugee camp tents to accommodate the larger numbers until they were finally able to build. We also spent time with the two sons in Pristina, helping them with some proposal writing for their vision of online theological training for the many young people they interacted with constantly. We said that their house was like grand central station, with dozens of pairs of shoes outside the door witnessing the many people inside at any one time.

We were excited to read that KPEC was given special recognition in the 2012 government monument to international and national organizations that have contributed to the peace and prosperity of the nation in the years from the end of the war to that time.[86]

The Kosovo school system—from the bizarre to the horrific

We gradually made our way around to the twenty-eight villages assigned to Samaritan's Purse to help rebuild homes, schools and clinics. I listened to stories from teachers who were trying to help traumatized children while dealing with their own grief from loss of their homes and loved ones. All the equipment and anything of value had been stolen from the schools and taken to Serbia, and the schools had been occupied by troops hoping that they would be safe there from NATO bombing. Many had been partially burned or bombed.

It was also surprising to hear that most of the Kosovar teachers, and the medical people as well, had not received regular salaries for nine years during the long standoff with the central government of Yugoslavia. Yet they had carried on as volunteers, knowing that their survival as a people depended on it. There was a Serbian school curriculum, which the Kosovars saw as 'revisionist history' and which they determined to supplement with much of their own curriculum. Most schools had been physically divided to segregate the Serbian from the Albanian students, with separate classrooms and even with walls down the corridors! In other schools the students took shifts, with Albanians and Serbs attending at different times. This extraordinary feature of the education system had existed since 1992 when the government fired all Kosovo Albanian teachers on the same day and closed all Albanian textbook publishing companies, thus shutting down all official Albanian language schooling. By the time of the war in 1999 there was a full parallel underground school system, with most high school and university education offered in private locations like homes. Attendance and the quality of education suffered. There was little or no professional development or in-service for the teachers. The same was true in medicine and likely every other profession, a fact that further eroded any hope of a unified country.

My driver, assistant and translator in these excursions to the country schools was Labinot, a fourth-year medical student in this parallel system, who was the same age as our own son. As a product of the educational system conducted mostly in homes, he was a wealth of information. He explained the great difficulty in such things as obtaining secondary and university level textbooks, as well as studying medicine without the benefit of classes or lab facilities. He was also a great source of stories of pre-war life growing up in Kosovo. The growing hardships and fear of the genocide intentions of Serbian President Slobodan Milosevic of the Federal Republic of Yugoslavia became clear. Serbia refused to recognize the rights of the ethnic majority Kosovars. The angry backlash against this meant that many of the Serbian Orthodox historical churches and sites sacred to Serbia were destroyed or damaged in the long conflict.

Labinot was determined that there would be better days ahead for all of them and was diligent to make sure that I saw as much war damage as possible to determine what would be needed to repair the schools. Seeing his attitude of total respect for his elders, in particular the school teachers who sacrificed for the children, I too saw them through different and very humbled eyes.

Some schools were small, one classroom for each primary grade, while others were much larger two storey buildings. Organizations bigger than Samaritan's Purse were focusing on the urban high schools. It was an interesting process to get together with all the NGO's (Non-Government Organizations) that were planning to rehabilitate schools and agree on who would repair which schools. I remember well a meeting chaired by UNICEF for school rehabilitation, where I had the feeling that we were all competitors in a turf war, vying for the projects that we wanted our organization to claim! Of the more than forty international NGO's in Kosovo by late summer, many wanted to help with school projects, with some working together on the bigger ones alongside UNICEF. This was my first realization that the aid industry really is like any other big business! Indeed, it has grown exponentially since the Kosovo crises.

I asked to be assigned the schools in the communities where SP was repairing homes, which meant more efficiency in getting materials to the sites. This included eight schools that needed some repair, along with two that needed complete rebuilding. Although I had looked at all of them, as a person with no experience in construction I remember feeling quite out of my element and nervous about how far the budget we were projecting for schools would really go! UNICEF did offer help with funding, but wanted the NGO's to coordinate and manage the projects. In the end it was amazing to see the groups come together to revitalize education as the state emerged from genocide and destruction unprecedented in Europe since World War II.

In a Sept 1999 information circular from UNICEF the post-war school summary assessment was almost unfathomable:

> *"According to a UNICEF survey covering all school districts, six hundred sixty-eight of Kosovo's one thousand schools were in need of repairs, with forty-five per cent severely damaged or destroyed, following the conflict. The majority have suffered looting or the destruction of school furniture. In addition, many schools have not yet been checked for landmines and unexploded ordnance.*
>
> *UNICEF is undertaking the rehabilitation and rebuilding effort with dozens of partner organizations. Work has already been completed on thirty-four schools and repairs are currently being carried out at two hundred sixty-three others. Reconstruction will soon begin at most of the remaining three hundred seventy-one facilities…aiming to have all three hundred ten thousand children with a fresh curriculum, repaired school buildings and new desks, chairs and blackboards… walls that previously separated Serb and Albanian children have been knocked down."*[87]

These Kosovars were resilient people, patriotic to the core, determined, industrious. Even though they welcomed our help, they were not about to play the victim role while waiting for others to rebuild their lives and their large extended family homes. We were surprised at how quickly the charred houses began to be refurbished, even though that first winter was hard. Being sixty per cent rural, many farmers stayed in their barns if they were intact, or huddled in one room of their broken houses. Because most houses were built of concrete block, the walls were standing, but no windows, doors, floors, ceilings, roofs or inside contents. SP and many of the other groups helping with housing, provided tarps to cover a section of the roof enough for one or two rooms until the roof was restored, as well as a wood stove to warm it. With winter in these mountainous villages bringing a meter of snow and freezing temperatures, this was critical. We were proud to report that by mid-December, SP with just a handful of international staff and many diligent Kosovar workers, had done repair on seven hundred eighty homes in forty-seven villages. As far as we know, nobody died from the cold that winter, which was a severe one.

I thought of the early settlers in Canada and the one-room sod houses where many spent their first winter, and of the one-room schoolhouses heated with one woodstove. The classrooms I visited in Kosovo were similarly heated in the winter by one wood heater in each room. Those that once had central heating had not yet repaired those systems. It did not seem to bother the children or the teachers to wear their coats and hats all day long inside the school. Nor did the fact that there were bullet holes in the walls of many classrooms that first winter, or whole sections with the walls or roof caved in. They were back home, and the restoration of school routines stabilized and normalized life, a huge part in the post-trauma recovery process.

Women usually bear the brunt of the aftermath of war. One day a nurse and I, along with a young woman as translator, went to check on the school damage in the community of Rabovec. It was a community of beautiful farming hamlets, with green rolling hills, apple trees, fertile fields, cow bells ringing from the necks of their milk cows, an idyllic scene—except that all the homes were burned and there were NO men over the age of twelve years! All the males over thirteen, well over two hundred of them, had been rounded up by the Serbian military and most were shot in front of the village, then every building burned. The women and children were forced to flee into the forest and then across the border into Albania and had now returned to this devastation with no men to help restore their lives.

Immediately when we drove up in our vehicle, several women and children came to meet us. They offered us a place to sit in the shade of a tree and quickly ran inside one of their burned-out homes. Apologizing that they had no Turkish coffee, the usual trademark of their hospitality, they came out with a two-litre bottle of coca cola! Where did that come from when they had nothing to eat apart from the aid-supplied rations, and why were they saving it for visitors such as us? We sipped it slowly, almost reverently, and listened to their horrific tales in near-disbelief. We brought them the only comfort we knew, again the gift of our concerned presence, teary-eyed hugs and prayers. Little did they realize the gift they were giving back to us, women touching other women and entrusting us with the raw vulnerability of their lives. I felt that our hearts broke and grew a bit larger that day.

I wondered how these women managed in the years after we left. Imagine my happy surprise when an internet search recently told about these courageous women making a deliberate decision to survive and succeed with what they had—their fertile farm land and their determination. They formed cooperatives and worked together to grow vegetables, first marketing their pickles and traditional relishes in Pristina. This success grew to expand to other processed vegetables marketed all around the country. While it took several years for their homes to be completely rebuilt and to raise their economic viability, they have done it. What a tribute to the women's will to survive and to see their children thrive, bearing witness to the fact that we can change our destiny.

When our initial assignment came to an end that fall, I was able to hand over my school assessment and rehabilitation role to another young Canadian woman, Laurie, who was amazing in the way she coordinated and carried out the plans to completion. She also had the benefit of Labinot's help, who eventually was able to return to university to finish medical school and carry on to become an orthopedic surgeon. His nation's trauma had carried a gift—exposure to the fine group of diligent and professional young international staff in the aid community. Likewise the lives of the aid workers were enriched by people like Labinot. The shared experience of rebuilding Kosovo created building blocks in the future lives of all concerned. One of these in the next phase of work there would be our own son.

Introducing medical connectivity to post-war Kosovo November 1999

The state of health care in Kosovo was abysmal. The Isa Grezda Hospital in Gjakove, where we were based, had been damaged but it was obvious that it had been very run-down even before the war, and medical standards were low. Both techniques and equipment were out-dated, and apparently not a single medical journal was to be found in any hospital library. This was not surprising given the description of the education system, and what Labinot had told us about medical education. Now with many staff killed or missing, their capacity was further reduced. Some NGO's took on physical repairs such as replacing all the broken windows in the hospital or painting wards, but SP decided to develop an emergency department, which had been assessed as practically non-existent. Western doctors and nurses worked with the staff on proper triage and protocols and brought much needed equipment. When we visited again fifteen years later, some of that equipment still had the Samaritan's Purse stickers on it, the poster with protocol for procedures was still on the wall and the staff all remembered with appreciation those who had come to help set them on course.

SP had also refurbished a rural clinic about half an hour away, where a doctor and several nurses worked with very little equipment or back-up support. That is when an idea came to Bill: years back in Papua New Guinea he had a radio system that connected all the rural health centres with his office (and in the evening to our home!) so the staff could always get help and advice when they were in difficult medical situations. What was needed here was something similar but using updated technology that Bill was well acquainted with in establishing the Health Plus Clinic in Calgary. During these years he made annual trips to Brussels as a consultant to the Telemedicine Initiatives of the European Union which gave him connections with people involved in this technology in places like nearby Greece. Why not build on all these past experiences and knowledge and use it here?

The idea grew into a passionate conviction that telemedicine could work here and might be a prototype for other post-war or less-developed places where specialist medical support was lacking. Selling the idea to the SP project coordinators was another matter! What on earth was telemedicine anyway? As Bill explained, it was simply using technology to provide clinical support from a distance, not far different from the health radio system of Papua New Guinea. It would make possible emergency consultations to isolated clinics or for medical education to students or practitioners. Fortunately, the Canadian SP director was a man of vision who was willing to put some funds towards the project, and the American hierarchy reluctantly went along with it.

"Why telemedicine in a post-war situation?" they all asked, with good reason. Bill had to have good answers, and we appreciated their prompting us to explain the rationale, which would be needed for the medical community of Kosovo, and later to European Union partners.

What problems could telemedicine address? The shortage of medical expertise coming out of the previous decade of suppression; the lack of up to date equipment for testing and procedures; the disorganization in medical education we found in the main hospital and medical school; the dire urgency to connect with the rest of the world that the medical practitioners had expressed to us. These reasons made the telemedicine approach seem like an obvious solution.

Some doctors told us that the majority of the ethnic Albanian Kosovo medical practitioners had been banned from the hospitals for the previous decade and were isolated to small health centres. The physical isolation of these rural doctors, especially in the winter, was another factor that made upgrading of skills critical, as was validated by the high infant mortality rates. The health centre that we chose to connect to the Gjakove hospital, called Ponashec, was only five kilometres distance, but sometimes it took an hour to get there even in a good vehicle because there was no snow ploughing equipment.

At the same time, a rheumatologist friend at the University of Calgary Medical Faculty, Dr. Edworthy, was involved with electronic health information systems and telemedicine. He was willing to come to Kosovo for a couple of weeks and share his knowledge. Our son Tim was able to take a three month leave from his job in electronic medical records software with Clinicare company in Calgary, as they were also interested in the project. It was a special privilege to work with Tim, with colleagues from Calgary and the new connections that Bill had made in Brussels and Greece. A couple of months later when the project was well underway, SP agreed to bring another young friend with aptitude and experience in computer technology, Brooks Bergreen. Between Brooks and Tim they trained Arben, a teenager who lived near the hospital and was a computer 'whiz kid', who maintained the system after they left. He later came to Canada for further training with the medical software company that Tim worked for and then settled in the IT industry in the US.

The human component was the easy part—but where would all the technical equipment be sourced in a country that had little of it even before the destruction they had gone through? It seemed that Thessaloniki, Greece was the closest access for most of the equipment, but the satellite system came from a company called Web-Sat in Dublin, Ireland and the Breezecom wireless radios from Israel! With low cost two-way transmission from the hub station on the roof of the Gjakove Hospital, wireless radios could shoot a distance of thirty kilometers.

This was definitely not all as smooth or easy as it sounds now! The trip to Thessaloniki in Greece which Tim and Brooks made several times, meant eight hours or more of driving plus long waits to cross two unfriendly borders. Both Macedonia and Greece had been sympathetic to Serbia rather than Kosovo during the war, and every time we crossed the borders there were lots of questions and long lines. Bringing back equipment into Kosovo elicited further interrogation. Tim and Brooks tell of driving back from Greece late at night in the SP vehicle, when they were accused at the border of stealing an NGO vehicle. They both appeared very young to have the kind of responsibility they were describing. After much talking and accusation back and forth they were released, but Tim promised the border guard he would never return even as a tourist after receiving that kind of treatment from Greece!

The first web-sat system had to be returned to Dublin with a long wait for the new one to come, and much 'tweaking' to get it to work. This was all being done in January, mostly outside in one of the coldest and heaviest snowfall winters in a long time. One day Tim was working on the hospital roof installing wire cables when the knife he was using with his cold stiff hands just carried on slicing right through the base of his thumb. He was not far away from the newly updated emergency department, so held his bleeding thumb and ran downstairs to have it sutured. He carries that scar as a permanent memory of that cold winter in Kosovo!

Connection to the medical faculty of the Pristina University was less difficult and there was no blood shed there! Dean Belegu and the other faculty were very motivated to get the telemedicine connection for the medical students and for research potential. They fully cooperated as Tim ran cables around the building and onto the roof, and put a hole in the window for a cable to run through. After some negotiation with the International Rescue Committee who had put in an internet service provider (ISP) in their building already, it was agreed that we could connect to that via microwave. IRC provided the conduit for internet connection for all government, UN and NGO use, and this project qualified.

Meanwhile... Operation Christmas Child!

I had been a bit anxious as to what my role would be when we returned in late 1999 for the telemedicine project, as my previous school project was being well managed by others. I need not have worried...four hundred thousand shoe box gifts, the trade mark of Samaritan's Purse to many in North American, had been promised for Kosovo! This represented one for every primary school child in the country. Now that was a massive undertaking that needed more hands on deck than we had. The armed forces from many countries still had peace-keepers, so in Kosovo, so I visited the bases and talk to the chaplains. We thought it would be a great way for soldiers to be involved in an exciting and happy event with the school children near their bases, or at least to help us with the trucking of boxes. Amazingly, some did not see it that way at all, including the Canadian Forces! That was disappointing. The Americans were helpful, but the Dutch were over-the-top enthusiastic! They became our best allies, trucking boxes and unloading them at the schools, and in some cases doing the actual distribution.

We first had to get all the numbers and ages of the boys and girls in each school, as the boxes are labeled with those categories. I had the task of connecting with school principals and other partners who provided the information and later would help with distribution. It was not until later that we became concerned for the accuracy of those numbers, as it seemed some reasoned that by inflating their numbers, they got extra boxes! In one school I realized something was amiss when I got there as it looked smaller than their numbers had indicated. Tension mounted as a group of outside teenage boys came to start 'helping' with the unloading and I realized they were being instructed to take the boxes away. I had only one or two helpers, and I remember an uneasy fear, as I knew things were not going to end well. Quickly I stopped the unloading, put everything back into the truck and hurriedly left before the school staff realized what was happening.

Most often it was pure joy to see the excitement and happy smiles of the children opening their boxes. Many of these children had witnessed much violence over the past months, and the images of murder and death would take years to heal. For a few minutes the children could forget, they could play, they could laugh. Many of them had never received a gift, so poor were their families. The boxes were packed with toys, school supplies, small items of clothing and candy. I have a vivid memory of one young boy about five or six opening his box, and pulling out a pair of blue snow pants, very appropriate for the cold snowy winter and the unheated school rooms. But the amazing thing was that he was wearing a jacket that was the exact same colour of blue—a matching set! My eyes popped wide, and I could only think, "That was a 'God thing!'" In another box that same day a young hearing-impaired boy received a Walkman radio with earphones! Witnessing the joy day by day as we moved between classrooms could only lead me to conclude that God too was smiling, just as His heart was breaking for the pain that these innocent children had experienced.

Family Christmas Kosovo-style, December 1999

Christmas 1999 in Kosovo will always stand out as one of the most unique festive seasons our family has experienced. Our daughter Tera, in her final year of university, was able to come and join Bill, myself and Tim. Instead of the familiar trappings of commercial Christmas at home or carols playing in the malls, there were calls to prayer from the local mosque hovering in the crisp air, cozy visits by candlelight in friends' homes because of the frequent power outages and family participation in the shoe box gift giving.

There were still a few school distributions left, so one day our family plus a couple of translators went to a school that had been repaired by SP Canada to distribute five hundred gift boxes, most packed in Canada. The school age kids brought their pre-school siblings that day, most walking a long distance through the cold and snow. With the excited small brothers and sisters in tow, it was quite a sight for us to watch the parade of kids bound for school as we bounced and slid over the icy road-trail in our warm four-by-four! A few were brought to school by their fathers with a horse and sleigh, reminding me of the stories my mother told of their similar winter rides to the school house with blankets tucked around them. We noticed that the majority of the kids had no mittens, even though it had snowed heavily the previous days and the temperature was well below freezing. We hoped there would be mittens in some of the boxes! Once inside the school, we realized that our plan to have two large sessions in the main hall would have to be adjusted as the only heat was from the small woodstoves in each classroom. So we moved from one class to the next, bringing a short greeting from the children of Canada, watching them open their boxes and having the pleasure of them showing us the contents before moving on to the next class. We were pretty high ourselves by the time the rounds were complete!

For me this day was especially significant. The joy was seeing the change both in the appearance of the school and the morale of the children and teachers, as this was one of the schools that five months earlier I had assessed for damage and agreed that SP Canada would repair. It looked beautiful now, as did the other eight schools we repaired and the one that had been totally rebuilt. The day before, Tera and I had helped give out boxes in another of these schools, and I could hardly believe it was the same place! However, while the buildings looked good and the children had notebooks and pens, there were still no textbooks, visual aids, libraries, reference books or other equipment. The teachers' dedication was obvious as they worked with so little resource material, and still without pay.

On the way back home that afternoon, we went to the home of a farm family we knew to take shoe boxes for their pre-school children. This was a particularly traumatized family, as both the father and his brother had been shot right outside the gate to their family compound. The wives were threatened that if they tried to move the bodies someone else would be killed, so they were forced to leave the bodies untouched even when they fled the country. The stains from the blood could still be seen on the pavement, a gruesome testimony to the pain they had suffered. We again felt honoured to be bearers of happiness as we huddled around the small woodstove drinking Turkish coffee and watching those children's smiles when they opened their gifts.

On Christmas Eve we participated in the first-ever Christmas concert in the local cultural centre. Muslims, Catholics, Orthodox and Protestants together enjoyed the choirs and carols in one of the first outward displays of unity. Then we invited some of our Kosovar friends around the ages of our kids to watch the movie "Cool Runnings" that had been filmed in Calgary during the 1988 Olympics. The hilarious laughter was great therapy! Christmas Day brought more visits to the homes of new friends, and others to our place in the evening to introduce them to an almost-traditional Canadian Christmas dinner of stuffed roasted chicken and apple pie.

The last piece of the telemedicine puzzle

The University Medical Faculty was wired, the Gjakove referral hospital ready, and now the third piece of the pilot project would be the rural health centre. This proved to be the hardest of all. The health centre at Ponashec was chosen because World Health Organization wanted to make it a model health centre for family practice residents in an effort to train two thousand family physicians in the next few years. Internet access for medical information fit very well with the development of this program, another indication that this was just the right time. The limiting factor of the wireless radios was that they needed to have direct line of sight between the hospital and the health centre, which in a mountainous country was tricky. It meant climbing trees on hilltops to try and sight the health centre, slipping on the snowy roof of the health centre to install the high receiver, numerous trips over the snow-covered roads looking for a site for a repeater. One good snowfall brought a meter of snow and -27 C temperatures, making road travel difficult even on main roads, not to mention that none of our vehicles had block heaters!

Another issue that complicated this last part of the project was that the back roads were still full of landmines on the edges of the roads, which the retreating Serbs had left to blow up NATO tanks as they crossed the border back into Kosovo. Once the snow covered the roads it was hard to see where the edges were and the danger of driving on a landmine was real. One day when Tim was driving the vehicle to the health centre with Bill the deep snow-covered road was particularly treacherous. Bill was getting more and more agitated. "If you slip off this road one more time I am going to drive," he told Tim.

"Dad, if I slip off this road one more time you are welcome to drive!" he retorted. "And there is just as much risk of land mines getting out of the vehicle as sliding around the road."

The task was finally done, an antenna installed on the top of the City Hall building which had direct line of sight to the hospital, then a repeater from there to a location on a farmer's property and finally to the Ponashec health centre! This last part Tim completed after we left.

Bill was also very proud of the way Tim interacted with everyone from farmers to the Pristina University professors, his cross-cultural skill coming very naturally. The farmer's family where he installed the repeater enjoyed his visits, showing the typical Kosovar hospitality with a nice hot breakfast of freshly baked flat bread, the homemade sausage specialty that each family took pride in hanging in links above their stoves, their tasty white feta-like cheese and of course the obligatory sweet Turkish coffee that by now we had all grown to like! Their 'second breakfast' was around 10:00 am after morning chores, about the time Tim would show up!

The Gjakove hospital provided a room for a computer resource centre on the third floor and we wanted that to be a comfortable lounge for study and rest. Furnishing that with workstations, computers, some easy chairs and rugs was one of our last tasks before returning home. The computers had links to several medical journals, as well as the Faculty of Medicine in Calgary and Boston. Tim stayed another month to complete the connections with Ponashec health centre, and Brooks continued for several more months.

Our visit six months later was encouraging, with Arben running the resource room, a young nurse aid trained to help, and doctors coming in and out all day long researching medical information online and sending emails. All the doctors in the hospital had taken ten hours of training to learn to use the internet, and the nurses were to be next. Whereas their past had been characterized by misinformation, no information and isolation, they now wanted the ability to study, to find out the truth and to taste the freedom that brings. The Medical Faculty in Pristina was using their internet connection to be in touch with other universities in Calgary and the USA to develop their curriculum for their new Family Medicine residency program.

Our excitement at seeing this project completed was laced with sorrow too, as political autonomy was not to be quickly forthcoming. Hundreds of men were still held in prisoner of war camps in Serbia, and while we were there two young friends received sad news; one, that she was indeed a widow, the other that her husband was sentenced to remain among those imprisoned in Serbia. With two small children, she was devastated by the news. We had all been so hopeful for their release. Sadly, the eventual trial of these men and others like them dashed hopes even further, giving them all seven- to thirteen-year sentences. Many were not even fighters but had been abducted from their homes and never seen again.

The story of our telemedicine pilot project did have a happy ending though. Bill spent time discussing with International Organization for Migration (IOM) the possibility of them continuing the pilot project throughout the country, a request he also took to their Brussels headquarters. It was the G8 Summit year, with Kosovo rehabilitation a priority. At that summit the European Union agreed to take the example of our small pilot telemedicine project, interject several million Euro into it and connect the other six main centres with Pristina University Hospital! They too saw the benefit in a post-war or post-disaster scenario where all communication infrastructure is destroyed and where health care must be one of the first to be resurrected. This was the exact result we dreamed about but did not dare think possible.

I was amused to read one of my final Kosovo letters home, qualifying our work there:

> Lest you think that we are well trained or naturally gifted in any of this stuff, the proverbial learning curve has been huge and I fear we have more stubbornness than brains! Indeed, as we think back over the past two years when we came to Albania to help in the planning of health and education for a refugee camp, the knowledge and experience we have gained, the skills

we have somehow acquired, and the phenomenal people who have enriched our lives is truly amazing. We can only say thank you to our Lord for giving us this privilege, to our friends for their encouragement and to Samaritan's Purse for trusting us to attempt such an innovative idea. We also thank Tim for his part in this project, still giving us online help and advice almost daily. All in all, we feel that we have gained much more personally than we have ever given.

In 2014 we visited Kosovo again for the first time since late 2000. Not only did we meet up with friends like Labinot and his family, Bessa

---

We feel that we have gained much more personally than we have ever given.

---

and Helman, Atafete and Njazi in the new town centre, but we went to the hospital to see if the telemedicine project was continuing. Yes! The doctor who heads up telemedicine was summoned, and she took us to a large conference room set up with internet connections and a large screen where they had regular in-service sessions. That very afternoon, she explained, they would be having a telemedicine seminar live from Boston University Hospital. We went away elated!

The telemedicine chapter may not be finished...it has now moved to a project we are currently involved with in post-typhoon Tacloban, Philippines! In working with their newly rebuilt regional hospital to provide Continuing Medical Education specialists for their doctors and at the same time build CHE in communities, 'out of the blue' Bill was asked, "Would you have any experience with telemedicine? We are trying to facilitate better connection between the isolated rural health centres and the regional hospital."

"Well, yes, we could look at that!" was Bill's surprised reply. Never close the book on any of your past experience!

DISCUSS AND REFLECT:

1. When have you taken the small resources you had, launched out in faith with something you felt you should do, and just started? Were there surprises at how it carried on or who came alongside to help?

2. What strengths, experiences or resources do you have that you may not have thought could be useful in your present circumstances?

3. Did anything in these stories touch you or remind you of a story of your own?

4. Are there ideas or visions that you have put on hold because you thought you did not have the means to accomplish them?

CHAPTER 10

Whole Person, Whole Community, Whole World: An integrated approach to transformation

We are not now what we shall be, but we are on the way...at present, everything does not gleam and sparkle, but everything is being cleansed.

--Martin Luther

It Was Only a Simple Health Education Lesson!

I recognized the voice on the other end of the phone immediately. Mama J is what we all called her. She was a competent registered nurse and CHE training coordinator for one of the larger provinces of Papua New Guinea. With excited animation she told of a committee training the previous week in a community outside the provincial capital.

As is so common in PNG, a person can never expect to conduct training in a community with only the invited participants! No, typically half the village shows up and hangs in every window of the open-style church or community centre. After all, there are not many events to break the sameness of their village life and certainly no television for entertainment. The gate- crasher participants are usually respectfully quiet, laughing at all the appropriate places or quietly snickering when someone makes a comment that they find embarrassing or surprising.

Children giggle as they hear serious statements from the mouths of the adults. Such was the scene of the story Mama J was relaying to me on the telephone that day.

"I was just doing the *Dr Akia* lesson when it happened," Mama J began. This lesson is a story of an overworked doctor whose patients really could prevent most of the illnesses that they are bringing to poor Dr Akia for treatment. The participants are asked to use their understanding of prevention to decide which of the patients in the story could have prevented their illness either at home or with the help of a nurse at the local health centre.

Mama J had told the story, then as usual handed each participant a cut-out picture of a person bearing the label of an illness: measles, typhoid, pneumonia, alcoholism etc. She had pictures of three possible treatment facilities at the front of the room—the doctor's office, the local health centre and a home. Each participant was asked to walk to the front, tell the illness of their patient and place it at one of the three pictures based on whether or not it was preventable.

As she described the scene to me, it seemed that all went as planned until a young man stood up with his picture figure. Instead of placing it at one of the three facilities he began to sob. Great big man-size tears were streaming down his face as the whole room, along with the window gazers went totally silent. Such a culturally unusual spectacle in a macho setting like this one—a grown man crying in front of his community!

After a few moments he began to speak. "I am holding in my hand a picture of a pregnant woman," he stated, eyes cast downward, face wet with tears. "I am feeling so sorry for her! I am one of those guys who has made young women pregnant but not taken any responsibility for the baby. I am so sorry, and I want to ask this community to forgive me."

"Well you would not have believed what happened next," Mama J continued. "And I tell you, honestly I did not say a thing!"

"What happened?" I asked, not sure what to expect from the volatile Highlander community where she was conducting the workshop. They could have lynched the guy right on the spot. Emotions run wild in situations like this.

"The whole room started to cry!" she said, hardly able to keep her own voice from breaking. "Everyone had something to confess and ask forgiveness for. Even the ones hanging in the windows were crying. Soon they were on their knees on the floor, asking God to forgive them and to heal the ugliness in their community. And I tell you the truth, Sharon, it was just a simple health lesson! There was nothing spiritual even said, no mention of God at all."

"Mama J," I said quietly, my tears flowing now. "You didn't need to say anything—God was already at work before you got there. You have by your very presence, brought the Kingdom of God into that community. Your humility and desire to do His work has given Him permission to speak into the hearts of these dear tender people. You have done a great thing for them, just being there and giving them opportunity to speak about important life issues."

"I guess this is an example of why we use the facilitation method," she added. "Being Learner Centered, is all about them, not me. My whole lesson was side-tracked by their need to deal with some deeply rooted community problems!"

"Yes, and by recognizing their own problems they will do something about them," I added.

From the inside out, that is the process of change. Learner Centered, Self Discovery, Action Oriented. Words that we had taught were now more than theory for Mama J and the other trainers she would go on to influence. Individuals impact their communities with small changes spilling over to create ripples of transformation that will gradually spread to other communities and bring societal change.

Pastor Joe: why didn't they tell us sooner?

The words of this simple but confident Papua New Guinean village leader had taken a few moments to sink in. As a lump rose in my throat I finally blurted out, "I am so sorry Pastor Joe. Please could I ask forgiveness on behalf of my generation of white people that came to PNG?"

Pastor Joe had been in a Training of Trainers workshop we conducted a few months previous and had become a Community Health Education trainer in his community. He was anxious to have us visit and see the changes and to commend them for the natural beauty their village now highlighted. It had taken no money to clean their common spaces, to plant vegetable gardens close to their homes, to fence the pigs outside the village, to grow colourful hedges of flowers. But the hard work of digging the fishponds that were fed by the clear stream meandering down the hill between large boulders was clearly impressive as well as beautiful. They were proud of the results of their labour and delighted to see our amazement.

As we strolled about the community, we asked Joe what he had observed of other changes in the health of the community. His face grew serious as he told us how diarrhea and respiratory illness had decreased among the children and how appreciative the mothers were to know the simple prevention measures. Their time was more productively spent now that trips to the clinic for medicine were infrequent. They were amazed that the simple changes had such impact.

Then out of the clear blue Joe dropped his own story. "You know," he confided as he paused in his steps, "I worked for twenty years as a pastor for the mission. The white family lived in the house I now live in right over there." He motioned towards the tidy white house not far from where we stood. "What puzzled all of us," he continued, "was that their children did not seem to get the same sicknesses as our children, and none of their children died while many of ours did. We wondered what the difference was. We talked about this all the time among ourselves. Finally, after much discussion, we decided that they had a secret they were hiding inside their house. We often looked for the secret, but we never found it."

He was looking sad now as he had shared something so brutally honest, and I felt my own tears coming to the surface. He was talking about me, about us. Is that how we had been perceived with our own happy, healthy children who we raised in this country?

"Sure, they helped us out when we were sick," he went on, "taking us to hospital or giving us medicine. But now we know there was no secret. It was simple prevention like how to drink clean water, hand washing, nutrition and immunization. Why did they not teach us these things twenty years earlier? Why did so many children have to die first?

Why was spiritual training seen as all that was important?" He was not speaking in anger, but genuinely questioning.

My mind raced as I replayed the years that we too, had been here in PNG, right nearby in fact, at the early part of those twenty years he was talking about. We had both been busy, Bill administering the health of the province with all the facilities and staff, I helping to organize continuing medical education for the rural health workers and raising our kids. All good, but top down, outside-in health fixes. Nobody was analyzing why the health education of the trained professionals never filtered down into the homes where the mothers needed it more desperately than anyone. Yes, we thought of training pastors, and started the Village Level Worker School around that time, but it was not a model that could readily multiply into the remote villages. A few like the Tainoraba village which the French consultant had termed the "good witch doctor village", were changed. But we had no system-wide approach as we did now with CHE, which Stan Rowland was quietly developing in Africa at about this same time, mid-1980's.

How I wished to give an answer, to justify. But there was no answer, just gut-wrenching silence. All I could offer was an empty apology, quietly spoken from a tight throat and a tearful face. I see the scene as clearly as I did then: the grave expression on his face, the beautiful village that was now what it should have been twenty years before, the former mission house still standing with its own secrets, the question hanging in the void between us—"Why did we have to wait so long to understand how to become physically as well as spiritually healthy?"

The God-Factor: the language of love

The questions that Pastor Joe asked will not go away because there are still churches and mission groups around the world that believe their mandate is just spiritual change, and that automatic physical or social transformation will follow. Jesus did not see it that way. His mandate?

> He has chosen me to proclaim good news to the poor (good news is not just spiritual)

To heal the broken hearted (that seems like emotional, social, mental health)

To announce pardon to prisoners (of all kinds)

And recovery of sight to the blind (blindness can be worldview as well as physical)

To set the burdened and battered free (this includes all who suffer from inequality)

To announce, "This is God's year to act!"[88] (There is urgency in His call)

One of the most famous of Jesus' stories is the Parable of the Good Samaritan[89]. It was told to illustrate the deeper meaning of a question asked by an expert in the Jewish law, "What must I do to inherit eternal life?" He knew the answer well, and recited it back to Jesus: "Love the Lord your God with all your heart (emotional), your soul (spiritual), your strength (physical) and your mind (mental), and love your neighbour as yourself (social)." This looks like the whole person in the World Health Organization definition of health: 'a state of complete physical, social, mental and spiritual well-being, not just the absence of disease.'

The lawyer appears to have known the answers well enough, so why did he ask? He knew the information, but he did not know how to apply it, how to let it transform the way he lived. He got stuck on the semantics, "so who is my neighbour?" Information, but no transformation. Head knowledge had not migrated to a heart change.

When Jesus had told him the story of the three responses to an injured man lying on the roadside, it was obvious which one was a neighbour. "The one who showed mercy," the lawyer correctly observed. But so deep was the animosity towards their 'enemy clan,' the Samaritans, that he did not even dare to speak the word. Like the Kosovo children in the refugee camp, the idea of helping an enemy was unthinkable. Yet this is what Jesus was asking the young lawyer to do as an indication that the Word of God had truly gone deep into his soul, deep enough to transform his mindset and then his actions.

We believe that Jesus' teaching is transformative. If we could only apply our belief—that 'health' really is harmony in all aspects of life. This is Hebrew *'shalom'* which includes not only harmony with God and with self and with our community, but extends beyond our own tribe to include every person, especially those different from us, and beyond that to the world of nature.

Faith-Based or Secular: collaboration not competition

Another piece of the multiplication puzzle is directed towards organizations—a variety of groups working cooperatively rather than as competitors. We see this cooperation sometimes during natural disaster rehabilitation or disease epidemics such as HIV/AIDS or the Ebola epidemic in West Africa. Such epidemics seem like war, and war is a time for collaboration and cooperation on all fronts—not arguing over motives or elitist attitudes but acknowledging with gratitude the efforts of the other. The necessity to work together to fight a common enemy becomes paramount. With each group working hard at what they do best, we are able to see with new clarity the continuum of relief to development, the need for both treatment and prevention, expertise in community engagement and organizational advocacy.

Yet during the Ebola response in 2015 we heard cynics questioning the motives of medical mission doctors who have committed their lives to serve the medically underserved of Africa and in so doing exposing themselves to the disease. Others wondered why the Christian groups were the main ones stepping up to the plate to help.

In an article in *Slate* magazine,[90] author Brian Palmer even queries the reliability of the mission doctors, who work in adverse and under-resourced conditions. The lack of trust seems to be justifiable, he infers, because they rarely publish their accomplishments in the journals of the ivory towers of academia! When they explain to patients that they are motivated by the love of Jesus rather than financial gain, somehow that is 'proselytizing'. Would it be nobler, I wondered, if doctors were there to seek danger pay or the desire for adventure or fame? These are unproductive and unfounded arguments by critics who clearly have their own axes to grind, and at a time when a world crisis calls for everyone to roll up their sleeves and get to work in solving problems plaguing us all.

Surely all the relief and development organizations that are out there in the world can come to the same conclusion on this one thing— everybody is needed in order to fight diseases such as Ebola, HIV/AIDS, Coronavirus or Tuberculosis, every agency has strengths that will add to the synergy of the whole. Whether faith-based, national government or secular NGO, all have been trained in similar techniques and scientific methods. Collaboration is what is needed in order for groups that are stronger to support those that are less resourced to achieve a common goal.

Faith-based organizations have a critical role to play in long-term development. From all quarters we are hearing that resilient communities must be the baseline from which health and development occurs. There must be community voice and ownership. This is where faith-based organizations like Medical Ambassadors shine. They walk long term with a community from the initial engagement until the community begins to understand its own issues and becomes proactive in finding solutions from within the community rather than from the outside.

In his recent book, *Shrewd Samaritan: Faith, Economics, and the Road to Loving Our Global Neighbor*[91], economist Bruce Wydick shares his academic research on the impact of all types of aid in poverty reduction. This includes research on the age-old question: does faith make a difference in economic outcomes? He cites a 2016 study, the first genuinely unbiased research conducted to determine any evidence of the impact of including spiritual values with health and livelihood training in increasing household income. International Care Ministries, with their four month 'Transform' program in the Philippines, agreed to randomly select communities for the experiment and conduct their program with and without the evangelical spiritual aspects. The 6,276 participating families were surveyed six months after completing the teaching program, and those receiving the spiritual along with the other teaching showed 9.2 percent increase in household income over the control groups. We recently had the pleasure of meeting their epidemiologist in Manila who confirmed the validity of the research. It also confirmed again to us the value of the similar work we have been focused on with the Medical Ambassadors' CHE approach.

These integrated approaches that address spiritual and social issues as well as physical and educational, provide for a firm base of development that encompasses the whole person and the whole community. While these represent prevention and development, other groups such as Samaritan's Purse and Doctors Without Borders (MSF) are experts in relief. Often the first responders on the ground in medical emergencies, we commend and support them for their professional work. They are resourced well and able to set up quickly to bring essential relief.

Groups that remain for the long haul, who know the leaders well and appreciate the culture and difficulties of everyday life, are in a good position to facilitate deeper community conversations. Mission hospitals and medical training institutions are in this category, with long histories of significant impact, dedication and passionate staff. It is true that these hospitals may suffer from lack of funds and equipment, but the government facilities in these countries are even less resourced. All of them could use encouragement and help from other groups, whether inside or outside the country. Especially since world expertise has emerged from such mission hospitals, as we mentioned earlier.

We are reminded of Catholic orders like that of Mother Teresa and her Sisters of Charity. It has been documented that the first large hospital was founded by St. Basil in 369, and thousands of Benedictine monasteries were known to treat the sick throughout the following centuries.[92]

Finally we must not forget the dedicated local community health workers and volunteers in communities all over the world. From the earliest written history of epidemics, such as the plagues during the time of the Roman Empire, we read about Christians who formed what became a recognized order, the 'Parabolani'. Known as 'the reckless ones', they stayed in the cities to voluntarily care for the sick and bury the dead in spite of the personal risks. Meanwhile, the more privileged citizenry fled to the countryside.[93]

Neighbours helping neighbours—these in the end will be the anonymous, but very essential heroes. From the highest levels of technology and medical science to the simple acts of neighbourliness, all are essential parts of this collaboration called health care.

In the eye of the beholder: Who determines the indicators of success?

The times are changing; words and their meanings are changing; understanding of appropriate development is changing; countries manage their health issues differently. How then can we ever hope to see collaboration among organizations or standardized methods for transformation?

World Health Organization tells us that the most important one thousand days of a person's life are from conception to two years of age, and we must focus more on all the complexities of this time period for the future generation to be healthy, intelligent and peaceful. The infant mortality rate and health status of the under-two age is a good measure of an effective health care system and predictor of a future stable society. Yet even though new programs like our 'First 1000 Days' CHE teaching module involve education and little money, health departments still pour most of their resources into clinical care and specialized referral hospitals. A disconnect? Indeed there is no quick return on investment when it takes twenty years for an infant to grow up, but if we know that poor nutrition and nurture at this critical stage will impair cognitive development and productivity of the next generation, can we afford to ignore it?

The HIV/AIDS crises, while far from over and seemingly on the rise in some countries like Philippines and Papua New Guinea, has been somewhat controlled by collaborative efforts from every sector of government, non-governmental organizations and faith groups. Education and the availability of anti-retroviral treatments have been given credit, but we know the long hours of work by countless volunteers are likely more significant. Government departments and agencies cannot possibly hope to achieve the results that they look for without those boots and bare feet on the ground. Community Health Educators, peer volunteers with their ears and eyes on their communities, can hold the key to the future health of their countries.

These are also the people who can tell us the real measurements of change. World Health Organization gave us Millennium Development

Goals and then Sustainable Development Goals, all with their indicators of success. But the people who know what really measures change in their places are those that live there. In Pastor Joe's community the missionaries had probably met their mission's criteria for success; the people knew that nothing had changed inside their own homes.

A Healthy Community: "it is the sounds we hear at night"

We have taught trainers, community leaders and committee members to write clear vision and mission statements, to state goals for their desired change as outputs, outcomes and impacts. But while the exercise is helpful, the statements are usually filed away and rarely looked at again. They seem to have little relevance to real life.

Communities know when they are truly flourishing, not just physically but socially, spiritually and emotionally. We were fascinated when we were told that how they feel at night is the real measurement of transformation—they know when they feel secure and when they feel fearful. In that most houses are not very strongly built, a trust of each other in the neighbourhood is essential. For the children, being part of a big extended family that watches out for them gives ease to both them and their mothers. If girls feel safe walking to school they will attend, if not they drop out. Freedom from fear of violence is the sign that a society is functioning.

We asked a researcher who was studying the CHE communities in PNG what was the first sign to her that a community had changed since pursuing the first phases of the CHE program. "Oh, it is very obvious," she answered. "It is the sounds we hear in the evening. In many places the night is filled with the sounds of arguing and fighting in the homes and from men out drinking in the village. Now we hear the soft voices of families talking together over their evening meal, or strumming a guitar and singing, or laughing children playing before bedtime. And now we can hear the sounds of the insects and birds."

In another village, a man told us "It is the smell of the air! It smells so sweet now with flowers everywhere, not the pig and people feces and garbage smells like before!"

And from an old man, "In the same way as we want our spirits to be clean, we realize we need our physical bodies and environment to be clean." Notice the link between the physical and the spiritual and the environmental—and the seamless, natural way that the old man integrated all of them! Who in our world would ever describe an indicator of spiritual change by talking about personal cleanliness? Or building latrines or planting flowers with sweet perfume for that matter? Maybe the quiet hum of dozens of families having evening prayers would be convincing, but the smell of the air? Not likely!

> *Who in our world would name personal cleanliness as an indicator of spiritual change? Or the smell of the air or the sounds at night? Yet how seamlessly these people have integrated them.*

We asked a similar question to a community in Cambodia. They listed a few things, mostly social, environmental and nutritional changes that they had noticed. We were amused but pleased by one comment: "Only two thick-headed men beat their wives now, while before they all did. We are all working on those two and they are sure to quit!"

In some countries, like Philippines and Papua New Guinea, governments have offered 'Clean and Green' or 'Healthy Community' awards as motivation for change. These come with specific achievements, such as the number of homes meeting the ten criteria for a Healthy Home, as described in the Sava story in Chapter two, along with evidence of environmental clean-up, beautification and addressing adverse social or cultural issues. A sign-board identifying the community as healthy or green is a great source of pride. The children grow up forming healthy habits that enable them to influence any community they move to as an adult. In Papua New Guinea the CHE trainers have endeavoured to make it a meaningful goal by making sure it takes group effort to attain. There, a rural highlands community is healthy if:

1. 85% of homes have healthy home certificates
2. All school age children attend school
3. Committee meets regularly and takes leadership
4. CHEs have regular training meetings, and share what they learn with other families
5. Safe drinking water is available, or drinking water is boiled

6. Community law enforcement
7. No cultivation of marijuana
8. Churches cooperate or have some joint meetings
9. HIV/AIDS teaching understood; compassionate care of persons living with HIV/AIDS
10. Animals are fenced out of homes or in pens
11. Clan disputes are resolved peacefully, no warfare
12. Negative cultural issues are addressed eg. Sorcery, burdensome funeral rites, polygamy
13. Reasonable access to a health care facility
14. Economic improvement; some cash crops

Whatever form of evaluation is used to measure results, the community must see it as their own. They have put in the effort to change, the statistics are theirs, the pride is theirs and they must also see that the benefit is theirs. If photos or numbers are used for reporting to donors or raising more funds for staff and administrative costs, this must be clearly explained. Many have felt used by outside organizations who move on to other projects and places because of the community's successful results. They are left behind, better off than before but often feeling once more forgotten. Outsiders need integrity and sensitivity to these dynamics, and care not to use the community's stories of success (or poverty for that matter) for their own or their organization's benefit. Even so, if the community motivators or champions remain and the committees or associations carry on, the positive changes we have described as 'place-building' will continue. Generations of children will grow into healthy and well-educated adults.

What about communities where initial great strides do not carry on, as described in chapter two? We know the memories of cooperative efforts and of achieving goals together for common benefit will keep coming back. For the many committee members and other leaders who have learned new social and management skills, the benefit spills over into other areas of work and life. Ideas like learning to set personal goals, critical thinking and decision-making skills are relevant to getting along in communities as well as in families. Efforts are not wasted when leaders learn to live peacefully in relationship with God, with each other and with their environment. No training is ever wasted, and while not all seeds will fall on good soil, many will. Those who prepare the soil and scatter good seed believe that God can make growth happen even in unlikely places. Indeed, this is the hope that keeps us from becoming disillusioned with slow responsiveness, apparent failure or false starts. It provides the grit that keeps us moving.

What have we learned that we will pass on?

As I summarize some of our life-long learning, there are now a few contexts and even faces to put on the words that follow. We have been privileged over the course of our lives to observe healthy change as we have walked with communities of the world. The stories we have given voice to encompass places like Papua New Guinea, Nepal, Kosovo, India and countries of Southeast Asia. Each is unique, but we have learned common themes:

1. Ideas matter. Their consequences reach beyond individuals to their community, society and ultimately the world. It is futile to fight against cultural beliefs to alleviate poverty, or to introduce healthy changes when a core belief system prevents change or says it is wrong to interfere with another's fate or to anger a spirit. We may challenge them to think through these ideas that block development, but in the end they decide.

2. Listening is far upstream from telling or doing. Learning to listen comes before any other communication. We need to listen with our hearts more than our ears, to every sector of society. Listen especially for the gentle whisper of God.

3. The gift of our presence, given consistently and at appropriate times, is of greater worth than money or words of advice. Never give up on people; become a friend of time.

4. Individuals and communities know most of the answers to their own problems, and even how to find the resources to solve them. What often lacks is the mindset to change, trust of each other and connections. Outsiders' roles are to respect them and to challenge them to move forward.

5. Communities must be willing to take ownership of change or our efforts are premature at best. Unless we see examples of

cohesiveness, of local champions to stir motivation from within, a respected leadership structure and an invitation to engage, we need to wait.

6. We should work behind the scenes but with willingness to go right to the top to advocate for those who cannot speak on their own. The credit is best given to others.

7. There are no 'unequal people'. All are made in God's image with equal worth and dignity, having unique contributions to make for the common good. No person should remain outside the margins of their own people. If we do not believe this or still live with the misconception of class or gender inequality, we do so to the detriment of our world.

8. We must not carry a load that belongs to another; do 'with others' not 'for them' to avoid dependency and to give agency and respect to the abilities and creativity that all possess.

9. There is power in the group process, the synergy of collective minds united to solve their own problems. This is more powerful than the intellectual solutions of the great planners of the world.

10. Collaboration among all groups, both faith-based and secular, is the only way we will see solutions to the massive problems of the world. Differences must be laid aside, problems tackled from an integrated perspective as we recognize each group's strengths.

11. Belonging is in the heart of all people. Making or having a place to feel secure is a basic human need. There is beauty and love to be found there—even slum dwellers strive to make beauty, to develop community and to see themselves as capable creative beings.

12. It is not access to resources that determines health, but a sense of belonging and a desire to live in harmony in the four essential relationships: self, God, others and the environment. A person's physical health can improve when embraced by a loving family and supportive community, adding quality and length of life to even the terminally ill.

13. We all possess far more than we think we do. No experience or ability is to be wasted; everything is a gift to be built upon

and ultimately to share. Generosity is within reach of anyone who would be liberated from the shackles of a poverty mind-set—both those who see themselves as poor and those who see themselves as rich.

14. When we feel we should do something, we need to make a start. Then persevere. Gaining momentum and inviting others aboard is easier when the vehicle is in motion.

15. We are integrated and relational beings, not just the sum of many parts. Physical, social, spiritual, emotional, economic, environmental realities are so intertwined they defy single-focus solutions. The communities we are part of are both diverse and uniform, and must be treated as a whole rather than working only with specific groups. Likewise, people and place intersect; the biodiversity of each environment is to be valued, protected and preserved in order to sustain our unique cultural and physical world.

16. Always go to the edges, to the margins of society, and reach those on the outside. Let there be no more exclusion of those we call 'marginalized' until all find a place inside.

Making sense of life through the lens of life

The stories of your life may not span the distances and cultures that ours have, but they are interesting, fun and worth reflection because they are important in the uniqueness of you. There were important junctions, footsteps to follow, intentional and unintentional decisions. In order to make sense out of our lives and to keep growing and contributing, an understanding of some of these dynamics is valuable. I encourage you to reflect on your life in these terms. One of my writer-mentors warned about "trying to make more sense out of our life than it really makes" as a precaution against over-analyzing! Good advice—be positive, focus on the helpful and healthy.

The learning, growing and contributing does not need to stop even when age might seem a limiting factor. Our focus may become smaller or closer to home, but sharper and more clearly defined by the lens of life. Being 'retired' need not mean perpetual holidays or simply living whatever the day happens to bring without purpose or focus. Strategic planning is hard enough when it comes to projects, but when it means ordering our lives it may seem impossible.

Without it though, some of the best years of our lives could be underutilized. Giving some time to intentional solitude each year to evaluate our strengths and plans within the parameters of our health, could bring to the surface exciting opportunities to utilize the gifts and experiences that should not be tucked away prematurely. Close friends are helpful with this exercise, as they often identify strengths we do not see.

I started out to write about what we have learned through living and working in communities around the world, ideas that might be important enough to pass on to the next generation. As I have returned to re-live these stories, I see all of life with more clarity. Even the seemingly disjointed parts are unified by common strands, like single differentiated threads running through a weaving.

The one unifying and motivating thread which Bill and I mutually strive for and which we hope comes through clearly yet simply, is "to love God and enjoy Him forever and to love our neighbours as ourselves."

"So do you feel you have been successful?"

This question was posed to me by Dr. John Payne, MAI past-president, after he had read the draft manuscript of this book. It prompted me to ask another question, "What really is success?"

Mother Teresa was apparently asked how she could feel successful in continuing to work in such abject poverty where many of her beneficiaries did not even survive. Her response? "God has not called me to be successful. He has called me to be faithful." That simple statement has had powerful impact on us over years of questioning what true success means.

It is not hard to define success by numerical data or attainment of results-based goals we set for ourselves. However, if our lifework is to pass on responsibility to others it becomes more complicated because we may never see the results. So the real question is not whether we have been successful in reaching our goals but whether we have been faithful in pursuing them. Have we simply been faithful to our commitments to do what we feel is right, with or without our pre-defined results? Are we faithful with the gifts of our time, our words, our ability to share what we have and know, faithful to encourage people around us?

I recently read a comment from an obscure but faithful worker among street youth. When asked about the admirable accomplishments of his efforts he replied, "It's not about what you accomplish, it is what you set into motion that matters. What you accomplish is short-lived. What you set into motion can last for generations." In other words, it is the ripples that are more important than the momentary splash, and we may never know where the ripples end.

If this focus seems backwards to how our world measures success, it might be a good indication that Mother Teresa had it right. And if faithfulness to our calling is truly what God values, that is ultimate success.

Discuss and Reflect:

1. Has this chapter given insight into looking at our problems from an integrated, whole-person perspective rather than only one piece at a time?

2. If you were asked to list ten criteria or indicators of 'whole health' in your own life and home, what would they be? How do you rate?

3. Which in the list of life lessons might you take away and apply in your life or world?

4. What do you value as important to be faithful in pursuing? How much do you consider or desire what God values in your present or future decisions?

ACKNOWLEDGEMENTS

I am grateful for the friends who have encouraged me to write these life-lesson stories, beginning with Scott Simpson, son of lifelong friends Steve and Vicky. On a visit to Papua New Guinea Scott suggested we should write a book on the ten most important cross-cultural lessons we have learned that might help younger people like himself.

Then came Karen Mains, whose own books have inspired many and who still coaches budding writers. She was on the Medical Ambassadors International Board and when exposed to our stories, urged me to write. She took the time to come from Chicago to visit us in Canada to motivate me to get started and then pushed me to keep at it. Our phone calls and emails have honed ideas and kept the inspiration alive, which surely would have waned as the seemingly endless project continued.

Bill Bunn is a local professor-writer who started a community writer's group where we live in Millarville, Alberta. The group has seen several published books each year. Without these encouragers telling me that the pieces I read to them were interesting and giving feedback on some of the sections, I may have given up.

To all the people whose lives have touched ours in all the countries where we have worked or visited, a simple thank you for what they have taught us seems totally understated. These are their stories, the heroes of this book and our life-shapers. My desire has been to amplify their voices that have much to tell our world.

Thank you to friends who read parts or all of the manuscript to give valuable feedback. First were Kathryn Hettler, then Sheila Rowe who read the whole manuscript, skilfully correcting and making insightful comments all the way through. Next Steve and Vicky Simpson also took the time to read it thoroughly. With their expertise in working both outside Canada and in post-graduate educational circles, they asked good questions and made suggestions for clarity and accuracy. Finally our good friends and colleagues in Medical Ambassadors International, Dr. John and Madelle Payne, both did a comprehensive read with John's art of asking good questions and Madelle's copy-editor thoroughness. I cannot say enough to thank such amazing friends.

As organizations, Medical Ambassadors International and Medical Ambassadors Canada have been a joy to work with over these years, sharing our own visions and planting new ones as a good team should. We could never have acquired the riches of such deep friendships spanning the globe that have resulted from interactions with the Regional Coordinators, staff and Board members.

Most of all, my husband Bill has been the stalwart supporter and contributor of ideas for these stories as he waited patiently for a book to materialize. Our partnership and friendship through the adventures of life has taught us interdependence as we draw strength from each other and from our Master teacher, Jesus. I have only penned the words, but together we have lived life along a road dotted with fellow travellers who all deserve our heartfelt thanks. Finally, our two children Tim and Tera-Lynn (Jones) have lived many parts of these pages alongside us, and we thank you for being patient with us as we dragged you into strange parts of the world. Thank you for telling us you enjoyed it!

To our grandchildren: Brodie, Penny and Nora Bieber, Jaidee and Zaia Jones. We have crafted these words for you and your friends, the future generation that can take the values and knowledge of God's Kingdom until it transforms the world.

Proceeds from the sale of this book will be donated to Medical Ambassadors International (see www.medicalambassadors.org) and Medical Ambassadors of Canada Association (see www.medambassadors.com)

Connect and interact with Sharon by email: bieber@platinum.ca

NOTES

Chapter One: Worldview Matters: Good witch doctor, bad witch doctor

1. Available online http://www.data.worldbank.org/indicator
2. *End of the Spear*, is a 2005 docudrama that recounts the story of Operation Auca (Auca meant 'naked savage', which is how this most feared and treacherous tribe was known). In 1956 five American male missionaries were speared to death while making first contact with the Waodani people group in the jungles of Ecuador. The story is told by Steve Saint, along with Mincaye, the man who had killed his father, Nate Saint. Steve was 5 years old at the time. He returned when he was 9 and each summer thereafter, to stay with his Aunt Rachel Saint, the older sister of his father. Her commitment and love for the Waodani was unquestioned, as she lived with them until her death in 1994. An earlier documentary movie, "Beyond Gates of Splendor," produced in 1967, was based on the best-selling book by Elizabeth Elliot, *Through Gates of Splendor,* 1957 and her second book, *The Savage My Kinsman.*
3. Zent, Stanford, "The Political Ecology of Ethnic Frontiers and Relations among the Piaroa of the Middle Orinoco." Available online http://www.academia.edu/466090/ In this paper Zent explains that despite sometimes being described as one of the world's most peaceful societies, modern anthropologists report that the external relations of the Piaroa tribe with neighbouring tribes are actually "unfriendly, marked by physical or magical warfare". Violent conflict erupted between the Piaroa and neighbours, for example, to control the clay pits of the Guanay valley, being the best clay for making pottery in the region. Constant warfare also exists between the Piaroa and Caribs, who invaded Piaroa territory from the east in search of captives. More recent history of the tribe includes the struggles for land rights and attempts to demarcate their traditional boundaries to register with the government.
4. Mangalawadi, Vishal. *The Book that Made Your World: how the Bible created the soul of Western civilization*. Nashville: Thomas Nelson Inc., 2011
5. Miller, Darrow. *Discipling Nations: The Power of Truth to Transform Cultures.* Seattle: YWAM Publishing, 1998.

6. Ibid. p 36
7. Ibid. p 38
8. Mark 12:29-31, NIV Translation.
9. *Sahih Muslim, Kitab al-Iman, 67-1,* Hadith no.45
10. Volf, Miroslav. *Allah: A Christian Response.* Harper Collins e-books. 2014. In the first chapter, Miroslav discusses the 'Open Letter' from Muslim scholars to Pope Benedict XVI after his 2006 Regensburg speech which had angered the Muslim community. They point by point refuted his statements, and concluded with a surprising "common essence" of both faiths as stated in the Two Great Commandments of Jesus. (page 27) A year later, he explains, a second letter by the same group, titled, 'A Common Word Between Us and You,' again reiterates this point. The issue of God-as-reason and God-as-pure-will, though, which the Pope says differentiate the two understandings of God, was sidestepped.

<u>Chapter Two</u>: Listen to the People: Engaging the community on its own terms

11. Bonhoeffer, Dietrich. *Life Together.* pp.42-44. New York: Harper & Row Publishers, Inc., 1954. First published in Germany in 1939 under the title Gemeinsames Leben
12. Documentary available online https://press.discovery.com/us/own/press-releases/2014/own-oprah-winfrey-network-air-10-part-documen-3014/
13. Acts 17:26-27 (NIV Translation). In describing God's involvement in shaping all cultures, Paul attests that there is significance in culture. "God did this so that they would seek for him and perhaps reach out for him and find him, though he is not far from any one of us."
14. Proverbs 31:8,9 NIV
15. World Health Organization Western Pacific Region, *Healthy Cities- Healthy Islands,* Document Series No. 11, WHO Publication, Manila, 2000.
16. "Church Health Services need support." *The National,* April 14, 2015. Available online www.national.com.pg
17. *PNG Vision 2050 Document.* Available online http://www.scribd.com.
18. StaRS. "National Strategy for Responsible Sustainable Development for Papua New Guinea 2nd Edition." PDF. Department of National Planning and Monitoring. Available online http://www.planning.gov.pg
19. Exodus 3:7-
20. Psalm 46:10
21. Matthew 5:8

22. Nicholson and Lee, eds. *The Oxford Book of English Mystical Verse*. 1917. From 'Aurora Leigh' by Elizabeth Barrett Browning (1806-1861).

23. Ernesto Sirolli: Want to help someone? Shut up and listen! TED talk/ TED.com

Chapter Three: Leader as Follower: We did it ourselves

24. Olson, Bruce. *Bruchko*. Creation House, 1978, pp 130-134. Print

Chapter Four: Living Beyond the Tribe: And the leaders that inspired us

25. Wilson, Dorothy Clarke. *Ten Fingers for God: The Life and Work of Dr. Paul Brand*. Publication City: Paul Brand Publishing, 1965.

26. *Clezy*, Ken. *Now in Remission: a surgical life*. Kent Town, Australia: Wakefield Press, 2011

27. Elliot, Elizabeth. *Through Gates of Splendor*. Harper and Brothers, 1957 first printing. The book tells the story of the murder of her husband and four companions in Ecuador in 1956.

28. Tawali, Kumalau. "Caring, sharing and society," in *The National*, March 1994.

Chapter Five: Equal Dignity: How much is she worth?

29. 1 Corinthians 14:34;

30. 1 Corinthians 14:34-35

31. CCunningham, Loren; Hamilton, David. *Why Not Women?* Seattle: YWAM Publishing, 2000, p 177.

32. 1 Peter 3:7

33. 3Ali, Ayaan Hirsi. *Heretic: Why Islam Needs a Reformation Now*. New York: Harper Collins Publishers, 2015.

34. Ibid. p 41

35. Wikipedia. "Polygamy in Islam." Available from http://www.wikipedia.org/ polygny_in_Islam

36. Ali, *Heretic*. p.129-131

37. http://www.theguardian.com/society/2014/feb/06/what-is-female-genital-mutilation-where-happen

38. "Religious views on female genital mutilation." Available from http://www.wikipedia.org

39. Ibid.

40. Jha, Preeti. "Southeast Asia's Hidden Female Genital Mutilation Challenge." *The Diplomat,* August 21, 2019.
41. UNICEF Data by topic, "Female genital mutilation (FGM)". Available from http://www.data.unicef.org.
42. Ibid.
43. Tlozek, Eric. "Papua New Guinea Mothers use baby bracelets to reduce newborn deaths." *ABC News,* 27 April 2018. Available from http://www.abc.net.au.
44. Ibid.
45. Selk, Avi. "A Nepali Teen died after she was banished to a hut for having her period." *The Washington Post,* December 20, 2016.
46. Ibid.
47. Kaur, Gagandeep. "Banished for Menstruating: the Indian women isolated while they bleed." The Guardian, 22 December 2015.
48. The Foundation for AIDS Research (amfAR)(2015). *"Statistics: Women and HIV/AIDS"*
49. Wikipedia. "European Witch-hunts", Origins. Available from Rationalwiki. org/wiki/European_witch-hunts.
50. Clark, Helen. "Sorcery and Sexism in Papua New Guinea". *The Diplomat,* June 2015.
51. *www.theguardian.com>World>PapuaNewGuinea.*
52. www.Amnesty.org/en/countries/asia-and-the-pacific/papua-new-guinea/report-papua-new-guinea.
53. https://www.hrw.org/world-report/2015/country-chapters/papua-new-guinea.
54. Bills and legislation archive.
55. "97 convicted in mass trial for PNG 'sorcery' killings. *Radio New Zealand News, Jan.16,2018.* Web.
56. Wakpi, Emma. "Haunted," *PNG Attitude, 2012.* This piece won the 2012 Crocodile Essay Award and the PNG Chamber of Mines and Petroleum Prize for Essays and Journalism.
57. Kristof, Nicholas and WuDunn, Sheryl. *Half the Sky: Turning Oppression into Opportunity for Women Worldwide.* Random House Books, 2009. Print.
58. Caprino, Kathy. "Why Women's Oppression is the Moral Dilema of our Time: Sheryl WuDunne Speaks Out." *Forbes Magazine, August 29, 2013.*
59. Molo, G., Kirby, B. "Discrepancies between national maternal mortality data and international estimates: The experience of Papua New Guinea." *Reproductive Health Matters.2013; 21(42):191-202.*
60. Kofi Annan opening address at 49th World Commission of the Status of Women, "Calls on International Community to Promote Gender Equality and Invest in Women," 28 Feb 2005. Available from www.un.org/press/en/2005/sgsm9738.doc

Chapter Six: People and Place: The importance of belonging

61. Details from personal interview with Egma in Oct 2016, but many other Pagahill newspaper articles confirming this are available online.
62. http://www.statecrime.org/testimonyproject/pagahill#*chapter1*
63. http://www.en.m.wikipedia.org. Blue Zone.
64. Buettner, Dan. *The Blue Zones: Lessons for Living Longer from the People Who've Lived the Longest.* National Geographic Society, Washington DC, 2008.
65. Buettner, Dan. *The World's Happiest People.* National Geographic Society, Washington DC, November 2017.
66. http://www.abundantcommunity.com.
67. McKnight, John and Block, Peter. *Abundant Community.* San Fransisco: Berrett-Koehler Publishers, Inc. 2010.
68. www.atimes.com/atimes/Southeast_Asia/KH21Ae01.html The catalyst for the rat invasion that put 100,000 Chin village people along the western border of Myanmar at risk of starvation, was an ecological phenomena that last occurred in 1958-59. When the bamboo flowers in the fifty-year cycle, the nutritious food supply causes the rats to multiply. When they have finished the bamboo, they eat every other food crop in the farmers' field. Even the food in the homes is not spared. While the government on the India side of the border prepared for it, the ruling junta of Myanmar did not, and in fact disallowed and denied access into the area to many international aid agencies.
69. Gilbert, Lela. *Baroness Cox, Eyewitness to a broken world.* Oxford UK: Monarch Books, 2007.
70. Luke 10:25-37
71. Pascale, Sternin & Sternin. *"The Power of Positive Deviance: How Unlikely Innovators Solve the World's Toughest Problems."* Harvard Business Press, 2010.
72. CCarmel, Laurence. "Besieged by the rising tides of climate change, Kiribati buys land in Fiji," *The Guardian,* July 1, 2014.

Chapter Seven: Work as a Gift: Meaningless drudgery as enslavement

73. www.psa.gov.ph/overseasworkers. *"Total Number of OFWs Estimated at 2.2 Million",* April 27, 2017.
74. Hincks, Joseph. "In the World's most expensive city, one in ten maids..." *TIME World/Hong Kong.* May 17, 2017.
75. Hossine, Md Mukul. *Me Migrant.* Singapore: Ethos Books, 2016, excerpt from "Expatriate Dreams," *16.*
76. Elkington, John. *Cannibals with Forks: The Triple Bottom Line of 21st Century Business.* Capstone/Wiley, Oxford, 1997.

77. Haugen, Gary and Hunter, Gregg. *Terrify No More: Young Girls Held Captive and the Daring Undercover Operation to Win Their Freedom.* Nashville: W Publishing Group, a Division of Thomas Nelson, Inc., 2005.

Chapter Eight: Give a Person a Fish: Or teach an entrepreneur?

78. Corbett, Steve and Fikkert, Brian. *When Helping Hurts: How to Alleviate Poverty without Hurting the Poor...and Yourself.* Chicago: Moody Publishers, 2009.
79. Seager, Greg. *When Healthcare Hurts: An Evidence Based Guide for Best Practices in Global Health Initiatives.* Bloomington, IN: AuthorHouse, 2012.
80. "Transforming our World: the 2030 agenda for sustainable development." *UN.* Available from https://sustainabledevelopment.un.org/post2015/transformingourworld/publication
81. Kretzmann, John; McKnight, John. *Building Communities from the Inside Out: A Path Toward Finding and Mobilizing a Community's Assets.* Chicago: ACTA Publications, 1993.
82. McKnight, John; Block, Peter. *The Abundant Community: Awakening the Power of Families and Neighborhoods.* San Francisco, CA: Berrett-Koehler, 2012.
83. www.edmonton.ca/abundant-community.

Chapter Nine: Use What You Have Been Given: Build on what has gone before

84. www.wikipedia.org/wiki/Bosnia_War.
85. Isaiah 61:3
86. http://wikipedia.org Kosovo Protestant Evangelical Church.
87. www.unicef.org/newsline/99pr35.htm.Luke 4:18-19, as read by Jesus from the scroll of Isaiah 61:1-2, The Message Bible.

Chapter Ten: Whole Person, Whole Community, Whole World

88. Luke 4:18-19, as read by Jesus from the scroll of Isaiah 61:1-2. (The Message).
89. Luke 10:25-37
90. Palmer, Brian. "In Medicine We Trust: Should we worry that so many of the doctors treating Ebola in Africa are missionaries?" *Slate Magazine*, Oct 2, 2014
91. Wydick, Bruce. *Shrewd Samaritan: Faith, Economics and the Road to Loving our Global Neighbor.* Nashville, Tennessee: W Publishing (Thomas Nelson), 2019, 147-148
92. http://www.cmf.org.uk/publications/content.asp?context=article&id=827.

93. http://wikipedia.org/wiki/parabalani.
94. Cusick, Sarah and Georgieff, Michael. *"The First 1000 Days of Life: the Brain's Window of Opportunity,"* Available from https://www.unicef-irc.org/article/958-the-first-1000-days-of-life-the-brains-window-of-opportunity.html

CPSIA information can be obtained
at www.ICGtesting.com
Printed in the USA
LVHW010233180720
661001LV00006B/475